White Men's Law

Books by Peter Irons

The New Deal Lawyers

Justice at War: The Story of the Japanese American Internment Cases

The Courage of Their Convictions: Sixteen Americans Who Fought Their
    Way to the Supreme Court

Justice Delayed: The Record of the Japanese American Internment Cases
    (edited, with an introductory essay)

May It Please the Court (four volumes of edited and narrated excerpts of
    Supreme

Court oral arguments from original audio recordings, with accompanying
    books of transcripts)

Brennan vs. Rehnquist: The Battle for the Constitution

Jim Crow's Children: The Broken Promise of the Brown Decision

A People's History of the Supreme Court

War Powers: How the Imperial Presidency Hijacked the Constitution

God on Trial: Dispatches from America's Religious Battlefields

The Steps to the Supreme Court: A Guided Tour of the American
    Legal System

WHITE MEN'S LAW

The Roots of Systemic Racism

PETER IRONS

OXFORD
UNIVERSITY PRESS

OXFORD
UNIVERSITY PRESS

Oxford University Press is a department of the University of Oxford. It furthers
the University's objective of excellence in research, scholarship, and education
by publishing worldwide. Oxford is a registered trade mark of Oxford University
Press in the UK and certain other countries.

Published in the United States of America by Oxford University Press
198 Madison Avenue, New York, NY 10016, United States of America.

Photo on page xx by Photo12/UIG/Getty Images

CIP data is on file at the Library of Congress
ISBN 978–0–19–091494–3

DOI: 10.1093/oso/9780190914943.001.0001

1 3 5 7 9 8 6 4 2

Printed by LSC Communications, United States of America

This book is dedicated to

Eleanor Holmes Norton
Henry "Hank" Thomas
John Lewis
Rev. James Lawson
Philip Randolph

These remarkable people each offered me guidance and inspiration during a critical period of my life, setting me on a course for social justice on which I am still traveling. Mentors and models, they each exemplify the challenge set by Horace Mann in 1859, exhorting the graduates of my alma mater, Antioch College, "Be ashamed to die until you have won some victory for humanity." Their many victories for humanity should inspire us all, as they have me.

Contents

Preface: Some Words about Words

What Does "Systemic Racism" Mean?

FAIR QUESTION FOR a book on the topic. My short answer (a longer answer is this book itself, to be not quite facetious) stems from the fact that every social system (often defined by national boundaries, as in "the American system") is made up of separate but interlinked and interdependent institutions, both public and private, that are designed to meet one or more needs of the public; the most important include education, business enterprises and employment, government at all levels, healthcare, the legal system (including policing, courts, and imprisonment), and even religion.

Each of these institutions, from their inception in colonial times (and modeled, with adaptations, on the English institutions the colonists brought with them) was established, maintained, and perpetuated by White men, who have never constituted a majority of the American population; as of January 2021, non-Hispanic White males numbered 102 million in a total population of 330 million, less than one-third. White men, of course, had completely dominated the parallel institutions in England, and the colonists had no thoughts of relinquishing their control of power; it hardly entered their minds. One institution, however, prompted the White men who controlled colonial governments to codify in law their complete control of an important form of "property" on which the colonial economy relied, especially in the agricultural South: Black slaves who could, as the Supreme Court later ruled, be "bought and sold as an ordinary article of merchandise." Every social and political institution in colonial America either excluded Blacks entirely, or subjected them to discrimination in the allocation of benefits such as education, without which Blacks could never escape poverty. Barring the education of Blacks by law, as most southern states did, was the paradigm of systemic racism, continuing with inferior Jim Crow schooling, exclusion from jobs requiring verbal and numerical skills, and consignment for many to lives in decaying inner-city ghettos, with "law and order" enforced by often racist police, prosecutors, and judges. This virtual millstone around the necks of generations of Black Americans has made the effects of systemic racism a continuing national crisis.

Even the adoption of a Constitution and Bill of Rights designed to govern "We, the people of the United States" did not change any of the institutions that excluded or discriminated against Blacks (and White women). And not even the end of slavery and promises in the Reconstruction constitutional amendments of "equal protection under the law" elevated Blacks to the legal or social status of Whites, as victims of a social system and its component institutions that rewarded Whites and punished Blacks for their skin color alone.

Social institutions, of course, are not "real" in any material sense. They are composed of individuals who set their policies and practices, and others who implement them. Over time, as individuals come and go (through death or retirement), and as social and political movements arise in response to factors such as immigration, technology, and economic upheaval, the goals of institutions change. But long-established and entrenched policies and practices remain, particularly at lower levels of decision-making, in which racial bias, both implicit and explicit, is common (and often unremarked) in dealings with customers, clients, and students. The many studies that have documented the discriminatory effect of these biases rebut the claims that shift blame to "a few bad apples" (such as racist cops) who violate the professed "color-blind" policies of their institutions. But the "bad apples" are in fact the poisoned fruit of institutions that fail to recognize the racism at their intertwined roots and whose institutional cultures (like the "blue wall of silence" that protects racist cops from exposure and discipline) are slow to change, even as the broader society responds to the demands of racial and ethnic minorities for equal status with the shrinking White majority. Growing in size and strength since the 1950s, the civil rights movement launched legal and political attacks on school segregation and racist denials of voting rights that forced most institutions to shift from exclusion to inclusion of Blacks and other minorities, at least as official policy.

But the damage inflicted on Blacks by these institutions, and the social system as a whole, had already been done. Despite the good intentions of reformers, systemic racism had placed Blacks well behind Whites in measures such as education, employment, life expectancy, and access to healthcare. Redressing those disparities will require, in my opinion, a multigenerational effort to "root out systemic racism" in all public and private institutions, as

President Joe Biden has stated as a primary goal of his administration. As this book recounts, the grip of "White men's law" on Black Americans has persisted over four centuries and will be difficult to dislodge. This challenge was well-expressed in 2018 by the U.S. Conference of Catholic Bishops, an institution that has pledged to combat racism in all its forms: "Today's continuing inequities in education, housing, employment, wealth and representation in leadership positions are rooted in our country's shameful history of slavery and systemic racism." But with Americans now bitterly divided over issues of racial justice, systemic racism will continue to disadvantage those who were once legally designated the "property" of White men. To be blunt, the cold hands of dead White men still maintain, through the laws and institutions they created and perpetuated, their grip on power and their legacy of White supremacy, however much disavowed by today's vote-seeking politicians. To deny the persistent reality of systemic racism, as traced in this book over four centuries of American history, makes the deniers part of the problem, not of its long-term solution.

Who Is "White" and Who Is "Black"?

Every author who addresses racial issues faces (but most often ignores or evades) the question of terminology. If I use the terms "White" and "Black" as racial categories, some readers may assume that I'm talking about two discrete, and identifiable, "races," based on the skin color of their members. Most authors use those terms for convenience, as I will, but few notify their readers that there is no such thing as a "White" or a "Black" race.

Most people know that racial categories are not totally discrete. And some recognize that such categories are socially constructed, acknowledging the obvious overlap between races, such as mixed-race people, but allowing people (particularly in filling out census forms) to identify themselves as "one-race" persons. For example, in the 2010 U.S. census, 97.1 percent of respondents checked the "one race" box. The census found that 72.4 percent of respondents claimed to be only White, 12.6 percent identified as Black, 4.8 percent as Asian, 0.9 percent as Native American or Alaskan Native, and 0.2 percent as Native Hawaiian or Pacific Islander. In addition, 6.2 percent checked "Other," with no indication of what "other" race they might be. That leaves 2.9 percent (roughly one out of thirty-three respondents) who identify as "two or more" races, or mixed-race.

But there are at least two problems with these numbers. One is that most of those who identify as mixed-race base that on going back just one or two generations, that is, to their parents or grandparents, with more than one race among them. However, studies by geneticists, going back many more generations, show that some 6.9 percent of Americans are mixed-race, although 61 percent identify as one-race on census forms. Another study showed that 12 percent of Whites in South Carolina and Louisiana had African ancestry, and that 23 percent of Blacks in those states had White ancestry, obvious consequences of either consensual or forced sex between Whites and Blacks.

In fact, going back nine generations, or roughly two hundred years, gives each of us 512 direct ancestors. Studies show that the average White American has at least one Black ancestor among these 512, and at least one Native American. Dig the generational tree to its roots, of course, and we are all "out of Africa." The point of these numbers is that virtually every American is technically mixed-race, even those who proudly call themselves "pure" White. Actually, although I'm designated as White, my skin is brown and so is yours, in varying hues from light to dark, with no agreed-upon midpoint to separate races. So why use terms that don't actually describe our skin colors, none of which is "pure" white or black? Those who adopted them, some four centuries ago, were "White," the color they associated with virtue, purity, innocence, while "Black" warned of danger, impurity, depravity—terms much preferred by racists rather than, say, "lighter" or "darker" people. And much easier for them to portray dark-skin people as completely lacking in the qualities associated with Whiteness. Racism, in fact, requires this binary division to avoid "pollution" and "mongrelization," terms often flung by race-baiting politicians of the Jim Crow era (and even beyond). But, to repeat, the colors black and white do not match anyone's skin color.

A second problem with terminology is that the terms "White" and "Black" to denote racial categories were first used in the late seventeenth century, with the racialization of slavery, to distinguish White slave owners from their Black chattel property. Before that time, hardly anyone considered it necessary to describe differences between people by skin color. After that time, especially in drafting laws governing owner-slave relations, these racial terms became important in ensuring the complete distinction between races, a necessary distinction for slavery's defenders.

Most racially prejudiced people, I'm sure, have no interest in studies by physical anthropologists and geneticists. But these scientists show that light-skin (read "White") people emerged only some eight thousand years ago, just a drop in the bucket of the emergence of modern humans of the species *Homo sapiens*, roughly 350,000 years ago in Africa. In other words, there have been "White" people for only a bit more than 2 percent of the entire time our species has been around; for 98 percent of that time, all humans had dark skin of various shades. I'm not a geneticist, so I won't delve into the very few genes, out of the roughly twenty thousand we each have, that determine skin color, except to note that geneticists have identified two (SLC24A5 and SLC45A2) that play major roles. These genes, which decrease production of the dark-skin pigment melanin, mutated as people from the Central Asian steppes migrated to northern Europe and Scandinavia. The light-skin genes help to maximize vitamin D synthesis; those migrants didn't get enough ultraviolet radiation-A (UVA, which comes from the sun) to do that, so natural selection over many generations favored those northerners with light skin, and also favored lactose tolerance (which darker-skin people had less of) to digest the sugar and vitamin D in milk, which is essential for strong bones.

So, in the end, our "race" depends largely on how close our ancestors lived to the equator: those closer to that line got more UVA, and those farther from it made up for getting less UVA by developing lactose tolerance to benefit from the vitamin D in milk. That's a pretty thin reed with which to construct an ideology of "White supremacy" and to justify the kidnapping and enslavement of darker-skin people through force of arms. But that's what happened, all because of a handful of genes that determine visible attributes such as skin and eye color, hair texture, and facial features, and despite the fact that White people share 99.9 percent of their genes with Black people and those of other socially constructed races. Unfortunately, privileged White men have seized on that handful of genes to develop an ideology and create institutions whose tragic consequences in racial violence and inequality have prompted this book.

As an addendum, let me note that, just as there are no "Black" or "White" races, the terms "Hispanic" and "Latino" do not denote a "racial" group. In fact, members of this group in Mexico and Central and South America have a wide range of skin color, from very light to very dark, a consequence of sexual mingling between White Europeans, Black Africans brought to South America and the Caribbean as slaves, and indigenous people: Aztecs, Maya, Incas, and Amazonians. In Brazil and Cuba, to which many more slaves were imported than to the United States, many residents are distinctively black in skin color. And many in Argentina and Chile, to which many Germans emigrated, are blond and have fair skin. This book does not primarily focus on Hispanics, but prejudice against them is obviously based on their "brown" skin color as much as language and culture, which vary widely. But whether White, Black, or "other," Hispanics in the United States encounter prejudice and discrimination, and the resultant inequality, as a direct consequence of the need of many White Americans to reserve racial supremacy and "purity" for themselves. Skin color has long been the defining characteristic by which most people view themselves and others. There would be no need for this book if it were not. But sadly, it still is.

What about the "N-Word"?

The news has recently been filled with articles about journalists, professors, and commentators whose use of what we today refer to as "the N-word" has been called into question. Many of these episodes revolve around issues of authorial agency, of impact and sensibility, and of the different contexts in which that word lands when spoken and written.

I'd like therefore to explain my approach to the use of the word, reproducing it in full in several chapters of this book. Everyone, of course, knows what that word is and what it has meant historically, as a hateful slur on Black people. But that is where agreement ends and where those who agree on its history sometimes disagree on its usage today. For instance, is it any less hateful and hurtful if it's used in a book, in quotations from people—including Black people—who have used it at some time, even in the distant past? Or is histor- ical exactitude—and insistence on reproducing the historical record exactly as it exists—a sufficient reason to include it as spoken or written when it lands even in this context—and perhaps especially in this context—so harshly to contemporary ears? Should the word be referenced or elided (e.g., "N-word" or "n-----") since, after all, the reference will be clear to everyone?

That word appears in this book, especially in chapter 2, most frequently in transcripts of interviews of formerly enslaved people recorded in the 1930s, people then in their eighties and nineties. The agency that conducted these interviews—some 2,300—was the Federal Writers Project, the New Deal agency designed to give employment to jobless writers, artists, photographers, and historians. The collection of what was called the Slave Narratives was followed by transcribing the tapes for publication by the Library of Congress. Most of these transcriptions were done by White people, with instructions to replicate as closely as possible the vernacular and pronunciation of the subjects, many of them illiterate and unschooled. This effort at verisimil- itude produced results that may strike many people today as offensive and patronizing, but to put them into standard English would, it seems to me, greatly alter and diminish the voices of people who were never schooled in standard English and would be a presumptuous act on my part. Most of the former slaves refer in their interviews to themselves and other Blacks as "niggers," long before terms such as "people of color" or "African Americans" became standard and preferred. As Harvard Law professor Randall Kennedy shows in his 2002 book, *Nigger: The Strange Career of a Troublesome Word*, although slaves used the word among themselves, by the 1840s it had become a pejorative slur by racist Whites about, or even to, Blacks. I don't believe it's my role as historian to reduce the impact of the word through euphemism or elision; this would in my opinion be to reach back into history and in effect edit the words of these historical figures to fit contemporary usage. Furthermore, it would almost certainly diminish the pain—palpable, acute—that emerges from these stories, which is one of the features that makes them so irreplaceable as testament and history.

A Word of Introduction

I suspect many readers of books like this would like to know more about the authors than book-jacket lists of degrees and academic positions. For such readers of this book, a few words of introduction about who I am and why I felt compelled to write this book.

For those who don't already know me, I am a privileged White male, born in 1940 and raised in upper-middle-class, virtually all-White, mostly Protestant, and staunchly Republican towns across the county, as my father's work as a nuclear engineer took our family from Massachusetts to Washington state, with my high school years in a country club Cincinnati suburb. My family tree includes a *Mayflower* pilgrim, William White, and his son Peregrine, born on the ship in Plymouth Harbor; on another branch, I share a long-ago English grandfather with Abraham Lincoln. My education includes a Ph.D. in political science from Boston University and a J.D. from Harvard Law School; I'm also a member of the U.S. Supreme Court bar. I taught constitutional law at the University of California, San Diego, from 1982 until my retirement in 2004. Along the way, I've written a dozen books on the Supreme Court and constitutional litigation, some winning prestigious awards. All told, that's about as privileged and credentialed as you can get and has given me an insider's vantage point near the top of both the legal and educational institutions, with decades of experience in how they operate to perpetuate White male privilege. (Perhaps that's why I focus on these two social institutions and their interaction in establishing and maintaining systemic racism.)

With this background and credentials, I could well have turned out like the people I grew up and went to school with: conservative, Republican, and also racist. The most common terms my high school classmates used to describe Blacks were "jigaboos" and "jungle bunnies," which always provoked derisive laughter. That's not just stupid teenage behavior but a reflection of the thoughtless racism that permeated our privileged White culture.

But I didn't turn out like my classmates. Instead, I have long been an outsider, a civil rights and antiwar activist, a democratic socialist, and a critic of incursions on the constitutional rights of all Americans. Three factors, I think, contributed to my apostacy. First, I got from my dad a reverence for facts and a critical (in the best sense) and skeptical attitude toward supposed authority and orthodoxy of all kinds, and from my mom (an accomplished poet) a love of words and the impact they can have on how people think of themselves and others. And from both of them, a rejection of racism in any form. Second, my six younger siblings and I were raised in the Unitarian (now Unitarian-Universalist) Church, which values tolerance, inclusiveness, and engagement in society; my favorite Sunday school teacher was a wonderful Black woman who took us to Black churches in Cincinnati to experience their exuberant gospel music and prophetic message of the hard but rewarding journey to the Promised Land.

Third, and perhaps most important, was my choice of Antioch College in Yellow Springs, Ohio, then and now a bastion of progressive (radical, in fact) politics and cultural nonconformity. Founded by abolitionists in the 1850s, Antioch was only the second college (after its Ohio neighbor, Oberlin) to admit Blacks, in 1853. Its first president was the noted educator and former abolitionist congressman Horace Mann. On my first day at Antioch, in 1958, I toured the campus and stopped at a marble obelisk that honors Mann; carved into its base is a sentence from his final commencement speech, weeks before his death in 1859: "Be ashamed to die until you have won some victory for humanity." That is Antioch's motto, and I adopted it for my own.

Early at Antioch, I joined the campus branch of the Youth NAACP, headed by a charismatic Black student, Eleanor Holmes, a mentor and inspiration (now the long-time D.C. delegate in Congress), who led a contingent of Antiochians to my first demonstration in Washington, a youth march for integrated schools on the fifth anniversary of the *Brown* case in May 1959. The next year, working at a cooperative-education job in D.C., one of my coworkers, Henry "Hank" Thomas, invited me to join the Howard University chapter of the Student Non-Violent Coordinating Committee (SNCC, known as "Snick"). I joined in picketing segregated theaters and restaurants in the Maryland and Virginia suburbs; my first arrest and night in jail was from a "bowl-in" at a Whites-only bowling alley in Maryland. (Hank later joined the Freedom Rides to integrate buses and terminal facilities in the Deep South; his bus was set afire by racists outside of Anniston, Alabama, a Klan stronghold, and Hank was bashed in the head with a baseball bat as he escaped the flames; a photo of that assault, with Hank covered in blood, was on the front page of newspapers and magazines covers across the country.)

Most important was my trip with Hank and other Howard students in October 1960 to Snick's first national conference at historically Black Morehouse College in Atlanta, at which Snick activist John Lewis outlined a strategy of sit-ins across the country to break lunch-counter segregation. But I was most impressed, and spurred to action, by Rev. James Lawson, a young Methodist minister who had been expelled from Vanderbilt University's seminary for leading sit-ins in Nashville, and who had earlier served a two-year federal prison sentence for refusing military service as a pacifist. At the Morehouse conference, Lawson implored us to break all our ties to a government that practiced and condoned Jim Crow segregation; shortly after returning to Washington, I sent my draft card back to my local board in Cincinnati, with a letter explaining why I would refuse induction as a pacifist and civil rights activist. Back at Antioch, I wrote and circulated antidraft pamphlets on midwest campuses, earning a visit from FBI agents who threatened me with arrest for sedition but never returned. I was finally ordered to report for induction in 1964, as American troops began flooding into Vietnam; after I refused to report, I was indicted by a federal grand jury in Cincinnati and tried in 1965 before a very hostile federal judge, who found me guilty and imposed a three-year sentence. (I later learned he had a son serving in Vietnam.)

After losing an appeal on a two-to-one vote, and advised that a Supreme Court review would be futile, I began serving my sentence in 1966 at a federal prison in Michigan; I was later transferred to the prison in Danbury, Connecticut, where I got to know Mafia bosses, Black Muslims, and crooked politicians. While at Danbury, a friend sent me several books by Howard Zinn, the radical historian and political scientist at Boston University; Howard and I began a correspondence that led to my graduate work at BU right after my release in 1969, with Howard as mentor and close friend. After I completed my Ph.D. in 1973, Howard arranged a job for me as a researcher with the lawyers defending Daniel Ellsberg in the Pentagon Papers case. (The charges were later dropped due to governmental misconduct.) I found this legal work fascinating, and in 1974 I applied to Harvard Law School, although I feared my felony conviction would lead to quick rejection. But Harvard was then boiling with antiwar activism and surprised me with a seat in the Law School's hallowed halls. Spurning the corporate-law and tax courses my classmates endured as tickets to eventual partnerships in Big-Law firms, I took all the constitutional law and legal history courses Harvard offered. While still in law school, I obtained (through the Freedom of Information Act) my FBI and draft board records, discovering that I had been drafted a year earlier than regulations permitted, as punishment for my antidraft organizing. Searching the Law School library, I found an obscure and rarely used provision of federal law (called a Writ of Error Coram Nobis) that allows former inmates to challenge their convictions with newly discovered evidence of governmental misconduct. I drafted a brief petition, attached the incriminating documents, and sent it to the federal court in Cincinnati. Much to my surprise, the U.S. attorney agreed I had been unlawfully charged, and a judge vacated my conviction; I was later granted a full pardon by President Gerald Ford, restoring my rights to vote and practice law, making me probably the only ex-convict member of the Supreme Court bar. I like to joke that I've been on both sides of the bars in prisons and courtrooms, but those experiences have given me insight that few others have into the systemic racism that both institutions still reflect and grapple with. And these experiences—as both an insider and an outsider in American society—have spurred me to devote much of my academic work and political activism to issues of race and inequality.

As a lawyer, I used the coram nobis writ in the 1980s to initiate the successful efforts to vacate the World War II criminal convictions of Fred Korematsu and Gordon Hirabayashi for violating military curfew and internment orders, convictions upheld by the Supreme Court in widely denounced opinions. During research for a book on their cases, I uncovered records showing that government lawyers had knowingly lied to the Court about the dangers of sabotage and espionage posed by Japanese Americans on the West Coast; this was evidence of egregious governmental misconduct. Aided by some thirty young lawyers and law students, most of them children or grandchildren of Japanese Americans imprisoned in concentration camps (120,000 in all, two-thirds of them native-born citizens), I was honored to represent Fred and Gordon in their long quest for vindication, culminating with both men receiving the Presidential Medal of Freedom, the nation's highest civilian award. Sitting in the East Room of the White House while President Bill Clinton placed the medal around Fred's neck, linking him to Rosa Parks and Homer Plessy as civil rights pioneers, was moving and immensely gratifying to me.

Let me close this introduction—in this time of a deadly global pandemic—with another admonition that inspires me, from the legendary labor organizer of a century ago, Mary Harris "Mother" Jones: "Pray for the dead, and fight like hell for the living."

I hope this brief account of my experiences gives readers a sense of who I am and why I felt compelled to write this book, which I view as a vicarious conversation with you, asking questions and pointing to sources from which you can learn more about the history and impact of systemic racism and persistent inequality in American society. And thanks for joining me in this conversation.

Fort Lauderdale, Florida, July 19, 1935

Prologue

FRIDAY, JULY 19, 1935, was a typically hot, muggy summer day in Fort Lauderdale, Florida. Decades before the Atlantic Coast city became a thriving metropolis—its white beaches and inlets luring 13 million visitors each year, docking forty-five thousand boats, the third-largest cruise ship port in the world, the seat of surrounding Broward County, with a combined population just under 2 million—Fort Lauderdale in 1935 was a town of some twelve thousand residents, with extensive citrus groves and vegetable farms in the western section, stretching through the county to the wetlands and swamps of the Everglades.

That Friday, a young woman was in the front yard of her home on Las Olas Boulevard, then a dirt road and now the main tourist drag of Fort Lauderdale, running inland from the beachfront to the city's western edge. Her husband was also out, mowing the lawn. The town had been buzzing since Tuesday with rapidly spreading rumors that a Black man had raped a White woman, who escaped after her screams brought neighbors rushing to her aid. Summoned by the Broward County sheriff, Walter Clark, a posse of one hundred men had been conducting a manhunt since then. Clark was elected sheriff in 1931 at the age of twenty-seven. By 1935 he had already become notorious among the county's small Black population as a virulent racist, demanding that Blacks stand up when he entered a room; one who didn't was arrested and found dead in his cell the next morning, supposedly having "fallen out of [the] bunk and hit his head." Clark also reportedly shot and killed a Black man who urinated within sight of an affronted White woman; the sheriff's younger brother and chief deputy, Robert, was widely known to have shot and killed a Black woman who spit on him during an argument. Confined to an area known as "Short Third," Blacks in Fort Lauderdale seldom ventured into White neighborhoods except to work, many as farm laborers and fruit pickers, and kept "in their place" around Whites, adopting the southern mores of servility and deference.

Newspaper reports of the alleged assault on Tuesday, although making no mention of a rape, completed or attempted, further inflamed the public as the manhunt spread throughout the county. On Thursday, July 18, the Sarasota *Herald Tribune*, under the headline "Woman Beats Off Assailant," ran a large photo of a woman sitting on a porch, her hands wrapped in white cloth, one arm around a small boy. Under the photo, two sentences explained the scene: "Accosted by an unidentified Negro who attempted to assault her, Mrs. J. L. Jones of Fort Lauderdale, Fla. put him to route [*sic*] by her struggling and screaming—but not until he had slashed her hands with a knife. She is shown after the attack with her 5-year-old son Jimmie who kept his wits and ran for help." Any attack by a Black man on a White woman, of course, was bound to produce cries for extreme punishment.

The young woman in her front yard on Las Olas Boulevard, watching a cloud of dust approach her home, soon made out a car in which she recognized Chief Deputy Sheriff Bob Clark. In the back seat she saw a Black man sitting between two White men. Clark's car was followed by several others and a uniformed officer on a three-wheeled motorcycle, which slowed down in front of the young woman's house, the officer shouting, "They've got him!" Assuming he meant the reported and sought-after rapist, she grabbed her husband, and they jumped in their car, joining the procession as Clark's car turned onto Old Davie Road, pulling up at its intersection with Southwest 31st Street, into a clearing with a pine tree near the center. The site for what followed had been picked in advance; it lay just behind the back yard of the home of Marion Jones, the alleged victim of an assault by a Black man. As the rest of the caravan arrived, with White men spilling out of cars, some carrying pistols and rifles, the young woman saw Deputy Clark lead a young Black man, his hands cuffed in front, dressed in denim overalls and a white, long-sleeved shirt, from the car toward the tree.

Fifty years later, in 1985, that young woman, now in her seventies and speaking anonymously, recounted what she had seen that Friday to Bryan Brooks, a writer for the Fort Lauderdale *Sun Sentinel,* who researched and wrote a fifty-years-after feature on what happened to that young Black man. Her story is the only first-person account—then or since—by anyone at the scene that day, told with the graphic details that people who have witnessed some horrific event can often recall many years later, indelibly impressed into their memories. She told Brooks that Deputy Clark turned his prisoner over to a member of the crowd, by then a couple dozen, then walked into the back yard of the Jones house, returning with a length of clothesline. Shouting, "You black son of a bitch!," he wrapped one end around the prisoner's neck, tying it tightly under his jaw, then tossed the other end over a tree limb about ten feet above the ground. The Black man, knowing his fate, said nothing and did not resist. Clark then pulled the rope until the man's neck snapped, his head lolling to the left, his body dangling about a foot off the ground.

The lynching—for everyone there knew what they had witnessed—was over, but Clark was not done. Pulling his pistol from its holster, he fired a round into the victim's body, followed by shots from mob members who had brought their own guns. Clark handed his gun to several people—including the woman who later spoke with Brooks—who also took shots, some missing and spraying pine bark, but most hitting their mark, the swaying body shuddering with each impact. Clark made it clear to the shooters that they were now accomplices to the lynching and had good reason to deny having taken part in it, or even being at the scene, in case an investigation ensued.

Word of the lynching quickly spread, drawing more than a hundred spectators, many of them families with small children. A local reporter, toting a camera, also arrived and took photos of the crowd and of those standing within a few feet of the hanging body. The woman who spoke with Brooks identified herself in one of those photos. Included in the photo were several children, among them a blonde girl of about seven, in a white dress, her hands clasped in front, perhaps in unconscious imitation of the cuffed body, gazing at it with an enigmatic smile on her face.

Deputy Clark left the body hanging for more than three hours, while a steady stream of spectators filed by the tree. Some cut swatches from the Black man's overalls, pieces of the hanging cord, even chunks of pine bark as souvenirs. The body remained hanging until about 7:30 p.m., when George Benton, the county's only Black undertaker and part-time coroner, arrived with his hearse. Deputy Clark cut the cord, letting the body drop into a heap. (Benton's son later told Brooks that Sheriff Clark once pulled up at the mortuary with the body of a Black man strapped across his car's hood, like a ten-point buck. Dropping the body to the ground, the sheriff had said, "Here's another dead nigger for you, George," then sped off.) Peeling the blood-stained clothing from the latest dead Black man, Benton counted seventeen bullet holes in the body, which was soon buried in an unmarked grave in the town's Black cemetery. His coroner's report listed the cause of death as "broken neck or bullet wounds." The death certificate filed with the county identified the deceased man as Rubin Stacy.

* * *

The aftermath and impact of Rubin Stacy's lynching was brief and frustrating. South Florida newspapers ran editorials condemning the bypass of the legal system in which Stacy would undoubtedly have been convicted of aggravated assault or attempted rape and sent to the state penitentiary for perhaps twenty years or even life imprisonment. But the editorial tut-tutting also painted him as a vicious criminal, attacking an innocent White woman in front of her three children, grabbing her around the neck and slashing her hands and arms with a pen knife when she fought back, screaming for help as Stacy threw her to the ground in the yard, running off into the surrounding woods and wetlands.

Responding to these editorials and calls to his office in Tallahassee from church leaders and antilynching advocates, Florida's governor Dave Scholtz promised a thorough and honest investigation. He instructed Louis F. Marie, the Broward County state's attorney, to convene a grand jury, which he did just three days after the lynching. Needless to say, all its members were White men from the county's business community, hand-picked by Marie, as were almost all southern juries for decades before and since. Sheriff Walter Clark pledged his full cooperation with the inquest. Marie called twenty-nine witnesses, including Clark and his brother the chief deputy. The Clarks both testified that Stacy had been apprehended about twenty miles north of Fort Lauderdale, after a passing trucker reported spotting a "suspicious looking" Black man ducking behind some roadside bushes, and that a police officer and two citizens had detained him after a chase that ended with shots fired at the suspect.

Sheriff Clark testified he had then taken Stacy to the home of Marion Jones, the woman who claimed she had been assaulted and slashed with a knife. A thirty-year-old housewife, she and her husband, James Lee Jones, lived in a comfortable home next door to Marion's parents, William and Catherine Hill, who owned and operated a surrounding truck and fruit farm. James, who was not home during the alleged attack, had a steady job as a lumber handler and planer at Gate City Sash and Door, one of the city's leading businesses. The Joneses' three children—Catherine was nine, Lorraine was seven, and James Lee "Jimmie" Jr. was five—had been home and raised cries for help as the assailant fled. Sheriff Clark testified that when he brought the suspect to the Joneses' door, Jimmie shouted, "That's the man, for sure," as the children ran from the room in fear.

Stacy, of course, could not contest what Sheriff Clark told the grand jurors or present anyone who could defend him. And there is no record of anything Stacy may have said during any "interrogation" by Clark or his deputies. Accounts did circulate, however, that he had admitted to police officers that he had, in fact, knocked on the Joneses' kitchen door to ask for a glass of water on that hot day. Marion Jones confirmed this request. But Stacy apparently said that the woman, with three young children at home, had panicked seeing a strange Black man at her door and began screaming, scaring him into running away. He denied threatening or slashing her with a knife. Asked by an officer why he had run to avoid arrest after being spotted by the truck driver, he replied, "Well, I just can't stand it. You know how Negroes are. They just can't stand for anyone to chase them."

Sheriff Clark further testified that after he took the suspect to the small Broward County jail, he started hearing of plans to form a lynch mob. Concerned about the prisoner's safety, Clark said, he consulted a local judge, who advised him to take the suspect to the larger jail in Miami, some twenty-five miles south of Fort Lauderdale. Assisted by several deputies, Clark went on, he loaded the Black man into a police car and set off for Miami. However, they encountered a roadblock of more than a dozen cars. Trying to get past them, Clark's vehicle was forced off the road into a ditch, where masked men seized the handcuffed Black man and sped away. By the time Clark and his deputies reached the clearing on Old Davie Road, he testified, the lynching was over and the masked men had disappeared, leaving the scene to the growing crowd of spectators.

Not surprisingly, not a single witness before the hastily convened grand jury could identify any member of the lynch mob, although the faces of several men who had been there were clear in the photos taken by the newspaper reporter at the scene. Two days later, on July 24, the grand jurors announced they had found "no true bill" of indictment against anyone, concluding that Rubin Stacy had died "at the hands of a person or persons unknown," a common phrase in reports of inquests into lynchings that found no one culpable.

Quite obviously, Sheriff Clark's account to the grand jurors was very different—and self-exculpatory—from the account told to Bryan Brooks by an eyewitness, who had no reason to fabricate, even admitting her participation by firing a bullet into Stacy's body. She, of course, would have no knowledge of what Clark and his deputies had done before she and her husband joined the caravan of cars passing their house. She did, however, recount that Deputy Clark had personally wrapped the clothesline around Stacy's neck and pulled him off the ground, perhaps with assistance, until his neck snapped. A plausible narrative of these events, in my mind, is that the sheriff's story was a ruse, planned and orchestrated by him to absolve him of any culpability in the lynching. But the upstanding White men of the hand-picked grand jury were unlikely to probe beyond Sheriff Clark's abduction story.

The pro forma grand jury inquest left several questions unanswered about what had actually happened between Tuesday and Friday. Most are impossible to answer now and were never asked then. First, how and why did Stacy get from his home to the Joneses' house that day? Newspaper reports at the time, and the few later accounts in short articles that mostly repeated the news stories, identified Stacy as "homeless" and perhaps itinerant; reporters then and later writers never checked to see if he had a residence or family in Fort Lauderdale. In fact, census reports reveal that Stacy had a home in the city, at 823 2nd Street, in the largely Black neighborhood known as "Short Third" for its main street. The Florida state census of 1935 (completed shortly before his lynching) listed Stacy, his wife, Willie Mae, and their three-year-old son, Willie, as residing at that address with Willie Mae's parents, Hampton and Nancy Stradford, who owned the house. Hampton Stradford's occupation was listed as "farmer," meaning he owned the land he cultivated, and Stacy's as "laborer." Under "years of school" on the census form, Stacy's education was recorded as "none" and Willie Mae's as "grammar." Stacy had never attended school while growing up on a Georgia farm, laboring in the fields as a child. Illiterate and unskilled, like many southern Blacks at the time, farm work was all he could do.

So how and why did he wind up at Marion Jones's door that hot Tuesday? It was about a three-and-a-half-mile walk from his house in the city to the rural farmhouse. Had he walked from his house to hers, or come from some other place? Perhaps he had been looking for work on one of the farms or citrus groves and stopped by her house to ask about field work at her parents' surrounding farm. We don't know, and no one ever asked. More important, did he in fact force his way into her house on the pretext of asking for a glass of water, and then assault her with a pen knife, as Marion and little Jimmie claimed, her bandaged hands as photographic evidence, although no one spoke of actually seeing her wounds? Perhaps Stacy came into the kitchen to get the water, and she panicked, grabbed a kitchen knife to defend herself, and was cut in a struggle with him, before he fled and disappeared. But, assuming the wounds were real and that he slashed her with a knife he brought, why would a Black man decide to assault *this* White woman; certainly he saw Jimmie in the kitchen with his mother, and his sisters close by? It seems suicidal in light of the virtual certainty that he would be hunted down and, if captured, either go to prison for many years or suffer the fate he did. Perhaps Stacy had been suddenly seized with the irrational urge to hurt Marion Jones, or even rape her. We don't know what was in his mind, of course. But he had been a ten-year-old Black boy in Thomas County, Georgia, in 1917, when a Black man named Linton Clinton was lynched for "scaring white girl," and he would likely have been told about that deadly lesson: Black men must keep "in their place" around White women and girls, preferably staying away from them as much as possible. Had Stacy forgotten this lesson, or had he simply decided to ignore that warning? Again, we do not know what was in his mind that Tuesday.

Another question: Where had Stacy gone when he fled the Jones house? Did he go home and tell his wife and her parents that he was being sought for something he denied doing? Had they urged him to leave town quickly, perhaps head for his family's farm in Thomas County, Georgia, some five hundred miles away? His in-laws would likely have heard that a Black man was being sought for assaulting—perhaps raping—a White woman; word of the manhunt for the assailant certainly spread through the Black neighborhood. Or did Stacy hide out for three days in the surrounding woods and marshes, until the passing trucker spotted him, then scooted behind bushes to avoid being seen? Most important, of course, what happened to him between his capture and lynching, while he was in the hands of Sheriff Clark and his deputy brother? Did they plan and organize the lynching from the start, or were they actually trying to protect their prisoner from the masked (and thus unidentifiable) White men who supposedly seized him from the sheriff? Any of these scenarios is possible; none can be verified.

These are questions that police officers, prosecutors, defense lawyers, and judges would ask today about a defendant—Black or White—charged with assault with a deadly weapon (although the pen knife was never found) on any person of any race. But that was 1935, in the state with the highest per capita rate of Black lynchings over any others, including Mississippi, Georgia, and Texas, the three states with the highest number of lynchings but with far greater Black populations. Lynchings avoid having to ask such questions, with the perpetrators assuming the victim's guilt, often through "confessions" made after beatings and other forms of torture. The legal process takes too long and sentences are too short, many people thought then, and some still do, perhaps including the children and grandchildren of the little White girl in the photo of Stacy's lynching, or of others who witnessed other lynchings as children; photographs of lynchings often included children, staring at the dead Black victim. The urge for retributive violence is never far from the surface of many people's attitudes toward "others" they perceive as threats, especially those whose skin is darker than theirs. That was true then and remains true now.

Finally, what if Rubin Stacy actually *was* guilty of assaulting and slashing Marion Jones? Would that in any way justify his lynching? The veracity of the maxim "Two wrongs do not make a right" depends, of course, on the balance of the wrongs: the deliberate murder of another person for a real or suspected crime, even murder or rape, is an affront to the rule of law upon which our entire social system rests for its legitimacy. Without respect for that rule, no one is safe from summary execution by persons with no authority to inflict it. But no one who participated in or witnessed Stacy's lynching, carried out by sworn law enforcement officers, made any effort to prevent it; in fact, given the temper of the mob, anyone who expressed qualms would have placed themselves in danger. Stacy's guilt or innocence made no difference to his executioners. He was Black; Marion Jones was White. That was all the evidence the mob needed to watch Deputy Clark pull the cord until Stacy's neck snapped.

I have recounted Rubin Stacy's lynching with as much detail as possible from the available records, including the unanswered questions of why he went to Marion Jones's house, what happened there, and what happened to him after he was captured. As with other lynchings, we will never have a full account, because Stacy was never able—by himself or through a lawyer—to give his own account in a courtroom, letting jurors decide whether there was proof beyond a reasonable doubt that he had committed an assault on Marion. (Needless to say, it would then have been an all-White jury, and he would certainly have been convicted.) But I need to make a point here: I picked just one lynching with which to frame this book largely because of the photograph that I think encapsulates the history of racism in this country. However, I could have picked another lynching, from more than 6,500 that have been documented during the period between 1865 and 1950; a report by the Equal Justice Initiative in June 2020 added at least 2,000 lynchings to its earlier listing of 4,400 in the period from 1882 to 1950. The more recent EJI tally includes lynchings, some of them outright massacres, during the Reconstruction years from 1865 to 1877, when Blacks were stripped of their hard-won right to vote after a backroom deal that gave the Republican presidential candidate, Rutherford Hayes, a one-vote Electoral College victory over Samuel Tilden, the Democrat who actually won the popular vote. Hayes secured his necessary electoral vote with a promise to end the federal military presence in the South, unleashing a wave of terror and death among Blacks, often led by former Confederate troops who vowed to exact revenge for their humiliating surrender in the Civil War. I urge readers to imagine a book that provided 6,500 stories of people like Rubin Stacy, murdered solely because their skin was dark. These stories would vary considerably in details, but Stacy's strikes me as exemplary of their common roots in White racism.

* * *

The Broward County grand jury's "no bill" report ended any official inquiry into the circumstances of Rubin Stacy's lynching, but not the efforts of civil rights groups to use his case to push for congressional passage of the Costigan-Wagner antilynching bill, then before Congress, which proposed to make lynching a federal crime. It was notorious that no all-White southern jury would convict a White person of participation in a lynching, no matter how clear the evidence. Congressional efforts to outlaw and punish lynching in federal courts had begun in 1918, when Rep. Leonidas Dyer, a St. Louis Republican, introduced a bill that failed in that session of Congress but was reintroduced and passed by the House of Representatives in January 1922. Predictably, it was blocked in the Senate by a filibuster (to end which then required a two-thirds vote) led by the southern Democrats in that chamber who railed against federal meddling in state and local law enforcement affairs, holding the Senate floor until the Dyer bill's supporters conceded defeat.

Not until 1934, after Franklin D. Roosevelt became president having promised voters a "New Deal" to lift the country from the ravages of the Great Depression that left millions of workers jobless, did antilynching advocates try once again to accomplish what the Dyer bill had proposed. Led by Colorado senator Edward Costigan, a former Republican who bolted the GOP for its big-business control and was elected in 1930 as a Democrat, and joined by New York senator Robert F. Wagner, leader of the Senate's mostly northern and western progressive bloc, the antilynching effort was revived in Congress with the Costigan-Wagner bill. Surprising to some, the bill did not make lynching itself a federal crime; the Supreme Court, ruling in 1876 in *United States v. Cruikshank*, decided unanimously that White citizens who murdered Blacks, by lynching or even massacres, could not be prosecuted in federal courts, construing the Due Process clause of the Fourteenth Amendment to reach only unlawful "state action." The *Cruikshank* case, stemming from the horrific Easter Massacre in 1873 of some two hundred Blacks in the small town of Colfax, Louisiana (discussed in more detail in a later chapter), held that only formal law enforcement officials, including southern sheriffs, could be prosecuted for acts they took "under color of law." This judicial decision put an effective end to enforcement of Reconstruction-era federal laws—including the Ku Klux Klan Act of 1870—designed to protect Blacks from the White terrorism that swept across the South after the Fifteenth Amendment, ratified earlier that year, gave Blacks the right to vote and Congress the power to enforce that right.

Recognizing the judicial barrier of the *Cruikshank* decision, the Costigan-Wagner bill limited federal prosecutions to state officers who directed or participated in lynchings, even by neglecting their duties to protect Blacks in their custody from lynch mobs. Those officials who were convicted under the proposed law faced a maximum of five years' imprisonment; in addition, anyone—including private citizens—who cooperated with or was in collusion with such officials was subject to prison terms of five to twenty-five years. About half of all lynchings between the 1880s and 1930s involved county sheriffs or local police who often willingly turned over Black prisoners to lynch mobs or participated in the extralegal killings themselves.

Some of those who questioned the need for the Costigan-Wagner bill reasoned that lynchings had been declining in recent years. According to figures compiled by the Tuskegee Institute in Alabama, between 1882 and 1901, with only one exception, at least 100 lynchings took place each year, with a high of 230 in 1892. Not all victims were Black; roughly a quarter were White, particularly in the early years, mostly lynched for murders or rapes of other Whites. And in the still wild and mostly lawless western states and territories, horse thieves and train robbers were strung up without benefit of law. In 1932, the year of FDR's election, only eight lynchings were recorded. But they ticked up during the first three years of his presidency, with twenty-six in 1933, fifteen in 1934, and twenty in 1935, Rubin Stacy among that year's victims in nine southern and border states; Mississippi led the toll with nine.

Hoping to capitalize on the new Democratic majorities in both chambers of Congress, and on Roosevelt's stated opposition to lynching, the Costigan-Wagner bill's supporters began a concerted campaign to enlist the president in pressuring Congress to enact it. Headed by the National Association for the Advancement of Colored People, a coalition of civil rights groups, churches and synagogues, and elected officials urged Roosevelt to make a public declaration of his support for the bill. Their hopes were dashed when he explained privately that he needed the support of the Senate's southern

Democrats, all of them staunch advocates of racial segregation and all opposed to the Costigan-Wagner bill, to push through his New Deal legislative program. The Dixie bloc in the Senate included such vocal and vituperative racists as Pat Harrison and Theodore Bilbo of Mississippi (the nation's lynching capital), Ellison "Cotton Ed" Smith of South Carolina, Harry Byrd of Virginia, and Joe Robinson of Arkansas, then the powerful Senate majority leader. Roosevelt owed them for their votes to pass the highly controversial National Labor Relations Act, ensuring the right of workers to organize and join unions, a bill sponsored by and bearing the name of Senator Wagner. He also had their support for passage of the less controversial but sweeping Social Security Act, still under consideration in Congress, before its final passage in August. Alienating the Dixiecrats over the antilynching bill was something FDR, always the political pragmatist, wanted to avoid. Without his public endorsement, the southern senators launched another filibuster to block any votes on the bill, which died in late May when its sponsors conceded defeat. In response, the New York *Amsterdam News*, a widely read Black newspaper, ran an entirely blank front page, with this chiding caption: "Here's Mr. Roosevelt's Message on Lynching."

Dejected and bitter after this presidential snub, the bill's supporters vowed to reintroduce it in the 1936 congressional session, an election year in which FDR hoped to increase the Democratic majority through his coat-tail popularity. In preparation for a renewed antilynching campaign, the NAACP prepared and circulated a poster in the form of a petition. It featured at the top a reproduction of the photograph of Rubin Stacy's recent lynching—the one with White children gazing at his lifeless, bullet-riddled body—with this text below it:

Do not look at the Negro. His earthly problems are ended. Instead, look at the seven WHITE children who gaze at this gruesome spectacle.

Is it horror or gloating on the face of the neatly dressed seven-year-old girl on the right? Is the tiny four-year-old on the left old enough, one wonders, to comprehend the barbarism her elders have perpetrated?

Rubin Stacy, the Negro who was lynched at Fort Lauderdale, Florida, on July 19, 1935, for "threatening and frightening a white woman," suffered PHYSICAL torture for a few hours. But what psychological havoc is being wrought in the minds of the white children? Into what kinds of citizens will they grow up? What kind of America will they help to make after being familiarized with such an inhuman, law-destroying practice as lynching?

The manacles, too, tell their own story. The Negro was powerless in the hands of the law, but the law was just as powerless to protect him from being lynched. Since 1922 over one-half of the lynched victims have been taken from legal custody. Less than one percent of the lynchers have been punished, and they very lightly. More than 5,000 such instances of lynching have occurred without any punishment whatever, establishing beyond doubt that federal legislation is necessary, as in the case of kidnapping, to supplement state action.

What, you may ask, can YOU do?

In May 1935, a filibuster in the United States Senate, led by a small group of senators, most of them from the states with the worst lynching record, succeeded in side-tracking the Costigan-Wagner Anti-Lynching Bill. This bill will be brought up again in the 1936 session of Congress.

The NAACP poster urged readers to write to their congressmen to support the bill; get their churches, fraternal organizations, and civic groups to pass resolutions in support; write letters to newspapers and magazines urging them to editorialize in support; and contribute to the NAACP. But once again, the antilynching campaign failed to break the power of the Senate's entrenched southern Democrats, aided by the filibuster rule and presidential silence. Not until February 2020 did either chamber of Congress pass another antilynching bill, this one named after Emmett Till, a fourteen-year-old Black boy who was tortured, mutilated, and thrown into a river by Mississippi racists in 1955 for allegedly whistling at a White woman; photos of his bloated and mutilated body in an open casket shocked the nation. Although the bill passed the House by a 410–4 vote, it died in the Senate without a vote after Republicans argued it was an overreach of federal authority in state matters; that, of course, was the point of the bill, when state prosecutors failed or refused to prosecute those who murdered Blacks from racist animus.

* * *

The NAACP poster did not sway the Senate to outlaw lynching, but its photo of Stacy's hanging, bullet-riddled body, and the text below the photo, help to explain why I chose it to introduce a book on systemic racism. As a historian of American law and politics, I've often read histories and wished they had pictures—paintings or photographs—to show me a place or person or event the author is portraying in words. Some histories do include graphics, often quite revealing ones. Some time ago, I was writing an article for an online magazine about the Red Summer of 1919, during which race riots swept the country and hundreds of Blacks were lynched or massacred; I was comparing those events to race relations a century later, especially the recent wave of police killings of unarmed Black men and women. To illustrate the article, I scrolled through hundreds of photographs of lynchings on the internet, many showing large crowds gathered to witness the killing; I was surprised at how many lynchings had been photographed. But one in particular struck me, and I sent it to my editor, who replied that it was "too gruesome" and might offend or upset readers. I saved the photo until I started this book, which is in fact a history of the United States seen through its treatment of racial and ethnic minorities and the systemic racism that has burdened them with permanent inequality.

Any full-scale history of America must deal with race; otherwise, it could just skip over slavery, the Civil War, Jim Crow, and Black protests against racism and inequality. Needless to say, that can't be done. Race is, beyond doubt, the most divisive and long-lasting issue in America's history. Racism, as we all know, has sparked many episodes of violence against Blacks and other minorities, including Asians, Hispanics, Jews, and Native Americans. The most extreme and barbaric expression of racist violence is clearly lynching, which often was advertised in advance by newspapers and drew as many as fifteen thousand onlookers, gathered to watch the victim writhe and die by hanging, burning, or drawn-out tortures, a few even forced to eat their own genitals before they died. There are plenty of even more gruesome and repellant photos of lynchings, including one in Omaha, Nebraska, in 1919, showing the charred body of its victim, Will Brown, smoldering on the pile of wood on which he had been doused with gasoline and set on fire, surrounded by several dozen grinning White men. I could have used that photo to illustrate the most ghastly method by which lynch mobs killed their victims. But I chose this book's photo for a reason: to me, it perfectly encapsulates and stands as a visual metaphor of the history of race in the United States. In particular, the stark contrast between the Black and bloody body of Rubin Stacy and the virginal white dress of the little White girl, protected by the White men around her from harm, reflects the primal fear behind many lynchings, of Black men "violating" helpless White women and girls. We do not know this little girl's name, although she looks about the same age as Marion Jones's seven-year-old daughter, Lorraine. It was children like them to which the NAACP poster referred, asking "What psychological havoc is being wrought in the minds of the white children? Into what kinds of citizens will they grow up? What kind of America will they help to make after being familiarized with such an in-human, law-destroying practice as lynching?" Those questions, posed in 1935, are equally—perhaps more—relevant and pressing today as then.

* * *

This book will explore these questions through a historical prism that places racism and the unequal treatment of minorities in the broader context of the social, economic, political, and legal factors that have shaped American society over the past four centuries. Vast increases in population and terri-tory, advances in technology and manufacturing, floods of immigration from around the world, and civil and foreign wars have radically changed the environments in which we have lived in the past and live in today; these will all be addressed. A basic premise of this book, one beyond question, is that a minority of privileged White men have established and controlled every major institution of American society, public and private. What I call "White men's law" is the institution with the coercive power of the state to enforce its decisions. The laws of race relations, from colonial Virginia's Slave Codes to current laws that foster the mass incarceration of Black and Brown men, have always been made and enforced by White men, even as White women and racial and ethnic minorities are finally—after more than a century of protest, struggle, and organizing—approaching parity with the White men who still control our institutions and perpetuate the inequality that still pervades them.

But this broader context is rooted in the stories of individual people of all races and ethnicities and the communities in which they grow up and learn all the rules and mores that signify their place in society, rules and mores that differ from one community, one state, and one region to another, often sharply and contentiously. In framing this book around the lynching of Rubin Stacy in 1935, I will first look backward from that event to the conflicts and divisions over race that began with the first Virginia settlements of White people and the first importation of slaves into Jamestown in 1619, which found one expression in Stacy's horrific death. I then move forward as lynchings decreased—but did not end—while racial violence, physical segregation, and economic inequality not only persisted but have in fact increased in recent years. That story is illustrated by tracing the forebears of Rubin Stacy and of the Jones family, as far as records allow, looking at where those ancestors were born and grew up, their occupations and education, and their migrations, coming together in Fort Lauderdale on July 19, 1935.

* * *

The stories of the Stacy and Jones families lie almost entirely in the southern United States, in Virginia, North and South Carolina, Florida, the Deep South states of Georgia, Alabama, and Mississippi, and across that river into Louisiana and Texas. That's not to slight any other states or regions of which the book will take account, but simply because slavery and its Jim Crow aftermath—which spawned the most bitter and bloody conflicts in American history—began in those southern states and most affected both the Black and White residents on opposite sides of the color line that has existed since 1619.

Rubin Stacy was born in 1907 in Thomas County, Georgia, on the border with the Florida panhandle and the state's capital, Tallahassee. The 1910 federal census put the county's population at twenty-nine thousand, the vast majority Black and poor, most scratching out a living on tenant farms; those Blacks over fifty years old had been slaves before emancipation, passing on stories of their often brutal treatment by White slave owners to their children and grandchildren, themselves often brutally treated by the White children and grandchildren who grew up believing they were superior in every way to the county's impoverished and mostly illiterate Blacks, who outnumbered them but had no voice in its governance.

The ultimate enforcement of White power was through lynching. No state of the former Confederacy had fewer than one hundred lynchings each year. Second only to Mississippi's 654, Georgia had 589 lynchings; Thomas County and neighboring Brooks County were the sites of eight and twenty, respectively. No one who grew up in these counties—White or Black—could have been ignorant of these lynchings. One of the most horrific took place in Brooks County in 1918. A Black man, Sidney Johnson, shot and killed Hampton Smith, a plantation owner known for his brutality against Black tenants. Before Johnson was captured and lynched, another thirteen Blacks were killed as Whites took out their anger in a rampage through the county. Two of those victims were Hayes Turner and his wife, Mary, who was then eight months pregnant. After Hayes was hanged, the mob grabbed Mary, who had loudly protested her husband's murder, tied her to a tree limb by her feet, doused her with gasoline, and set her on fire. A member of the mob, still unsatisfied, drew a knife and sliced her open, dropping her unborn child on the ground, weakly crying. Another mob member then stomped on the child's head with his boot, crushing any life that remained. Rubin Stacy, eleven at the time, may not have heard of the outrage in the next county, although the country as a whole reacted with shock and revulsion at stories of the

lynching in the press. There were no photos taken of this gruesome immo-
lation, butchering, and infanticide, but graphic press accounts prompted the
NAACP to persuade Rep. Leonidas Dyer to introduce his first antilynching
bill in Congress.

Rubin was the fourth child of Annie Gilley and John Stacy Jr., whose
brood reached nineteen children in twenty-one years. They were farmers,
born in 1873 and 1874 in Thomas County, cultivating land willed to Annie's
mother, Patsy Gilley, by the man listed as her husband, James Moses Gilley,
born in 1813. No one knows Patsy's parents, who were both slaves. But, surprising to me, James Gilley was not only White; he owned Patsy and her
sister, Ann, both born in 1840 and probably twins.

His White grandfather and slave grandmother made Rubin and his
siblings "mulattos" under the law: mixed-race children, almost all with
Black mothers and White fathers. The term itself comes from the Spanish
for "mule," the (sterile) offspring of a female horse and a male donkey. The
law in southern states designated mulattos as Black, regardless of their White
parentage; Rubin himself was listed as "mulatto" in the 1920 federal census.
Some of these children had distinctly light skin and "White" hair, nose, and
lips; others, including Rubin, had dark skin and "Black" features.

Many White slave owners took no interest in their mulatto children, who
mostly wound up in the fields, tending crops and picking cotton. James Gilley,
however, was unusual in calling his Black concubines his "wives," giving them
his name and raising their children with his White children. He eventually fathered ten children with Patsy and eleven with Ann, including Patsy's
daughter and Rubin's mother, Annie. (He reputedly had a total of sixty-two
children with six "wives.") He was also unusual in bequeathing 125 acres of
farmland in Thomas County to Patsy and Ann at his death in 1879, giving
them and their children a relatively decent living.

Records of Rubin's father's background go back only to John Stacy Sr. and
his wife, Phillis Rogers, born in Georgia as slaves in 1842 and 1845. However,
James Gilley's ancestry can be traced back to the earliest Virginia colonists
from England in the 1620s. Because many of these settlers were themselves
descended from English aristocracy (who kept detailed records of births,
marriages, children, and deaths to establish their roles in the title-conscious
landed gentry), Rubin Stacy's White ancestors can be traced back at least to
Sir Edmund de Gaye in 1470, more than four centuries before Rubin's birth
and certainly unknown to him.

Finding these unexpected White ancestors did more than satisfy my genealogical curiosity. Stacy was at least one-quarter White, through Gilley and

his grandfather John Stacy Sr., listed in the 1870 census as "mulatto." Under southern law and mores, Stacy was Black, no matter his proportion of "White blood." His White ancestry, had anyone known of it, would have made no difference to the White men who lynched him. Skin color alone sealed his fate. And skin color alone remains the one visible feature that still places Black men (and women) in peril during encounters with White men (and women) who take out their fears and sense of racial superiority on Blacks they perceive as threatening, from verbal insults to murder at the hands of White police and vigilantes.

We don't know whether James Lee Jones witnessed or participated in Rubin Stacy's lynching, which took place just outside his back yard. It seems likely, however, that he joined the posse of men who spent three days searching for his wife's suspected assailant; perhaps he was one of the supposed "masked men" who Sheriff Clark said had seized Stacy from the sheriff's car and lynched him before Clark could intervene, if that in fact happened as Clark testified. It would be surprising if Jones had not at least viewed Stacy's lifeless body, perhaps with his children in tow, before Deputy Sheriff Clark cut it down, to be hauled away in George Benton's hearse. Jones, who was born in Georgia in 1904, was descended from a line of farmers in Alabama, Mississippi, and Texas that stretched back to his great-great-great-grandfather Zachariah Jones in 1726. Marion Jones, who was born in 1905 and married James Lee in 1923, also came from farming families, beginning in Virginia, that grew relatively prosperous; her parents, William Hill and Catherine Braddock, owned a fairly large farm with citrus groves and vegetable plots in Fort Lauderdale, on which they all lived.

It's fair to assume that the Joneses' forebears were among the yeoman White farmers in the South who, while rarely owning slaves themselves, grew up believing themselves far superior to Blacks. They likely supported the Confederacy during the Civil War and, after the bitter loss in that war ended the institution of slavery, supported the Jim Crow system of racial segregation that consigned Blacks to second-class citizenship. Among those ancestors, it's possible that some raised their children free of the entrenched racism of the South, but they would have been in a distinct minority; "nigger-lover" is an epithet long hurled at Whites who display any degree of sympathy toward the plight of Blacks.

I've ended this prologue with histories—as much as records allow—of the families on both sides of Rubin Stacy's lynching, Black and White. With the exception of his White grandfather, an unusual slave owner, they were all—Black and White—struggling to support their families through hard work on plantations and farms. They are among the vast majority of ordinary Americans whose names and lives are rarely recorded in history books. They include no generals or presidents, no business tycoons or flashy celebrities. But they have been, in fact, the people—both White and Black—whose sweat and toil made possible the prosperity and power of the few whose lives and exploits, good and bad, we now read about in most books on American history. And race is the one factor that has most divided the country for more than four centuries. As the earliest recorded ancestors on both sides of Rubin Stacy's family arrived in Virginia—some willingly and even eagerly, others bound in chains, traded with privateers for food—we will begin this American history in that colony of a few hundred settlers, now part of a powerful nation of more than 330 million, still divided by—and often fighting over—the one human characteristic that is only skin deep, the result of a few mutant genes that determine skin color, but the source of incalculable pain and suffering.

I

"Thirty Lashes, Well Laid On"

SIR JOHN ROLFE is most remembered—if at all—as the Virginia settler and planter who married the teenage Native girl Pocahontas in 1614,
hoping to ease relations between her father, chief of the Powhatans, and the
struggling Jamestown colonists who traded tools for food. ("Pocahontas" was
actually her nickname, meaning "little mischief" in the Algonquian tongue;
her real name was Amonute, which she concealed from the colonists. After
her Christian baptism and marriage, she was called Rebecca Rolfe).

First settled in 1607 by one hundred English men and boys, the tiny out-
post of English society struggled to house, clothe, and feed its residents.
During the "Starving Time" in the brutal winter of 1609–10, on the verge
of starvation and decimated by disease, settlers had resorted to eating shoe
leather, rats, and each other, in what anthropologists call "survival cannibalism." Colonial records describe one man who "slew his wife as she slept in
his bosom, cut her in pieces, powdered [salted] her & fed upon her till he had
clean devoured all parts saving her head & was for so barbarous a fact and cruelty justly executed." Archaeologists have confirmed that at least one settler,
a fourteen-year-old girl who had already died, had her skull smashed open to
extract her brain. Some 80 percent of Jamestown settlers died that winter of
starvation and disease, before food and supplies arrived from England, along
with more immigrants.

Fortified with boatloads of supplies, the surviving Jamestown residents
and the new settlers pushed out from their fortified village to clear and cul-
tivate land along the James River, displacing the Powhatan Natives and their
hunting grounds. Tensions rose and boiled over in 1622, when Natives attacked
those settlers outside the Jamestown fort, killing an estimated 350 to 400.
The settlers responded with extermination, ending only in 1677 with a treaty
that established reservations on which Powhatan descendants still gather in

commemoration of their ancestors. The sordid history of Indian extermination, forced relocation, land confiscation, confinement to reservations, Native
languages and sacred rites banned, and treaty violations dismissed is beyond
this book's scope, but the present-day consequences of poverty, unemployment, poor health, and staggering suicide rates among Native Americans are
another example of White men's laws and the persistent inequality they inflict on a minority racial group.

John Rolfe has another, unremembered distinction, as the Jamestown
settler who recorded the arrival in August 1619 of an English warship, the
White Lion, which "brought not any thing but 20 and odd Negroes, which
the Governor and Cape Merchant bought for victualls at the best and easiest
rate they could" to replenish the ship's food supplies before it left with another cargo of "Negroes" to the British Caribbean island plantations. Flying
the Dutch flag to conceal its English ownership, the *White Lion* was a pri-
vateer, allowed to attack any Spanish or Portuguese ships it encountered. It
overpowered a Portuguese slave ship bound from Africa to the Mexican port
of Veracruz, taking about forty of its slaves before letting the vessel continue
its voyage.

Rolfe did not record the names of any of the "Negroes" traded for food in
Jamestown, nor do any documents tell what happened to them. But if we assume that some or all of them survived, and had children who also survived, it
is likely that among their descendants—some sixteen or so generations since
then—are African Americans now living who could, if records had survived,
properly claim that their ancestors arrived in America before the *Mayflower*,
which dropped anchor in Plymouth Harbor in December 1620, a year after
slaves arrived in Jamestown. That's an irony probably lost on those Whites
who proudly claim membership in the Society of Mayflower Descendants.

From the beginning of the slave system, the White men who bought and
sold slaves faced the problem of deciding who actually was a slave. This became a difficult question that finally resulted in laws that were designed to
keep as many Blacks as possible as slaves, cutting off all roads to freedom that
had previously allowed some Blacks and mixed-race "mulattos" to escape
slavery. We tend to assume that Blacks in colonial America were all held in
slavery, and the vast majority were. However, during the first century of colonial settlement in Virginia, a small number of Blacks and mulattos, like many
Whites, lived in a state of quasi-freedom as indentured servants, freed from
servitude once they completed their terms of service, ranging from seven
to twenty years. The Blacks among this group were often brought into the
colony from the West Indies by White merchants and traders who did not

own plantations and had no need for slave labor; many of the indentured Blacks—most of them men—had useful skills that could earn them money to eventually buy their freedom: carpentry, blacksmithing, shoemaking. The fewer indentured Black women included dressmakers, midwives, and skilled cooks. These Blacks were often considered almost-family, and often stayed with their White "families" after completing their indenture or buying their freedom. A small number of slaves also gained their freedom through manumission, the owner's voluntary act of freeing a slave, most often elderly "house slaves" who had served loyally for years. Between purchasing freedom and manumission, however, the number of free Blacks (or "free persons of color" in legal terms) never amounted to more than 5 to 10 percent of the Black population, varying from colony to colony. And until 1649, the number of Blacks in Virginia was only 300, of a total population of 15,000. By 1700 the slave population had grown to 16,390, almost a quarter of the colony's population, as the number of plantations grew rapidly to produce tobacco for the European market, for which tedious labor was required for all the steps, from planting to harvest and curing; slave labor was less costly than wages for free, White laborers. By the end of the colonial period and the start of the American Revolution, the slave population in Virginia had grown faster than the White population; with 210,000 slaves in 1775 and 279,500 Whites, close to half of the colony's residents were slaves.

The rapid increase in the total numbers of slaves, and their growing proportion of the population, became a major concern of the White men in Virginia, plantation owners and members of governing bodies, from local parishes to the colony's House of Burgesses, the twenty-two-member, locally elected branch of the General Assembly, along with the royally appointed governor and six-member Council of State. The concern of the White men who governed the colony stemmed from the fairly loose relationships of Blacks and Whites during the early decades of slavery. The relatively small number of Blacks who lived in towns and settlements, not in the "slave quarters" on plantations, most often lived close by, or even with Whites, including even larger numbers of indentured White servants. They worked together and spent free time together, even socializing at gatherings with food and music. Not surprisingly, young adults of both races sometimes wound up in bed together, tied by affection or simply mutual needs. And from some of these interracial liaisons, not surprisingly, children were born, the "mulattos" decried by later racists as "mongrels" and stains on White racial purity.

The story of Elizabeth Key illustrates the ways in which White settlers in Virginia shaped (actually, reshaped) the English common laws of family relations to ensure that the mixed-race children of slave mothers and White men (especially wealthy and well-connected planters and politicians) remained in slavery. The number of such "mulatto" children was relatively small, but giving them freedom, at a time when the slave population was growing rapidly, opened a door that influential Whites were eager to slam shut, not least because they feared that some slave women might deliberately bear children with White fathers to aid their own "freedom suits" in colonial courts.

Elizabeth Key was born in 1630 in Warwick County, Virginia, the daughter of an African slave named Bess and Thomas Key, a wealthy plantation owner and elected member of the colony's House of Burgesses. In 1636, Key was charged in the civil court with fathering Elizabeth (known as "Black Bessie"); the fathers of illegitimate children, both White and mixed-race, were often sued, not only to establish paternity but also because courts could order fathers to provide support for their children, including requirements that children be placed in apprenticeships to learn skills for their later livelihoods. Key first denied Elizabeth's paternity, blaming it on an unidentified "Turk" whom no one remembered, but numerous witnesses identified Key as the father, which the court found to be true. He then took responsibility for Elizabeth and arranged her baptism in the Church of England. Key was in bad health, and before his death later in 1636, he placed Elizabeth with another wealthy planter, Humphrey Higginson, with a nine-year indenture, which would expire when she turned fifteen, at which time she would become free. However, Higginson decided to return to England and transferred her indenture to another planter, Col. John Mottram, whose lands were worked by a group of twenty young White indentured servants. One of them, sixteen-year-old William Grinstead, had likely been the son of an English lawyer before shipping to Virginia for his indentured service with Mottram. Recognizing the young man's talents, Mottrom delegated Grinstead to represent him and the plantation in legal matters as an "attorney in fact," since actual lawyers were in short supply. In the early colonial years, courts generally allowed laymen to represent clients in most proceedings.

Elizabeth and William were both indentured servants, living on the same plantation. The two young people became romantic and then intimate partners and had a son together, naming him John; with one-quarter-Black heritage (through Elizabeth's slave mother), the child was racially designated a "quadroon," a mixture that allowed some light-skin "free persons of color" to pass as White. Mottram died in 1655, at which time Elizabeth was twenty-five and had completed her nine-year indenture. However, the executors of Mottram's estate classified her and her son as slaves, notwithstanding Elizabeth's status as an indentured servant. Wishing to marry her, Grinstead filed a suit on her behalf, seeking to have her and their son judicially designated as free persons. Under English common law, children born outside England to English parents became English "subjects" at birth; the concept of citizenship had not been developed or utilized at that time, as status flowed from being subject to the reigning monarch. Grinstead raised three points in his argument to the court. First, under English common law, a child's status depended on that of their father. Elizabeth's father, Thomas Key, was a free English subject; therefore, she was free. Second, Elizabeth had been baptized as a Christian in the Church of England; Grinstead cited cases holding that Black Christians could not be held in lifelong servitude or as slaves. Third, her son's father was an English subject, even as an indentured servant. These arguments, based on a solid foundation of English common law, persuaded the trial court to grant Elizabeth her freedom. However, Mottram's estate appealed this decision to the General Court, then the colony's highest tribunal. Ruling that Elizabeth was a slave because her mother was a slave, the judges disregarded the common law principle that a child's status stemmed from that of the father; instead, they turned to ancient Roman law and its principle of *partus sequitur ventrem* ("that which is brought forth follows the belly" or womb), under which the child's status depended on the mother's. Although the General Court was the body that disposed of most lawsuits in Virginia, the General Assembly was authorized to take up cases that its members considered important to the entire colony; when Grinstead asked for reconsideration of the General Court's decision, the Assembly appointed a committee to investigate the case and decide whether further proceedings were warranted.

The lower court took notice of the Assembly report and reversed the finding of the General Court that Elizabeth was a slave because of her mother's status, granting her and her son their freedom. But as the slave population grew in Virginia, the prospect of further "freedom suits" prompted the governing House of Burgesses to enact a law in 1662 that gave every child born in Virginia the social and legal status of its mother. This act effectively reinstated the principle adopted from Roman law by the General Court in Elizabeth's case. Thereafter, all mixed-race children (most with White fathers) would remain in bondage for their entire lives; the much smaller number of children with White mothers and Black fathers were most often raised as slaves. (For readers who enjoy historical trivia, the actor Johnny Depp is the eighth great-grandson of Elizabeth and William Grinstead.)

What is notable, and significant, about the law passed in 1662 in response
to Elizabeth Key's successful "freedom suit" is that it was one of more than a
dozen Virginia laws, first enacted in 1639, that imposed barriers to free and
equal citizenship for Black and mixed-race residents of the colony, before the
adoption of a comprehensive Slave Code in 1705, which incorporated most
of the earlier laws. Over a period of six decades, the propertied and privileged
members of Virginia's legislature gradually tightened a figurative (and sometimes literal) noose around the necks of all those who were not completely
"White" in complexion and ancestry.

A listing of the racial and slave laws passed by Virginia's colonial legislature between 1639 and 1705 illustrates the measures deemed necessary to
protect Whites from the growing number of Blacks and mixed-race residents,
prompted in large part by fears of eventual "amalgamation" of the races and
of resistance to the slave system:

1639: The General Assembly excludes Blacks from law requiring firearm
possession.

1642: Black slave women are deemed taxable as property.

1662: Any child born to an enslaved woman will be and remain a slave for
life (a reaction to the 1656 decision freeing Elizabeth Key).

1667: Christian baptism does not free a slave, adult or child (another response to that decision).

1668: Free Black women are deemed taxable.

1669: The "casual killing of slaves" who resist their master will not be
considered acts of "prepensed [premeditated] malice."

1670: Free Blacks are barred from purchasing "Christian servants." (A
small number of free Blacks did own slaves.)

1672: It is legal to kill or wound a slave who resists arrest; the owner will
receive financial compensation from the colonial treasury for the
slave's market value.

1680: Limits are imposed on the number of slaves at gatherings, including
funerals. Slaves are also forbidden to leave their plantation without
written permission (punishable by twenty lashes on the bare back);
to "lift up [their] hand against any Christian" (thirty lashes); a
White person married to a Black or mulatto is banished from the
colony; a White woman who has a mulatto child is fined 15 pounds
sterling; if the mother is an indentured servant, five years will be
added to the term of servitude; a mulatto child born to a White
indentured servant will serve a thirty-year indenture.

1692: Slaves have no right to a jury trial in capital cases; slaves are not permitted to own horses, cattle, or hogs.

1705: This comprehensive statute—known as the Slave Code—provided, among other provisions, that free Blacks and slaves cannot testify as witnesses in any trial or judicial proceeding; that Black and mulatto slaves are considered real property; that slaves cannot serve in the colonial militia; that a White man or woman who marries a Black will serve six months in jail; and a minister who marries an interracial couple will be fined ten thousand pounds of tobacco. Restating earlier laws, the code included this language: "If any slave resist his master, or owner, or other person, by his or her order, correcting such slave, and shall happen to be killed in such correction, it shall not be accounted felony; but the master, owner, and every such other person so giving correction, shall be free and acquit of all punishment and accusation for the same, as if such incident had never happened: And also, if any negro, mulatto, or Indian, bond or free, shall at any time, lift his or her hand, in opposition against any christian, not being negro, mulatto, or Indian, he or she offending shall, for every such offense, proved by the other of the party, receive on his or her bare back, thirty lashes, well laid on."

As these laws provided, slaves in colonial Virginia had no more rights than horses, mules, and cattle: they could, in fact, be killed by a White master or overseer with no consequence. Every aspect of their lives, including marriage and childbearing, was regulated, without giving them any voice in their status or treatment. They were bought and sold as articles of merchandise. Those Whites who owned slaves could literally rip children from their mother's arms for sale to other Whites, never to see each other again. Slaves could be, and often were, punished for any reason—or none—by lashings that left both physical and emotional lifetime scars. The fear and reality of punishment, not surprisingly, had the intended effect of producing in most slaves the outward docility and servile behavior that led Whites to consider them inherently incapable of independent thought and action, feeding the widespread (and still existing) stereotypes of Blacks as indolent and lacking the intelligence of Whites. At the same time, and in contradiction of these stereotypes, Blacks were feared as potential killers of their White masters, through mass rebellion or individual violence, their outward docility thought to mask inner rage. These White fears prompted the Virginia laws that banned slaves from possessing firearms and gathering in groups, even for attending funerals.

White fears of slave resistance and rebellion were not unfounded. This account of two of the earliest slave revolts during the colonial period is meant to illustrate both the desperate attempts of subjugated slaves to free themselves and other slaves from harsh and often cruel bondage and the almost inevitable response of threatened Whites, heavily armed and often on horseback, to track down the rebellious slaves, kill some on the spot, and execute others in public spectacles, sending a deadly warning to any slave who might harbor similar thoughts of violent resistance. These two slave revolts—one near Charleston, South Carolina, the other in New York City—show that slaves from south to north on the Atlantic coast were driven to wreak vengeance on Whites, especially their masters, with the violence to which they had been subjected.

By the early 1700s, Charleston, South Carolina, had become the largest port of entry for slave ships from the Caribbean and Africa and the center of the slave trade, with frequent public auctions attended by planters from several colonies. The city was also home to many slaves who had training in firearms and other weaponry, some in their former Angolan tribal wars. On Sunday, September 9, 1739 (a day of respite from forced labor), a group of about twenty slaves, led by a man named Jemmy, gathered at the Stono River Bridge near Charleston. They raided a store and warehouse, seized weapons, killed the Whites on the property, placing their victims' heads on the store steps, and spread through the area, killing twenty-three Whites, before they began marching south toward Florida, a Spanish colony where slavery was banned. Along the way, they exhorted other slaves to join them, numbering roughly one hundred at the end, when they were tracked down by a local militia. After battles that lasted a week, most of the rebel slaves had been caught and executed, although a few may have made it safely to Florida. Predictably, the Stono Rebellion was crushed, but also predictably, it failed to extinguish that initial spark; records show that during the succeeding year, South Carolina executed at least fifty slaves charged with various forms of rebellion.

Most people do not associate New York (or other northern states) with slavery, but in the early 1700s, more than 20 percent of New York City's population were slaves, along with a number of free Blacks, often themselves treated virtually as slaves. An outbreak of fires in 1741 caused widespread alarm, especially since almost all buildings in the city were wooden and firefighting equipment was rudimentary. The fires sparked rumors of arson, and suspicion fell on slaves, with other rumors of a larger plot to burn the city (then home to about 7,500 people, 1,700 of them Black) and kill as many Whites as possible. Based on a claim by a sixteen-year-old Irish indentured servant, facing a theft charge, that he could identify leaders of the alleged plot, police rounded up scores of suspected plotters, including some Whites thought to be sympathetic. After perfunctory trials, thirty Black men, two White men, and two White women were executed; another seventy Blacks were exiled to Caribbean slave colonies. Over the next few months, another seventeen Blacks were hanged and thirteen burned at the stake, perhaps as fiery retribution for supposed arson. Given the evidence that some slaves had joined free Blacks and Whites in burning some buildings, the New York arson conspiracy was a form of revolt, although many (perhaps most) of those who were hanged, burned, or exiled were simply victims of public hysteria in a highly flammable city.

Few Americans have learned anything in their American history classes about the Stono Rebellion or the New York City arson plot; the more well-educated may have vague recall of the slave revolts led by Denmark Vesey in Charleston in 1822 and Nat Turner in Southampton County, Virginia, in 1831, at times of a postcolonial growing public debate over slavery. But those few examples of organized slave rebellion are just the visible tip of an iceberg. In his definitive 1943 book, *American Negro Slave Revolts*, historian Herbert Apthecker defined a slave revolt as an action involving ten or more slaves, with "freedom as the apparent aim [and] contemporary references labeling the event as an uprising, plot, insurrection, or the equivalent of these." Based on these criteria, Apthecker "found records of approximately 250 revolts and conspiracies in the history of American slavery." Spread over the 250 years of legal slavery, from 1619 to adoption of the Thirteenth Amendment in 1865, that comes to just about one recorded slave revolt each year, perhaps a small number to some people. But considering the consequences of almost certain capture and execution, it seems more remarkable that the thousands of slaves who took part in these revolts against oppression knowingly risked their lives in the almost impossible quest for freedom.

The Virginia Slave Code of 1705, incorporating and codifying the earlier slave laws, was itself a model for similar codes in the other slaveholding colonies. The members of the Virginia House of Burgesses in 1705 included men with such surnames as Washbourne, Armistead, Randolph, Taylor, Beverley, Mason, Byrd, and Fitzhugh, all of them the progenitors of descendants who became known as the FFV, the First Families of Virginia, whose wealth and influence lasted well into the twentieth century. Having attained their privileged status through birth, successive generations (with some exceptions) held onto it even through and after the Civil War, particularly in winning election to Virginia's legislative bodies, where they made sure that the Slave

Codes remained intact and, after the Confederate defeat and the shameful end of Reconstruction in 1877, imposed a series of Black Codes, the Jim Crow system, that subjected Blacks to forced labor as well as laws establishing segregation in public facilities.

The significance of the antebellum Slave Codes and the later Black Codes to the subject of inequality in American society is both obvious and profound. The laws were designed to keep Blacks in their place, voiceless and vote-less, while Whites, even those on the lower rungs of the economic ladder, gained enough education and skills to provide a decent life for their families; their children in successive generations began life with advantages no Black person could possess. Those barriers to Black achievement, once impenetrable, were first constructed and then maintained and enforced by White men much like the wealthy and privileged burgesses in colonial Virginia.

Perhaps the most pernicious of the colonial-era laws, imposing damages on Blacks that persist today, were those that made it a criminal offense to teach a slave to read and write. Here, it's worth listening to the stories of former slaves:

> None of us niggers never knowed nothin' 'bout readin' and writin'. Dere warn't no school for niggers den, and I ain't never been to school a day in my life. Niggers was more skeered of newspapers dan dey is of snakes now, and us never knowed what a Bible was dem days.

These are the words of Georgia Baker about her life as a slave, growing up on a Georgia plantation before the Civil War. Both the land and her body were owned by Alexander H. Stephens, a planter who became vice president of the Confederate States of America and whose defense of slavery and secession we'll read shortly. Like most Black people who were born into slavery, Georgia was illiterate because it was both illegal and dangerous for a slave to learn how to read and write in the days before Emancipation.

Arnold Gragston told of his master in Macon County, Kentucky: "Mr. Tabb was a pretty good man. He used to beat us, sure, but not nearly so much as others did." When the master suspected that his slaves were learning to read and write, he would call them to the "big house" and grill them. "If we told him we had been learnin' to read," Arnold recounted, "he would near beat the daylights out of us." Sarah Benjamin, who was born on a Louisiana plantation, recalled the fate of fellow slaves whose masters discovered that their "property" had secretly learned to read and write: "If yer learned to write dey would cut yer thumb er finger off."

But some slaves took the risk of beatings or amputations. Mandy Jones described the ways that slaves in Mississippi would educate themselves. "Dey would dig pits, and kiver the spot wid bushes and vines," he said. "Way out in de woods, and de slaves would slip out of the Quarters at night, an' go to dese pits, an' some niggah dat had some learnin' would have a school." But not all learning took place in "pit schools" in the woods. The children of slave owners sometimes became the teachers of slave children. "De way de cullud folks would learn to read was from the white chillun," Mandy Jones recalled. "De white chilluns thought a heap of de cullud chilluns, an' when dey come out o' school wid deir books in deir han's dey take de cullud chilluns, and slip off somewhere an' learns de cullud chillun deir lessons, what deir teacher had jus' learned dem."

The full impact of depriving Blacks of education can only be measured against the historical record of slavery and segregation. From the very first importation of Blacks into the British colonies, education of this servile class was both feared and forbidden. The Virginia legislature enacted a law in 1680 that prohibited gatherings of Blacks for any reason, punishable by "Twenty Lashes on the Bare Back well laid on," a law designed to keep slaves from holding clandestine schools as well as meeting to plot rebellion against their masters. In 1695, Maryland imposed a fine of one thousand pounds of tobacco on teachers who instructed Blacks. As time passed, other states followed suit. South Carolina made it a crime in 1740 for anyone "who shall hereafter teach, or cause any Slave or Slaves to be taught to write, or shall use or employ any Slave as a Scribe in any manner of writing, whatsoever."

The legal bans on teaching slaves to read and write did not prevent all Blacks from becoming literate, at least at a basic level. Some masters found it advantageous to have a few slaves who could read instructions and keep records of production. On many plantations, trusted and favored slaves acted as overseers of "field slaves" and needed to keep records of who worked, became ill, or was injured. One former slave recalled that his master had a "special slave" who could "read and write and figger." Other masters believed in converting their slaves to Christianity and felt that teaching them to read the Bible would not only save their souls but make them more amenable to their state. Christian missionaries sent teachers among the slaves, particularly in cities like Charleston, with support from their owners.

What many slave owners feared even more than their "property" learning to read and write was the greater danger of slave revolt and insurrection, which might take the lives of their wives and children. The connection between literacy and slave uprisings was not an imaginary one. Turner and Vesey, who organized slave revolts that failed but that terrified many Whites, were both literate; after Turner's bloody rebellion in Virginia was crushed in 1831, Black children were expelled from the White Sunday schools in Washington, D.C., where many had been taught to read the Bible. One prominent defender of slavery asked in 1855, "Is there any great moral reason why we should incur the tremendous risk of having our wives and children slaughtered in consequence of our slaves being taught to read incendiary publications?" Before the Civil War began, the border states of Maryland, Kentucky, and Tennessee were the only slave states that did not prohibit the teaching of slaves. Reading and writing, most southern Whites believed, were the matches that lit the fires of rebellion and revolt that supposedly "happy" slaves were constantly plotting against their masters. Without literacy, of course, Blacks—slave or free—could rarely advance past menial labor. To a large extent, as we will later see, many Blacks are still consigned to low-skill, low-wage jobs because their schools do not expect any more of them than the most basic literacy and numeracy, tossing many Black (and Brown) young people into the pool of cheap labor without which many businesses cannot function. Who, after all, is going to wash the dishes in the upscale, expense-account restaurants, pick the crops that go into meals for wealthy diners, or change the sheets in luxury hotels, working for minimum wages? In that respect, things have not changed very much since the days of legally imposed illiteracy. That centuries-long barrier to better lives for many of today's Black and Brown young people is the very definition of systemic racism.

* * *

Virginia was also the spawning ground for the most significant event in eighteenth-century America, and the entirety of the nation's history: the American Revolution and its celebration of victory in the drafting and adoption of a constitution to govern the former colonies and now-united states. Among its planter aristocracy were George Washington, Thomas Jefferson, and James Madison, who joined in advocating a strong union from the fractious states that each held veto power over any efforts at cooperation. The primary and precipitating impetus for revolution, historians concur, was growing resentment among the colonies at cross-Atlantic British rule and the imposition of taxes the colonists had no voice in setting or spending. Another factor, much less discussed by historians, also pitted some of the leading political figures of the pro-independence movement against other advocates of independence: the issue of slavery.

By 1770, the slave population of the colonies had grown to about 500,000 (the first national census was not conducted until 1790, so colonial figures are estimates); four out of five slaves lived in just four states: Virginia, Maryland, and North and South Carolina. As revolutionary ferment grew in the colonies, southern slave owners were split; they relied heavily on trade with Britain, sending tobacco for the burgeoning English market and getting tools, machines, and consumer goods in return. Some remained loyal to the Crown; others—especially those whose education had exposed them to the writings of Locke, Montesquieu, and other liberal political theorists—had a dislike of monarchy and rule by descent and edict. Among slave owners, divisions between Loyalists and Patriots did not extend to the institution of slavery, on which their wealth and influence rested.

Schoolchildren now learn that most of the Founding Fathers—Washington, Jefferson, and Madison among them—owned slaves to plant, grow, and harvest the crops and tend the livestock from which they profited and which supported the lifestyle of the landed gentry. In fact, displays at Mt. Vernon, Monticello, and Montpelier have recently been redesigned to show the reconstructed "slave quarters" and to depict the lives and labor of slaves on these estates; tour guides have revised their scripts to include mentions of the slaves. At Monticello, for example, Jefferson's slave mistress, Sally Hemings, and the four children he fathered with her (who were born into slavery) are acknowledged in exhibits and tour presentations. One question that confronts visitors to these presidential plantations is central to the whole discussion of race and inequality in American society: How could men (for they were all men) who professed the egalitarian belief that "all men are created equal" and have an "unalienable" personal right to "liberty" justify denying that equality and liberty to fellow human beings solely on the basis of their race? Logically, these propositions cannot be reconciled. To use current psychological theory, the disparity between one's beliefs and one's actions creates a condition of "cognitive dissonance," a term coined in the 1950s by psychologist Leon Festinger. To resolve this dissonance, a person must either change their behavior to match their beliefs or change their beliefs to match their actions. Failure to do one or the other of these choices, and eliminate the dissonance, will result in feelings of mental discomfort. Normally, many people live with some form of cognitive dissonance (smokers, for example, who know that smoking causes cancer, heart disease, and other maladies but refuse to quit), but a high level of cognitive dissonance about an important issue (slavery, for example) will often expose that mental discomfort to one's peers or the entire public.

Jefferson is perhaps the best example of unresolved dissonance during the late colonial and early federal periods. He owned slaves and profited from their unpaid labor, but he also considered slavery an unjust system, a violation of the "liberty" for all persons that he professed. The mental discomfort Jefferson felt, and acknowledged, was reflected in the initial and final drafts of the Declaration of Independence. Jefferson initially listed among the grievances against the king the imposition of slavery in the colonies for the economic benefit of England:

> He has waged cruel war against human nature itself, violating its most sacred rights of life & liberty in the persons of a distant people who never offended him, captivating & carrying them into slavery in another hemisphere, or to incur miserable death in their transportation thither. This piratical warfare, the opprobrium of infidel powers, is the warfare of the CHRISTIAN king of Great Britain, determined to keep open a market where MEN should be bought & sold, he has prostituted his negative for suppressing every legislative attempt to prohibit or to restrain this execrable commerce; and that this assemblage of horrors might want no fact of distinguished die, he is now exciting this very people to rise in arms among us, and to purchase the liberty of which he has deprived them, by murdering the people upon whom he also obtruded them; thus paying off former crimes committed against the liberties of one people, with crimes which he urges them to commit against the lives of another.

This initial draft expressed in moving terms the "horror" of slavery and Jefferson's belief that this "execrable commerce" in human beings should end. However, this section of the Declaration was removed by the drafting committee of John Adams and Benjamin Franklin. Jefferson later wrote a *mea culpa* in his autobiography:

> The pusillanimous idea that we had friends in England worth keeping terms with still haunted the minds of many. For this reason, those passages which conveyed censures on the people of England were struck out, lest they should give them offense. The clause, too, reprobating the enslaving [of] the inhabitants of Africa was struck out in complaisance to South Carolina and Georgia, who had never attempted to restrain the importation of slaves, and who, on the contrary, still wished to continue it. Our Northern brethren also, I believe, felt a little tender under

these censures, for though their people had very few slaves themselves, yet they had been pretty considerable carriers of them to others.

Another of the Founders who suffered mental discomfort over slavery was James Madison, known by later generations as "the Father of the Constitution," as the instigator of the Constitutional Convention in 1787 and primary drafter of the document—which went through numerous drafts and amendments—that ended with the bold statement that its provisions would now be "the supreme Law of the Land; and the Judges in every state shall be bound thereby, any Thing in the Constitution or Laws of any State to the Contrary notwithstanding." In simpler terms, this provision subjected every state government and official to a federal constitutional standard. Madison, like Washington and Jefferson, was a prosperous planter, and like them owned slaves, roughly one hundred, to labor on his four-thousand-acre estate, Montpelier.

Madison expressed his feelings of moral discomfort about slavery in a telling letter to his father in 1783, while serving a term as a Virginia delegate to the ill-fated and toothless Confederation Congress, which then met in Philadelphia. He had brought with him a twenty-four-year-old slave named Billey to act as his manservant. Philadelphia then had a sizable population of free Blacks, and Billey mingled with them and developed a taste for freedom. He expressed this desire to Madison, whose awareness of the lure that Blacks living as free men and women in the nation's then-capital had for slaves like Billey obviously discomforted him. "I am persuaded his mind is too thoroughly tainted [by association with free Blacks] to be a fit companion for fellow slaves in [Virginia]," Madison wrote to his father. "I do not expect to get near the worth of him [by selling Billey], but cannot think of punishing him by transportation merely for coveting that liberty for which we have paid the price of so much blood, and have proclaimed so often to be the right & worthy the pursuit, of every human being." Madison's belief that Billey's mind had been "tainted" by association with free Blacks is telling; a slave with a taste of freedom would likely not be a "fit companion" with other slaves, trained for submission to their masters, enforced by laws that allowed harsh punishment by lashing, branding, and shackling. "Tainting" their minds with stories of free life in northern cities might prompt attempts to escape to free states like Pennsylvania and Ohio, or even to Canada, beyond the reach of professional slave-catchers. In Billey's case, Madison somewhat assuaged his mental discomfort by arranging his sale to a Philadelphia Quaker, guaranteeing his freedom after a seven-year indenture; after that term, Billey became a prosperous merchants' agent and adopted the name William Gardener.

Madison faced the greatest test of his mental discomfort over slavery during the Constitutional Convention in 1787, a four-month marathon of speeches, drafting sessions, and votes by the fifty-five delegates who met in Philadelphia, not all of whom stayed until the final vote, and one state— Rhode Island—boycotting the convention altogether. The convention was Madison's third effort to bring the states together to supposedly amend, but actually to replace, the ineffectual Articles of Confederation. The Confederation Congress was a debating society, with no power to bind any state to obey its resolutions, with no executive to administer the nonexistent federal government, and with no judiciary to resolve disputes between the sovereign states. Madison arrived in Philadelphia with a fourteen-point plan for a new federal government; its structure included a legislative branch to make laws, an executive to administer the congressional laws and conduct the nation's foreign affairs, and a judicial branch to resolve disputes between states (largely over commerce among them, and suits against the federal government). This three-branch plan was designed to create a functioning federal government in which each branch had its powers delineated by constitutional grant, and with each branch a check on overreaching by another: the "checks and balances" of high-school civics instruction.

From the outset of the convention, over which Washington presided by unanimous vote, competing proposals over the structure and powers of each branch were hotly debated: Should the national legislature have two bodies or one? How would seats be apportioned between the states? Should there be a single executive or some form of collective governance (to abate fears of a "monarchical" uncrowned king)? What kind of "supreme" federal judiciary should be created, and with what jurisdiction? These questions sparked a plethora of proposals and jockeying by various and shifting factions and coalitions. The most contentious dispute reflected fears by the states with smaller populations that their voices and interests would be ignored or given short shrift by the larger states, particularly if both legislative bodies (the more numerous lower house and the smaller upper body) were elected by popular vote, in which case larger states would easily outvote the smaller ones. Related to this division by population size was another, based on geography, pitting northern states with larger mercantile and manufacturing enterprises against largely agriculture-based southern states. The reluctance of both sides in these twin divisions—small and large states, northern and southern states—to find an acceptable resolution of their differences was complicated by even sharper divisions over an issue that threatened to end the convention in disarray, with no governing charter to replace the Articles of Confederation: the issue of slavery.

Determined to save the convention and draft a new constitution, Madison took upon himself the difficult task of framing some sort of compromise, knowing that it would not satisfy all the states and their delegates but would give each the metaphorical "half a loaf" as better than none. He faced opposition from several delegates, William Paterson of New Jersey the most vocal and prominent. Like Madison a graduate of Princeton (then called the College of New Jersey), he epitomized the elitism that Madison (also a member of the elite class) professed to scorn; Paterson wrote favorably of the "good breeding" that produced the "true gentlemen" (including himself) who were best fitted to govern the masses. Paterson had no deep-rooted opposition to slavery, but he appealed to its opponents in seeking to maintain the powers of the smaller states. Madison, who recorded the convention proceedings almost verbatim from his front-row seat, quoted Paterson as stating that "he could regard Negro slaves in no light but as property. They have no free agents, have no personal liberty, no faculty of acquiring property, but on the contrary are themselves property, and like other property entirely at the will of the master." He posed a rhetorical question: "Has a man in Virginia a number of votes [in state and local elections] in proportion to the number of his slaves?" The answer was obvious: he did not. "And if Negroes are not represented in the states to which they belong," he continued, "why should they be represented in the general government?" Paterson's opposition to counting slaves in apportioning seats in the lower house was self-interested: he wanted to prevent states with small White populations but large numbers of slaves, such as Georgia and South Carolina, from outvoting states like New Jersey and New Hampshire in the federal Congress.

Madison was acutely aware of the appeal to smaller northern states of Paterson's proposal for counting no slaves and also of the implacable opposition of the southern states to this plan. In his reply to Paterson, he "suggested as a proper ground of compromise, that in the first [lower] branch the states should be represented according to their number of free inhabitants; and in the second, which had for one of its primary objects the guardianship of property, according to the whole number, including slaves." As a compromise, Madison's proposal satisfied no one, since the lower branch would be dominated by the states with larger White populations, while the upper branch (modeled by some on the nonelected British House of Lords), with Paterson's "true gentlemen," as a check on the transient

passions of the masses. After sending the issue to a committee, it came
back to the delegates with another compromise proposal, drafted by Hugh
Williamson of North Carolina. Williamson, a genial moderate in temper-
ament and trained as a physician, proposed that "a census shall be taken of
the free white inhabitants and three fifths of those of other descriptions"
and that "representation [in the lower house] be regulated accordingly."
Pierce Butler and Charles Cotesworth Pinckney of South Carolina, slave
owners and adamant defenders of slavery, promptly "insisted that blacks be
included in the rule of representation, equally with the whites," and moved
to strike the words "three fifths" from Williamson's motion. But only two
other states voted with South Carolina on this motion. (Votes were cast by
states, according to a majority of their delegates; ties within a state were not
counted in the final tally.)

Still searching for a compromise that would satisfy a majority of states,
and after much passionate, often heated, debate, Madison finally brokered
what became known as the Great Compromise: the three-fifths clause was
reinstated for apportioning House seats, giving slave states a 60 percent
advantage in seats over northern states, while the smaller states each were
allotted two seats in the Senate, placing Georgia and South Carolina on a
par with New York and Pennsylvania. Thus, the numbers of people in each
state—both free Whites and slaves—made no difference in giving small and
large states equal representation in the Senate, whose members were chosen
by the legislators in each state; not until ratification of the Seventeenth
Amendment in 1913 were senators elected by popular vote. Ironically, the
motion to adopt the Great Compromise passed by a single state vote: despite their opposition to slavery, delegates from Connecticut, New Jersey,
Delaware, and Maryland were joined by North Carolina, which stood to gain
several House seats under the "three-fifths of a person" provision, while the
smaller states were given equal votes in the Senate. Those five states outvoted
Pennsylvania, Virginia, South Carolina, and Georgia, whose delegates stood
firm in counting all slaves.

Many people—a vast majority, in my estimation—do not remember or
never learned that our "divinely ordained" Constitution was adopted and
sent to the states for ratification; that ratification by nine of thirteen states
was necessary for adoption; that final adoption was won by a single vote;
that four states did not vote because of ties among their delegates or (like
New York) because they lacked a quorum when two of three initial delegates
left early in objection to a total replacement of the Articles of Confederation.
What might have happened if the Great Compromise had failed is one of

those intriguing but unanswerable "what if" questions that historians enjoy quarreling about in obscure journals.

Having gotten "60 percent of a loaf" with the three-fifths clause, southern delegates forced two other provisions into the final draft; one, the fugitive slave clause, also pressed by Butler and Pinckney, provided that even in free states, slaves who were apprehended—often by professional slave-catchers—"shall be delivered up to the person justly claiming their service or labor." Perhaps worn out from debate over the three-fifths clause, delegates adopted the fugitive slave clause by voice vote after little debate. When it was later enacted into federal law, efforts by southern slave owners to reclaim their human "property" ran into fierce resistance by northern abolitionists and led to several lawsuits and a famous Supreme Court decision in 1842 (to be discussed later).

The third provision about slavery did provoke debate, much of it heated. Luther Martin of Maryland, himself the owner of "domestic" slaves as household servants, moved that Congress be allowed to prohibit the further importation of slaves into the United States, objecting that slavery "was inconsistent with the principles of the Revolution and dishonorable to the American character to have such a feature in the Constitution." John Rutledge of South Carolina, who owned sixty slaves, responded to Martin for the slave states. "Religion and humanity had nothing to do with this question," he said dismissively. "Interest alone is the governing principle with nations. . . . If the northern states consult their interest, they will not oppose the increase in slaves which will increase the commodities of which they will become the carriers." Rutledge issued an implied threat, reminding Martin that the convention had not yet adopted a constitution and that the "true question" was whether the slave states "shall or shall not be parties to the Union." This, and other threats to walk away from Philadelphia, succeeded in pushing the date on which Congress could ban further importation to twenty years after ratification, in 1808. Madison was the only voice in opposition to this final compromise on slavery: "Twenty years will produce all the mischief that can be apprehended from the liberty to import slaves," he warned, to no avail.

Like many politicians of that time, who privately opposed slavery but shrank from publicly advocating its abolition, Madison was attracted to the movement in the early years of the nineteenth century for "colonization," a plan that proposed to send Blacks, both free and slave, "back to Africa," a continent few of them had ever seen. This plan, Madison wrote to the secretary of the American Colonization Society in 1819, "merits encouragement from all who regard slavery as an evil, who wish to see it diminished and abolished by peaceable & just means." The colonization movement did have some limited success; the first republic in Africa, Liberia, was founded in 1822 by freed and freeborn Blacks. Between then and the Civil War, about fifteen thousand Blacks emigrated to Liberia, although this number was a tiny fraction of the roughly 6 million slaves who lived in the United States during this period. Supporting this movement, however, did help to reduce the mental discomfort suffered by well-meaning men like Madison, who, unlike Washington and Jefferson, did not free his slaves at his death, instead willing them to his wife, Dolley, who later sold many of them—even breaking up families—to relieve her financial distress.

These brief stories of the conflicts between beliefs and behavior of two of the nation's most revered Founding Fathers (all White, no mothers among them) is a sobering reminder that self-interest and political expediency often prevail over conscientious belief that something is damaging or evil; the victims of Jefferson's and Madison's equivocation and yielding on the subject of slavery were some 700,000 slaves in 1790, two years after the Constitution's final ratification, consigned to servitude under a law (for the Constitution *is* a law itself) that treated them like property. Perhaps, some historians argue, if Madison had not brokered the Great Compromise that protected slavery, the southern delegates would have carried out their oft-stated threats to leave the convention, with no federal government and with slavery still the most divisive issue between the states. This is, of course, another of those "what if" questions with no clear answer. In either event, compromise or fracture, the lives of slaves were not changed by the Constitution's adoption and ratification. The White men who provided that its provisions would be "the supreme law of the land" had agreed—with varying degrees of enthusiasm—on provisions that allowed slaveholding states to count their "property" in gaining extra seats in Congress, to enlist the federal government in returning escaped slaves to their masters, and to allow for the next twenty years the continuing importation of slaves, bringing in and auctioning off another 400,000 human beings—and kidnap victims—before that deadline. And, with ratification complete on June 21, 1788, a Constitution that left in force dozens of state laws designed not only to keep Black slaves in lifetime servitude but to allow their harsh punishment—even their murder—for real or imagined infractions of even the most petty rules imposed by their masters. The compromises and concessions that produced the pro-slavery Constitution, to the dismay of many Framers, did nothing to resolve the divisive issue of slavery. In fact, passions and tensions on both sides headed toward an inevitable conflict as the new nation entered the nineteenth century.

2

"Dem Was Hard Times, Sho' Nuff"

THIS CHAPTER, SPANNING the years between the Constitution's ratification in 1788 and the Confederate attack on Fort Sumter in April 1861, will be almost entirely in the words of two very different groups of people, with a minimum of commentary. The first group is composed of White men of the South who were well-educated, articulate, and influential. They were also adamant in their defense of slavery through widely circulated speeches and writings. The second group, in contrast, includes both men and women, all Black and all former slaves, who had received little or no education, whose speech was in a vernacular that many Whites had trouble understanding, and who wielded no influence at all over public affairs, or even over their own lives. Living in close contact with each other, neither group shared its culture with the other, the first holding fancy-dress balls and sumptuous dinners in spacious plantation mansions, the second cooking pork belly and greens over open fires, singing hymns and spirituals to lift their spirits, crowded into pine-board shacks in the plantation's slave quarters.

We will hear first from four White men, advancing their arguments for slavery, with dire predictions of southern secession if northern abolitionists gained a firm hold on public sentiment against slavery. Their arguments, often eloquent in phrasing and passionate in tone, were never heard or read by the former slaves who recalled the pain and brutality they suffered at the hands of White slave owners who did hear and read those arguments and who were willing to provoke a civil war to defend their "property" from northern "fanatics." But those Black voices, and the stories they tell, are as powerful a refutation of claims that "happy" slaves had no desire to become free as one could possibly make. Education, eloquence, and influence cannot mask the harsh treatment of the institution that allowed these privileged White men to enjoy the fine wines and prime ribs served to them by Black men and women who were, in effect, invisible to their masters.

I have included fairly lengthy excerpts from the speeches and writings of slavery's defenders to provide readers with a fuller context of their arguments. In reading them, I've been struck by how little understanding they reveal of the actual lives of the people held in bondage, although each of these men owned slaves, as many as three hundred on huge plantations. But keep in mind while reading these apologetics that not a single one of these White men, or any slave owner, would willingly trade places with those who toiled in their fields and homes and whom they could legally kill without compunction or penalty. I have not included writings and speeches of prominent abolitionists—men and women like William Lloyd Garrison, Wendell Phillips, Lucretia Mott, Frederick Douglass, Angelina Grimke, Harriet Beecher Stowe, and others whose pens and voices laid bare the horrors of slavery—because the former slaves themselves recounted those horrors in words whose eloquence lies in the pain and suffering they reveal.

* * *

We hear first from one of slavery's most fervent defenders and the most experienced in governance and public office. John Caldwell Calhoun was born in South Carolina in 1782 to a prosperous farming family and traveled north to study at Yale College and Litchfield Law School in Connecticut, returning to his home state and practicing law in Charleston before his election to the federal House of Representatives in 1810 as a member of Thomas Jefferson's Democratic-Republican Party and an advocate of popular sovereignty, serving until 1817. He then became secretary of war under President James Monroe, then vice president to John Quincy Adams from 1825 to 1832, resigning a few months before his term expired to become a U.S. senator from South Carolina. By this time Calhoun had shed his Jeffersonian views and party affiliation, joining the southern bloc known as Nullifiers, which argued that states had the right to "nullify" federal laws that supposedly trampled on their rights. After a decade in the Senate, now as a Democrat, he resigned to serve as secretary of state under Presidents John Tyler and James Polk, returning to the Senate in 1845, when he warned of a certain and impending fracture of the Union over slavery. Calhoun did not live to see the result of his warnings of secession—beginning in his home state of South Carolina in 1860—and the civil war that soon erupted. He died in March 1850 of tuberculosis, lauded by friends and foes alike as an eloquent spokesman of the

South. The speech excerpted, delivered in the Senate in 1837, is known by its informal title, "Slavery a Positive Good."

I do not belong to the school which holds that aggression is to be met by concession. Mine is the opposite creed, which teaches that encroachments must be met at the beginning, and that those who act on the opposite principle are prepared to become slaves. In this case, in particular I hold concession or compromise to be fatal. If we concede an inch, concession would follow concession—compromise would follow compromise, until our ranks would be so broken that effectual resistance would be impossible. We must meet the enemy on the frontier, with a fixed determination of maintaining our position at every hazard.

As widely as this incendiary spirit [of abolition] has spread, it has not yet infected this body, or the great mass of the intelligent and business portion of the North; but unless it be speedily stopped, it will spread and work upwards till it brings the two great sections of the Union into deadly conflict. . . . The consequence would be inevitable. A large portion of the Northern States believes slavery to be a sin and would consider it as an obligation of conscience to abolish it if they should feel themselves in any degree responsible for its continuance, and that this doctrine would necessarily lead to the belief of such responsibility. . . .

They who imagined that the spirit now abroad in the North, will die away of itself without a shock or convulsion, have formed a very inadequate conception of its real character; it will continue to rise and spread, unless prompt and efficient measures to stay its progress be adopted. Already it has taken possession of the pulpit, of the schools, and, to a considerable extent, of the press; those great instruments by which the mind of the rising generation will be formed.

However sound the great body of the slaveholding states are at present, in the course of a few years they will be succeeded by those who will have been taught to hate the people and institutions of nearly one-half of this Union, with a hatred more deadly than one hostile nation ever entertained towards another. It is easy to see the end. By the necessary course of events, if left to themselves, we must become, finally, two people. It is impossible under the deadly hatred which must spring up between the two great nations, if the present causes are permitted to operate unchecked, that we should continue under the same political system. The conflicting elements would burst the Union asunder, powerful as are the links which hold it together. Abolition and the Union cannot coexist. As the friend of the Union I openly proclaim it—and the sooner it is known the better. The former may now be controlled, but in a short time it will be beyond the power of man to arrest the course of events. We of the South will not, cannot, surrender our institutions. To maintain the existing relations between the two races, inhabiting that section of the Union, is indispensable to the peace and happiness of both. It cannot be subverted without drenching the country or the other of the races. . . . But let me not be understood as admitting, even by implication, that the existing relations between the two races in the slaveholding states is an evil; far otherwise, I hold it to be a good, as it has thus far proved itself to be to both, and will continue to prove so if not disturbed by the fell spirit of abolition. I appeal to facts. Never before has the black race of Central Africa, from the dawn of history to the present day, attained a condition so civilized and so improved, not only physically, but morally and intellectually.

I hold that in the present state of civilization, where two races of different origin, and distinguished by color, and other physical differences, as well as intellectual, are brought together, the relation now existing in the slaveholding states between the two is, instead of an evil, a good—a positive good. . . . There has never yet existed a wealthy and civilized society in which one portion of the community did not, in point of fact, live on the labor of the other. Broad and general as is this assertion, it is fully borne out by history. . . . I may say with truth, that in few countries so much is left to the share of the [slave], and so little extracted from him, or where there is more kind attention paid to him in sickness or infirmity of age. Compare his condition with the tenants of the poorhouses in the more civilized portions of Europe—look at the sick, and the old and infirm slave, on the one hand, in the midst of his family and friends, under the kind superintending care of his master and mistress, and compare it with the forlorn and wretched condition of the pauper in the poorhouse. . . .

All we want is concert, to lay aside all party differences and unite with zeal and energy in repelling approaching dangers. Let there be concert of action, and we shall find ample means of security without resorting to secession or disunion.

We hear next from George Fitzhugh, born in Virginia in 1806. Like Calhoun, he was a lawyer who practiced sporadically, spending most of his time and effort reading widely in political philosophy and economics. His defense of Black slavery was matched by his attacks on what he called the "White Slave Trade," asserting that free laborers, especially in the northern states, were in fact worse off than Black slaves because the capitalists who employed them were motivated only by the profit they could make from the toil of their laborers, who received only a "pittance" in wages with which to support their families. In contrast, Fitzhugh argued, Black slaves had all their needs—food, housing, clothing—met by their masters and were "the happiest, and, in some sense, the freest people in the world."

Advocating a form of agrarian feudalism, Fitzhugh was a fierce critic of the liberal, free-market views of Adam Smith, John Locke, and other Enlightenment thinkers who greatly influenced Jefferson, Madison, and those who drafted the Declaration of Independence, calling its claim that "all men are created equal" an "exuberantly false" doctrine. Sounding more like Thomas Hobbes, Fitzhugh responded that "[t]he principle of slavery is in itself right, and does not depend on difference of complexion," and that "Nature has made the weak in mind or body slaves.... The wise and virtuous, the strong in body and mind, are born to command," those, of course, being White men with the ambition, skill, and knowledge to employ those who lacked these qualities and to profit from their labor.

With much of Europe still mired in feudalism, Fitzhugh's writings resonated with like-minded southern apologists for Black slavery. On the other hand, Abraham Lincoln was said to have been more angered by Fitzhugh's writings than those of any other pro-slavery advocate. The excerpt below is from chapter 1 of his 1857 book, *Cannibals All! Or, Slaves without Masters.*

We are all, North and South, engaged in the White Slave Trade, and he who succeeds best is esteemed most respectable. It is far more cruel than the Black Slave Trade because it exacts more of its slaves, and neither protects nor governs them. We boast that it exacts more when we say that "the *profits* made from employing free labor are greater than those from slave labor." The profits made from free labor are the amount of the products of such labor which the employer, by means of the command which capital or skill gives him, takes away, exacts, or exploits from the free labor. The profits of slave labor are that portion of the products of such labor which the power of the master enables him to appropriate. These profits are less, because the master allows the slave to retain a larger share of the results of his own labor then do the employers of free labor. But we not only boast that the White Slave Trade is more exacting and fraudulent in fact, though not in intention than black slavery, but we also boast that it is more cruel, in leaving the laborer to take care of himself and family out of the pittance which skill or capital have allowed him to retain. When the day's labor is ended, he is free, but is overburdened with the cares of family and household which make his freedom an empty and illusive mockery. But his employer is really free, and may enjoy the profits made by others' labor without a care or a trouble as to their well-being. The slave is free, too, when the labors of the day are over, and free in mind as well as body, for the master provides food, raiment, house, fuel, and everything else necessary to the physical well-being of himself and family. The master's labors commenced just when the slave's end. No wonder men should prefer white slavery to Negro slavery, since it is more profitable, and is free from all the cares and labors of black slave-holding. . . .

The Negro slaves of the South are the happiest, and, in some sense, the freest people in the world. The children and the aged and infirm work not at all, and yet have all the comforts and necessaries of life provided for them. They enjoy liberty, because they are oppressed neither by care nor labor. The women do little hard work, and are protected from the despotism of their husbands by their masters. The Negro men and stout boys work, on the average, in good weather, not more than nine hours a day. The balance of their time is spent in perfect abandon. Besides, they have their Sabbaths and holidays. White men, with so much of license and liberty, would die of ennui, but Negroes luxuriate in corporeal and mental repose. With their faces upturned to the sun, they can sleep at any hour, and quiet sleep is the greatest of human enjoyments. . . . We do not know whether free laborers ever sleep. They are fools to do so, for whilst they sleep, the wily and watchful capitalist is devising means to ensnare and exploit them. The free laborer must work or starve. He is more of a slave than the Negro, because he works longer and harder for less allowance than the slave and has no holiday, because the cares of life with him begin when its labors end. He has no liberty, and not a single right.

Most people know that Jefferson Davis was president of the Confederate States of America from the Civil War's start in 1861 until its commanding general, Robert E. Lee, surrendered to the Union's commander, Gen. Ulysses S. Grant, on April 9, 1865. In this post, Davis headed a breakaway government whose political and military leaders launched a treasonous insurrection against the Union. "Treason" is a term too often hurled at political opponents, most of whom have simply criticized a thin-skinned officeholder. But it has a specific definition in Section 3 of Article III of the Constitution, which reads, "Treason against the United States shall consist only in levying War against them, or in adhering to their Enemies, giving them Aid and Comfort. No person shall be convicted of Treason unless on the Testimony of two Witnesses to the same overt Act, or on Confession in open Court." Davis certainly met this definition by levying war against the Union; trying to escape Union forces after fleeing the Confederate capital of Richmond, Virginia, he was captured and indicted for treason after the war, confined for two years in prison although not tried, and finally given amnesty by President Andrew Johnson, facts that most people don't know. But it's important, I think, to remind readers that the treasonous conspiracy Davis led could have ended with his execution; there is no way to put a gloss on crimes for which he was ultimately responsible.

In many ways, however, Davis had much in common with men whose troops fought against his. Born in Kentucky in 1808 to a moderately prosperous farming family, he grew up in Mississippi on a plantation with 113 slaves and received an appointment to the U.S. Military Academy at West Point, New York, in 1824. During six years in the army after graduation, he rose in rank to first lieutenant colonel and commanded Union troops in the American Indian Wars, the Black Hawk War, and the Mexican-American War.

Drawn to politics, Davis won election to the U.S. House of Representatives in 1845, moving to the Senate the following year to fill a vacant seat for two years, followed by four years as secretary of war under President Franklin Pierce, returning to the Senate in 1857 until his resignation in January 1861, leaving the Senate with the farewell speech excerpted here. After a lengthy illness, he died on December 6, 1889, honored at memorial services in many cities by former Confederate soldiers.

His legacy of armed rebellion against the Union, praised by many southerners then and since, endured a final humiliation in June 2020, when civil rights activists in Richmond, protesting police brutality across the nation, gathered on Monument Avenue, wrapped chains around the statue of Davis, and toppled it to the ground, where it was hauled away by a tow truck.

A fitting end, I think, for a man who would rather attack the Union he had served with some distinction than abandon the institution that held some 4 million slaves in bondage. His last words were said to be, "Oh, the South, the poor South." And it *was* poorer, both in wealth and status, because of Davis and men for whom their human property had no more rights than a mule.

> I rise, Mr. President [Vice President John C. Breckenridge, presiding over the Senate], for the purpose of announcing to the Senate that I have satisfactory evidence that the state of Mississippi, by a solemn ordinance of her people in convention assembled, has declared her separation from the United States. Under these circumstances, of course my functions are terminated here. . . .
>
> It has been conviction of pressing necessity, it has been a belief that we are to be deprived in the Union of the rights which our fathers bequeathed to us, which has brought Mississippi into her present decision. She has heard proclaimed the theory that all men are created free and equal, and this made the basis of an attack upon her social institutions; and the sacred Declaration of Independence has been invoked to maintain the position of the equality of the races. That Declaration of Independence is to be construed by the circumstances and purposes for which it was made. The communities were declaring their independence; the people of those communities were asserting that no man was born—to use the language of Mr. Jefferson—booted and spurred to ride over the rest of mankind; that men were created equal—meaning the men of the political community; that there was no divine right to rule; that no man inherited the right to rule; that there were no classes by which power and place descended to families, but that all stations were equally within the grasp of each member of the body-politic. These were the great principles they announced; these were the purposes for which they made their declaration; these were the ends to which their enunciation was directed. They have no reference to the slave; else, how it happened that among the items of arraignment made against George III was that he endeavored to do just what the North has been endeavoring of late to do—to stir up insurrection among our slaves? Had the Declaration announced that negroes were free and equal, how was the Prince to be arraigned for stirring up insurrection among them? And how was this to be enumerated among the high crimes which caused the colonies to sever their connection

with the mother country? When our Constitution was formed, the same idea was rendered more palpable, for there we find provision made for that very class of persons as property; they were not put upon the footing of equality with white men—not even upon that of paupers and convicts; but so far as representation was concerned, were discriminated against as a lower caste, only to be represented in the numerical proportion of three fifths.

Then, Senators, we recur to the compact which binds us together; we could recur to the principles upon which our government was founded; and when you deny them, and when you deny to us the right to withdraw from a government which thus perverted threatens to be destructive of our rights, we but tread in the path of our fathers when we proclaim our independence, and take the hazard. This is done not in hostility to others, not to injure any section of the country, not even for our own pecuniary benefit; but from the high and solemn motive of defending and protecting the rights we inherited, and which it is our sacred duty to transmit unshorn to our children. . . .

Mr. President, and Senators, having made the announcement which the occasion seemed to me to require, it only remains for me to bid you a final adieu.

Alexander H. Stephens, a Georgian who served as Confederate vice president during the whole of Davis's tenure as president, was a reluctant secessionist until the Civil War began, although a firm defender of slavery (he owned thirty-four slaves) and advocate of expanding slavery into the western territories. Born in 1812, he grew up poor, living with relatives after both his parents died when he was twelve. He did, however, obtain a law degree and practiced for some thirty years; he boasted that none of his clients (all White) had been executed after murder charges.

Stephens served in the U.S. House of Representatives from 1843 until 1859, counseling fellow southerners against secession, which he thought would prove economically ruinous to the South. But he was a loyal southerner and agreed at the convention that wrote and adopted the Confederate Constitution to serve as vice president, although he and Davis clashed over matters large and small. After the Confederate surrender, he spent several months in prison but was released without charges. The Georgia legislature elected him to the U.S. Senate in 1866, but the Republican majority refused to seat him. For a year before his death in 1883, Stephens served as governor of Georgia; unlike Davis, his name has faded into obscurity. But it's worth reading his defense of slavery in what became known as the "Cornerstone Speech," delivered in Savannah, Georgia, on the very eve of the Confederate attack on Fort Sumter.

[W]e are passing through one of the greatest revolutions in the annals of the world. Seven States have within the last three months thrown off an old government and formed a new. This revolution has been signally marked, up to this time, by the fact of its having been accomplished without the loss of a single drop of blood.

This new constitution, or form of government . . . amply secures all our ancient rights, franchises, and liberties. All the great principles of the Magna Charta are retained in it. No citizen is deprived of life, liberty, or property but by the judgment of his peers under the laws of the land. The great principle of religious liberty, which was the honor and pride of the old constitution, is still maintained and secured. All the essentials of the old constitution, which have endeared it to the hearts of the American people, have been preserved and perpetuated. . . .

The new constitution has put at rest, forever, all the agitating questions relating to our peculiar institution. African slavery as it exists amongst us is the proper status of the negro in our form of civilization. That was the immediate cause of the late rupture and present revolution. Jefferson in his forecast, had anticipated this, as the "rock upon which the old Union would split." He was right. What was conjecture with him, is now a realized fact. But whether he fully comprehended the great truth upon which that rock stood and stands, may be doubted. The prevailing ideas entertained by him and most of the leading statesmen at the time of the formation of the old constitution, were that the enslavement of the African was in violation of the laws of nature; that it was wrong in principle, socially, morally, and politically. It was an evil they knew not well how to deal with, but the general opinion of the men of that day was that, somehow or other in the order of Providence, the institution would be evanescent and pass away. . . . Those ideas, however, were fundamentally wrong. They rested upon the assumption of the equality of races. This was an error. It was a sandy foundation and the government built upon it fell when the "storm came and the wind blew."

Our new government is founded upon exactly the opposite idea; its foundations are laid, its corner-stone rests, upon the great truth that the negro is not equal to the white man, that slavery subordination to the superior race is his natural and normal condition. This, our new government, is the first, in the history of the world, based upon this great physical, philosophical, and moral truth. This truth has been slow in the process of its development, like all other truths in the various departments of science. It has been so even amongst us. Many who hear me, perhaps, can recollect well, that this truth was not generally admitted, even within their day. The errors of the past generation still clung to many as late as twenty years ago. Those at the North, who still cling to these errors, with a zeal above knowledge, we justly denominate fanatics. All fanaticism springs from an aberration of the mind, from a defect in reasoning. It is a species of insanity. One of the most striking characteristics of insanity, in many instances, is forming correct conclusions from fancied or erroneous premises; so with the anti-slavery fanatics. Their conclusions are right if their premises were. They assume that the negro was equal, and hence conclude that he is entitled to equal privileges and rights with the white man. If their premises were correct, their conclusions would be logical and just but their premise being wrong, their whole argument fails. . . .

Many governments have been founded upon the principle of the subordination and serfdom of certain classes of the same race; such were and are in violation of the laws of nature. Our system commits no such violation of nature's laws. With us, all of the white race, however high or low, rich or poor, are equal in the eyes of the law. Not so with the negro. Subordination is his place. He, by nature, or by the curse against Canaan, is fitted for that condition which he occupies in our system. The architect, in the construction of buildings, lays the foundation with the proper material—the granite; then comes the brick or the marble. The substratum of our society is made of the material fitted by nature for it, and by experience we know that it is best, not only for the superior, but for the inferior race, that it should be so. It is, indeed, in conformity with the ordinance of the Creator. It is not for us to inquire into the wisdom of His ordinances, or to question them. For His own purposes, He has made one race to differ from another, as He has made "one star to differ from another star in glory." The great objects of humanity are best attained when there is conformity to His laws and decrees, in the formation of governments as well as in all things else. Our Confederacy is founded upon principles in strict conformity [with] these laws. The stone which was rejected by the first builders "is become the chief of the corner," the real "corner-stone" in our new edifice. . . .

We hear much of the civilization and Christianization of the barbarous tribes of Africa. In my judgment, those ends will never be attained, but by first teaching them the lesson taught to Adam, "in the sweat of his brow he should eat his bread," and teaching them to work, and feed, and clothe themselves.

Stephens spent the remainder of his speech praising the "virtue, integrity, and patriotism" of those who supported the secession of slaveholding states from the Union. He stated proudly that formation of the Confederacy had "been accomplished without the loss of a single drop of blood." Three weeks later, Confederate forces in South Carolina fired upon the Union garrison of Fort Sumter on an island in Charleston harbor. The Civil War had begun, and it would not end before the blood of soldiers on both sides stained the battlefields where they fought and died.

* * *

The arguments of slavery's defenders could be, and were, answered by prominent abolitionists in words equally eloquent and far more compelling. But even more compelling are the stories of former slaves about their treatment on the plantations owned by slavery's defenders. Next are excerpts of tape-recorded interviews of former slaves conducted in the 1930s, when all were in their eighties and nineties and a few into their second century. These interviews were transcribed with instructions to reproduce as closely as possible the vernacular and pronunciation of people who never attended school during their bondage and were accustomed to refer to themselves and other slaves as "niggers."

From my reading of hundreds of interviews, I selected excerpts from thirteen narratives. Each is different, just as all people's lives are different, but they have common themes: the auctioning of slaves to plantation owners; the cruel breakup of families by their purchasers, selling wives from their husbands and children from their parents; the practice of "breeding" slave women with "sturdy young bucks" to produce more slave labor; and punishment of recalcitrant slaves, sometimes ending in their death. These were not isolated or aberrant practices, although not every slave endured them; brutal punishments—such as setting vicious dogs to rip flesh and limbs from helpless slaves—were intended as deterrents for any misbehavior, even as petty as a surly response to a master's or overseer's order. Anyone who views the lives of slaves as "happy" and their treatment as humane has only to read the words of people who lived in slavery. Those whose narratives are quoted here are identified only by name and residence; unlike slavery's defenders, they have no college or law degrees, no list of high public offices held, or prominence among their peers. All they have are memories, many of them painful to recount and painful to read.

Julia Brown, Commerce, Georgia

Slaves were treated in most cases lak cattle. A man went around the country buyin' up slaves lak cattle, and he was called a "speculator," then he'd sell them to the highest bidder. Oh! It was pitiful to see chil'en taken from their mothers' breast, mothers sold, husbands sold frum wives. One 'oman [that a slave owner] wuz to buy [was pregnant] and the baby came befo' he bought her and he wouldn't buy the baby; said he hadn't bargained to buy the baby too, and he just wouldn't. My uncle wuz married but he wuz owned by one master and his wife was owned by 'nother. He wuz 'lowed to visit his wife on Wednesday and Saturday. He went on Wednesday and when he went back on Saturday his wife had been bought by the speculator and he never did know where she wuz.

W. L. Bost, North Carolina

The speculators stayed in the hotel and put the niggers in the quarters jus' like droves of hogs. All through the night I could hear them mournin' and prayin'. I didn't know the Lord would let people live who were so cruel. The gates were always locked and they was a guard on the outside to shoot anyone who tried to run away. Lord, them slaves look just like droves of turkeys runnin' along in front of them horses. I remember when they put 'em on the block to sell 'em. The ones 'tween 18 and 30 always bring the most money. The auctioneer he stand off at a distance and cry 'em off as they stand on the block. I can hear his voice as long as I live. If the one they going to sell was a young Negro man this is what he say: "Now gentlemen and fellow citizens here is a big black buck Negro. He's stout as a mule. Good for any kin' o' work an' he never gives any trouble. How much am I offered for him?"

If they put a young nigger woman the auctioneer cry out: "Here's a young nigger wench, how much am I offered for her?" The pore thing stand on the block a shiverin' an' a shakin' nearly froze to death. When they sold, many of the pore mothers beg the speculators to sell 'em with their husbands, but the speculator only take what he want. So maybe the pore thing never see her husban' again.

Henri Necaise, Mississippi

I never knowed my mother. I was a slave an' my mother was sol' from me an' her other chilluns. Dey tole me when dey sol' her my sister was a-holding me in her arms. She was standin' behin' de Big House peekin' roun' de corner an' seen de las' o' her mother. I seen her go, too. Dey tell me I used to go to de gate a-huntin' for my mammy.

Mary Ferguson, Maryland

It was durin' cotton chopping time dat year [1860], a day I'll never fergit, when de speculataws bought me. We come home from the fiel' 'bout half after 'leven dat day an' cooked a good dinner. Oh, I never has forgot dat last dinner wid my folks! But some'ow, I had felt, all de mawning, lak sumpin' was gwineter happin. I could jes feel it in my bones! An' sho' nough, 'bout de middle of the even', up rid my young Master on his hoss, an' up drive two strange white mens in a buggy. Dey hitch dere hosses an' cum in de house, wich skeered me. Den one o' de strangers said, "git you clothes, Mary, we has bought you frum Mr. Shorter." I c'menced cryin' an beggin' Mr. Shorter to not let 'em take me away. But he say, "yes, Mary, I has sole yer, an' you must go wid 'em."

Den dese strange mens, whose names I ain't never knowed, tuk me an' put me in de buggy an' drive off wid me, me hollerin' at de top o' my voice an' callin' my Ma! Den dem speculataws begin to sing loud—jes to drown out my hollerin. Us passed de very fiel' whar Paw an' all my fokes wuz wuckin, an' I calt as loud as I could an' as long as I could see 'em, "good-buy, Ma! Good-buy, Ma!" But she never heard me. Naw, naw, daz white mens wuz singin' so loud Ma could'n hear me! An' she could'n see me, caze dey had me pushed down out o' sight on de floe o' de buggy. I ain't never seed nor heared tell o' my Ma an' Paw, an' bruthers, an' susters from dat day to dis.

John Cole, Athens, Georgia

If a hand were noted for raisin' up strong black bucks, he would be sent out to the other plantations. There he would be "married off" time and again. This was thrifty and saved any actual purchase of new stock.

Martha Jackson, Alabama

Wunner dese here 'omans was my Auntie and she say dat she skacely call to min' de master whoppin' her, 'cause she was a breeder woman, and brought in chillum ev'y twelve mont's jes' lak a cow bringin' in a calf. And she say, dat whut make her mo' val'ble to her Ole Marster. He orders she can't be put to no strain 'casen uv dat. But dem others he worked 'em day en night, Sad'dy en Sunday too.

Dora Franks, Choctaw County, Mississippi

My daddy was my young Marster. His name was Marster George Brewer an' my mammy always tol' me dat I was his'n. I know dat dare was some diff'ence 'tween me an' de res' o' her chillum, 'cause dey was all coal black, an' I was even lighter dan I is now. Lawd, it's been to my sorrow many a time, 'cause de chillum used to chase me 'round an' holler at me, "Old yellow Nigger."

Mos'ly, we stay on de plantation, but lots o' Niggers would slip off from one plantation to de other to see some other Niggers. Dey would always manage to git back 'fore daybreak. De wors' thing I ever heard 'bout dat was once when my Uncle Alf run off to "jump de broom." Dat was what dey called goin' to see a woman. He didn' come back by daylight, so dey put de Nigger hounds after 'im. Dey smelled his trail down to de swamp an' found where he was hidin'. Now, he was one o' de biggest Niggers on de place an' a powerful fas' worker. But dey took an' give him 100 lashes wid de cat-o'-ninety-nine tails. His back was somethin' awful, but dey put 'im in de fiel' to work while de blood was still a-runnin'. He work right hard till dey lef'. Den, when he got up to de end o' de row next to de swamp, he lit out again. Dey never foun' him dat time. Dey say he foun' a cave an' fix him up a room whar he could live. At nights he would come out on de place an' steal enough to eat an' cook it in his little dugout. When de war was over an' de slaves was freed, he come out. When I saw him, he look lak a hairy ape, 'thout no clothes on an' hair growin' all over his body.

Mattie Curtis, Orange County, North Carolina

Preacher Whitfield, bein' a preacher, wuz supposed to be good, but he ain't half fed ner clothed his slaves an' he whupped 'em bad. I'se seen him whup my mammy wid all de clothes offen her back. He'd buck her down on a barrel an' beat de blood outen her. Dar was some difference in his beatin' from de neighbors. De folks round dar 'ud whup in de back yard, but Marse Whitfield 'ud have de barrel carried in his parlor fer de beatin'.

Mary Reynolds, Black River, Louisiana

Slavery was the worst days as ever seed in the world. They was things past tellin', but I got the scars on my old body to show to this day. I seed worse than what happened to me. I seed them put the men and women in the stock with they hands screwed down through the holes in the board and they feets tied together and they naked behinds to the world. Solomon the overseer beat them with a big whip and massa look on. The niggers better not stop in the fields when they hear them yellin'. They cut the flesh near to the bones and some they was when they taken them out of stock and put them on the beds, they never got up again.

Aunt Janey was just out of bed with a suckin' baby one time, and she run away. Some say that was 'nother baby of massa's breeding. She don't come to the house to nurse her baby so they misses her and old Solomon gits the nigger hounds and takes her trail. They gits near her and she grabs a limb and tries to hoist herself in a tree, but them dogs grab her and pull her down. The man hollers them onto her, and the dogs tore her naked and et the breasts plumb off her body. She got well and lived to be an old woman, but 'nother woman has to suck her baby and she ain't got no sign of breasts no more.

When a nigger died they let his folks come out the fields to see him afore he died. They buried him the same day, take a big plank and bust it with an ax in the middle 'nough to bend it back, and put the dead nigger in betwix. They'd cart them down to the graveyard on the place and not bury them deep 'nough that buzzards wouldn't come circlin' 'round. Niggers mourns now, but in them days they wasn't no time for mournin'.

Seems like after I got bigger, I 'member more and more niggers run away. They's most all got cotched. Massa used to hire out his niggers for wage hands. One time he hired me and a nigger boy, Turner, to work for some ornery white trash name of Kidd. One day Turner goes off and don't come back. Old man Kidd say I knowed about it, and he tied my wrists together and stripped me. He hanged me by the wrists from a limb on a tree and spraddled my legs 'round the trunk and tied my feet together. Then he beat me. He beat me worser than I ever been beat before and I faints dead away. When I come to I'm in bed. I didn't care so much iffen I died.

Charlie Moses, Marion County, Mississippi

Oh Lordy! The way us Niggers was treated was awful. Marster would beat, knock, kick, kill. He done ever'thing 'cept eat us. We was worked to death. We worked all day Sunday, all day, all night. He whipped us 'till some jus' lay down to die. It was a poor life.

If one of his Niggers done something to displease him, which was mos' ever' day, he'd whip him 'till he most die an' then he'd kick him 'round in the dust. He'd even take his gun an' before the Nigger had time to open his mouth, he'd just stan' there an' shoot him down.

Slavery days was bitter an' I can't forget the sufferin'. Oh, God! God Almighty never meant for human beings to be like animals. Us Niggers has a soul an' a heart an' a min'. We aint like a dog or a horse.

Cornelia Andrews, North Carolina

Alex Heath, a slave was beat ter death, hyar in Smithfield. He had stold something, dey tells me, anyhow he was sentenced ter be put ter death, an' de folkses dar in charge 'cided ter beat him ter death. Dey gib him a hundred lashes fer nine mornings an' on de ninth morning he died.

Ferebe Rogers, Baldwin County, Georgia

When dey got ready to beat yo', dey'd strip you stark mother naked and dey'd say, "Come here to me, God damn you! Walk up to dat tree, and damn you, hug dat tree!" Den dey tie yo' hands 'round de tree, den tie yo' feets, den dey'd lay de rawhide on you. Sometimes dey'd rub turpentine and salt in de raw places, and den beat you some mo'. Oh, hit was awful! And what could you do? Dey had all de 'vantage of you.

Cato Carter, Wilcox County, Alabama

Long as I lived I minded what my white folks told me, 'cept one time. They was a nigger workin' in de fiel' an' he kept jerking the mules and Massa got mad, and he gave me a gun and said, "Go out there and kill that man." I said, "Massa, please don't tell me that. I ain't never kilt nobody and I don't want to." He said, "Cato, you do what I tell you." He meant it. I went out to the nigger and said, "You has got to leave this minute, and I is too, 'cause I is 'spose to kill you, only I ain't and Massa will kill me." He drops the ranes and we run and crawled through the fence and ran away. But today I is an old man and my hands ain't stained with no blood. I is allus been glad I didn't kill that man.

George Young, Livingston, Alabama

My brother Harrison ran away an' dey sot de "nigger dogs" on him. Dey didn't run him down till 'bout night but finely dey cotched him, an' de hunters feched him to de mistress do' an' say, "Mary Ann, here' Harrison." Den dey turned de dogs loose on him ag'in, an' sich a screamin' you never hyared. He was all bloody an' Mammy was a-hollerin', "Save him, Lord, save my chile, an' don' let dem dogs eat him up." Mr. Lawler said, "De Lord ain't got nothin' do wid dis here," an' hit sho' look like He didn't, 'caze dem dogs nigh 'bout chewed Harrison up. Dem was hard times, sho' nuff.

I don't see the need to add any words to those I've excerpted. Except to note that the White men whose words defended slavery were traitors to the Union and directly responsible for the deaths—some 600,000 from combat or disease—of their own soldiers, mostly young, simple farmhands and artisans, but also of the mostly young, simple farm hands and artisans in the Union troops, armies that killed each other simply to survive the bloody war they had no voice in declaring. Those who still cling to the misty and mythical nostalgia of the "Lost Cause," and those who still deny that defending slavery was the *only* motivation for the rebellion (high tariffs do not constitute a *casus belli*) need only read the speeches of its White defenders and the recollections of those whose dark skin was the *only* reason for their enslavement to decide whose hands are stained with the blood of millions of innocent fellow humans.

3

"Beings of an Inferior Order"

INTRANSIGENT SOUTHERN POLITICIANS like John Calhoun, Jefferson Davis, and Alexander Stephens pushed back against growing abolitionist sentiment in northern states with threats to dissolve the Union, much as their predecessors had done with threats to walk out of the Constitutional Convention in 1787 if slavery was not given protection in the nation's fundamental charter of government. As an institution, the political system was subject to periodic electoral upheavals, particularly during the fractious early years of sectional strife; the presidential campaigns of John Adams and Thomas Jefferson matched and even exceeded those of recent years, with allegations of "treason" and "mobocracy" hurled against opponents.

But no institution in American society did more to provoke the final rupture in 1860 than the legal system and its judiciary. In this chapter, we'll discuss and demonstrate the power that system exercised over slaves during the antebellum years. The legal system, in fact, has more power than any other institution because its decisions have the force of law and the armed force of the state to enforce them. Other institutions—schools and colleges, private businesses, churches of all denominations, even the political system of elected representatives—must abide by judicial orders. We call this "the rule of law," a term much discussed and debated over the past several years, with its twin guarantees of fairness and equality under attack by "populist" officials at every level of government. But unfairness and inequality have been the inheritance of Black people from slavery. The rule of law has never protected Blacks from the arbitrary rule of the White men in black robes who, until the civil rights revolution of the past century, exercised their power to decide which "persons" deserved equal treatment under the law, regardless of race or status. The justices who sat on the Supreme Court during the antebellum period wielded their unchallengeable power to make such decisions with a hand on the scales of justice that denied all Black people the personhood that would give them equal rights with White people.

Most reasonably well-educated people can—with a bit of prompting—recall the Supreme Court decision in the infamous *Dred Scott* case in 1857. Scott was not, however, the first slave whose bid for freedom was rebuffed by the Supreme Court. Fifteen years before the ruling in his case, in 1842, the Court heard an appeal from Edward Prigg, a professional slave-catcher charged in Pennsylvania with kidnapping Margaret Morgan, who escaped from slavery in Maryland. Prigg's appeal brought to the Court the reach of the Fugitive Slave Act of 1793, in which Congress gave the slaveholding states the enforcement power of that constitutional provision.

The story of Margaret Morgan and her children is a chilling reminder that the Constitution's Framers' inclusion of the fugitive slave clause in the Great Compromise over congressional representation provided slave owners with legal sanction for what was, in fact, kidnapping. Under the prevailing legal standard of "once free, always free," slaves who escaped and reached a free state were no longer enslaved and would have all the rights of White citizens. But if the slave-catchers employed to kidnap and return the escapers to their masters faced no legal constraints on the methods they used, slavery was now a fully national institution.

Despite the primacy of the Fugitive Slave Act over state laws, some of the northern states, pressured by the growing abolitionist movement, enacted laws designed to frustrate the slave-catchers by forcing them to prove the persons they had kidnapped were in fact slaves and the property of the slave owner who paid for their return. Pennsylvania passed what was called a "personal liberty" law in 1826, which placed a greater burden of proof on slave-catchers, forcing them to appear before a state judge to obtain the removal certificate required by federal law, and also giving the fugitives the right to challenge their captivity.

Eleven years passed between enactment of Pennsylvania's law and the first judicial test of its constitutionality. In 1837, a professional slave-catcher named Edward Prigg tracked down Margaret Morgan, seized her and her three children, and brought them before a state judge, seeking a removal certificate to return his captives to slavery. The judge refused to grant the certificate, but Prigg took them back to Maryland anyway, returning them to Margaret Ashmore, who paid him for returning her human property.

Prigg was later indicted in Pennsylvania for kidnapping, tried and convicted in state court, but released pending his appeal to the Supreme Court. The record in *Prigg v. Pennsylvania* suggests that officials in the two states colluded in this case, hoping to resolve the growing conflicts over enforcement of the Fugitive Slave Act. The abolitionist movement had lost support in Pennsylvania, and state officials did not defend their "personal liberty" law with much enthusiasm.

During the Supreme Court arguments in the *Prigg* case, Maryland's lawyers pointed to the Great Compromise in the Constitutional Convention to support their claim that the Framers intended Congress to have exclusive jurisdiction over the "rendition" of escaped slaves to their masters. During the period of confederation, they argued, many northern states allowed no aid to the owners of fugitive slaves, and sometimes they met with open resistance. Faced with this situation, the Framers—and later Congress—turned the whole issue over to federal authority.

On their part, the state's lawyers put up a feeble defense. They "admitted" Maryland's claims that "slaves are not parties to the Constitution" and that " 'we the people' does not embrace them." Pennsylvania only wanted to protect its Black "freemen" from unlawful capture. These "freemen" included a small number of former slaves freed by their masters, and some "free persons of color" who had never been enslaved. The state's lawyers spoke directly to Maryland: "Pennsylvania says: Instead of preventing you from taking your slaves, we are anxious that you should have them; they are a population we do not covet; and all our legislation tends toward giving you every facility to get them; but we do claim the right of legislating upon this subject so as to bring you under legal restraint, which will prevent you from taking a freeman." Pennsylvania did not claim that Margaret Morgan was free on her soil, only that Edward Prigg had not followed the rules for her capture under state law. If he had, the state would not have objected to her return to slavery in Maryland.

Justice Joseph Story, a Massachusetts native who served thirty-three years on the Court, was an opponent of Jacksonian populism and the "oppression" of property rights by legislative majorities. Writing for the Court in 1842, his personal objections to slavery were overcome by adherence to federal power over state laws that limited those powers. In this respect, Story illustrates the willingness of privileged White men to subordinate their sympathy for enslaved fellow humans to the "property rights" of slave owners, members of their own race and class. For Story, the case was simple. Margaret Morgan and her three children—one born in a free state—were slaves in Maryland. The Framers had recognized the lawfulness of slavery in the Constitution, and Congress thus had the right to adopt the Fugitive Slave Act, whose provisions the states must follow. In praising the "courteous and friendly spirit" in which the neighboring states—supposedly adversaries in the case—appeared before the Court, Story expressed his hope that the "agitation on this subject, in both states, would subside, and the conflict of opinion be put at rest." But this was a vain hope, as the conflict over slavery that gripped the nation was mirrored in the Court. Although the justices agreed on striking down Pennsylvania's law, Story's opinion hinted that states were under no obligation to aid the enforcement of the federal law, even though barred from hindering its execution. This suggestion encouraged abolitionists and upset Chief Justice Roger Taney, who argued in a concurring opinion that laws allowing state court judges to interfere with "renditions" stepped on federal toes.

Whether intended or not, Story's hint prompted several northern states to pass laws that prohibited their officials from aiding slave-catchers in any way. Two episodes show not only the reaction to the *Prigg* decision but also the capitulation of state judges to the force of federal enforcement. In the first, a "mulatto" slave in Virginia, George Latimer, whose father was a slave owner, escaped to Boston in 1842 with his pregnant wife (who posed as her light-skin husband's servant). Unfortunately, that same day Latimer was recognized by a friend of his master, James Gray, who reported his find to Gray. Latimer, unaware that he had been spotted, was soon arrested and brought before Justice Story, then on circuit duty in Boston to handle federal district cases. Story ordered him held on a spurious charge of larceny, but abolitionists filed a habeas corpus petition in state court, arguing his detention was unlawful, citing Story's recent *Prigg* opinion and its hint that state officials were not obliged to assist in the rendition of fugitive slaves. The state's chief judge, Lemuel Shaw, ruled that he was bound to follow *Prigg* and ordered Latimer returned to Gray. Crowds of abolitionists and free Blacks tried but failed to "rescue" Latimer from jail, and the public uproar prompted Gray to "sell" him for $400 to a group of abolitionists, who then freed him from both jail and slavery. Responding to a petition with sixty-five thousand signatures, the Massachusetts legislature passed the "Latimer Law," prohibiting state judges and local police from taking any part in the rendition of fugitive slaves. The victory in freeing George Latimer from slavery was tempered, however; had Gray been unwilling to "sell" him, federal officials would have returned him to his master.

Contrary to Justice Story's hopes, his *Prigg* opinion did not end the sectional conflict over slavery; in fact, it placed the federal government even more firmly on the side of slave owners and encouraged their representatives to enact an even more stringent fugitive slave law in 1850, which was enforced with a vengeance. The arrest of Anthony Burns in Boston in May

1854 prompted a massive abolitionist protest. Burns had escaped from slavery in Virginia and was seized by a federal marshal, who held him for his owner. When Burns was taken before a state judge for a rendition hearing, his owner's lawyers argued that the Latimer Act was an unconstitutional intrusion on federal power. After the judge agreed and ordered Burns's rendition to Virginia, federal troops and the state militia trained a cannon on a crowd of twenty thousand that gathered on the Boston Common to protest the decision. William Lloyd Garrison, the nation's leading and most outspoken White abolitionist, seized the moment with a dramatic gesture. Holding up a copy of the Constitution, he denounced it as "A Covenant with Death and an Agreement with Hell." With those incendiary words, he put a torch to the Constitution and burned it to ashes. "So perish all compromises with tyranny!" he cried, echoed by the shouts of the assembled crowd.

* * *

The apotheosis of White Men's Law in casting Black people from the body politic, and virtually from the human race, came in 1857 with the Supreme Court's decision in *Dred Scott v. Sandford*. Before we take a close look at the Court's most infamous case, it's instructive to first look at Dred Scott himself and how he wound up before the Supreme Court and became a chapter in American history books and a lesson plan for high school students. One thing we learn about Scott is that, like most slaves, his identity and history are riddled with historical gaps. This fact tells us a great deal about an institution that robbed its victims not only of rights but often of their names. This was true of Scott, who may have been known simply as "Sam" for most of his life and acquired the name Dred Scott after his sale in 1833 to Dr. John Emerson in St. Louis, Missouri. His previous owner, Peter Blow, arrived in St. Louis from Alabama in 1830 with six slaves, five male and one female. He set up a boardinghouse but died in 1832. After Blow's death, his executor sold two male slaves to settle claims against the estate, one named Sam and the other with no recorded name. No one knows which of these two slaves was purchased by Dr. Emerson, whether Sam became Dred Scott or whether the unnamed slave was in fact named Dred Scott. No one knows for sure when or where Scott was born. He was literally a man without a past, or at least one known to White people. We do know the Blow family remained close to their former slave and supported Scott during his long struggle for freedom. Three months after the Supreme Court ruled in March 1857 that Scott was still a slave, Peter Blow's son Taylor regained title to him and promptly freed him.

But Scott lived only fifteen months as a freeman, working as a hotel porter in St. Louis; he died of consumption in September 1858. He never sought the limelight, although he did talk with several newspaper reporters about his case. One report, published in 1857, described him as "illiterate but not ignorant" and as a person with a "strong common sense." An article in 1858 called him "a small, pleasant looking negro" with an "imperial" beard, wearing a "seedy black suit" and looking "somewhat the worse for wear and tear."

Life imposed a great deal of "wear and tear" on Scott, particularly after Emerson purchased him from the Blows. By all accounts, Emerson was a poor doctor and a chronic malcontent. He finagled a position in 1832 as an army medical officer and was posted in 1834 to Fort Armstrong in the free state of Illinois. Scott—then in his early thirties—accompanied his new owner, who disliked life on the frontier and asked to return to St. Louis for treatment of a "syphiloid" disease. After several rebuffs by the army brass, Emerson finally secured a new post in 1836 when Fort Armstrong was closed. He and Scott moved to Fort Snelling, located in Wisconsin Territory (later renamed Iowa Territory and now part of Minnesota).

These chapters in Scott's life have great significance. Fort Armstrong and Fort Snelling both lay in free territory, north of the line drawn by the Missouri Compromise in 1820. Slavery was illegal in both Illinois and Wisconsin Territory, and Scott could not lawfully be held as a slave in either place. While he lived at Fort Snelling, Scott met Harriet Robinson, a teenage girl, also held as a slave by the resident Indian agent, Major Taliaferro. He either sold Harriet to Emerson or gave her to Scott as a wife; they were married by the major as a local justice of the peace. The Scotts had four children; two sons died in infancy, but two girls—Eliza and Lizzy—grew up and joined their parents' suit for freedom.

Emerson returned to St. Louis in 1837 but in 1840 was ordered to Florida, where the army was engaged in the Seminole War against the Indians, while his wife remained in St. Louis with the Scotts. Perhaps with the assistance of Peter Blow, Dred and Harriet, along with their daughters, filed suit in 1846 in Missouri state court in St. Louis, seeking their freedom. Emerson's wife had earlier moved to New York and had supposedly given the Scotts to her brother, John Sanford, but no records of this "gift" have been found. Nonetheless, Sanford claimed ownership of the family during the eleven years before the Supreme Court ruled on the suits.

Missouri law was on the Scotts' side, at least when they filed their suits. The state's highest court had repeatedly held that masters who took slaves into free territory thereby emancipated them, and that slavery did not reattach when they returned to Missouri. The legal doctrine of that time was "once free, always free," but Dred and Harriet Scott had the misfortune to find their suits caught in the shifting currents of Missouri and national politics. That misfortune stemmed from the snail's pace at which their cases proceeded through the state courts.

Whoever put up the funds for the Scotts' lawsuit picked a prominent lawyer in Samuel Bay, Missouri's former attorney general; John Sanford was defended by an equally prominent lawyer, George Goode, a Virginian with strong pro-slavery views. The two lawyers sparred before a jury in 1847, but the trial became entangled in questions of evidence and procedure, leading the Missouri Supreme Court to order a second trial in January 1850. The Scotts' residences in both Illinois and Wisconsin Territory and the doctrine of "once free, always free," then the prevailing standard in Missouri law, persuaded a jury to find them freed from slavery.

Unfortunately for the Scotts, Sanford's appeal from this verdict was not decided by the state supreme court until 1852. By that time, Missouri voters had placed two new judges on the court; one of them, William Scott (no relation) was a fervent pro-slavery Democrat and convinced his colleagues that they were bound by an 1851 U.S. Supreme Court decision in a case called *Strader v. Graham*. This case involved two slaves in Kentucky who were hired out by their owner as musicians and were allowed to perform in Ohio, a free state. However, the slave musicians skipped a beat in Ohio and kept traveling to Canada, beyond their master's legal reach. He retaliated by suing the Ohio resident who hired them for damages, claiming he had encouraged the slaves to abscond to Canada. Chief Justice Taney wrote for a unanimous Court in dismissing the case for lack of federal jurisdiction. However, Taney took the opportunity to hold that, if the missing slaves had returned to Kentucky— which they never did—their status would have "depended altogether upon the laws of [Kentucky] and could not be influenced by the laws of Ohio." This part of Taney's opinion was what lawyers call "dictum," a statement in an opinion that was not necessary to the decision. But Taney was intent on the judicial burial of the "once free, always free" doctrine.

Having reached the end of the road in Missouri state courts, Scott's lawyers filed a new suit in federal district court in St. Louis, claiming the court had jurisdiction because Scott was a "resident" of Missouri while Sanford, who claimed his ownership, had left Missouri and now resided in New York. Under the so-called diversity clause of the Constitution, federal courts can decide state law suits between "citizens" of different states. Citing the Supreme Court ruling in the *Strader* case, the district judge held in

1854 that, since the Scotts—unlike the slaves in that case—had returned to Missouri from Wisconsin Territory and Illinois, they remained slaves under Missouri law.

After this setback, the Scotts filed an appeal with the Supreme Court; they were now represented by an eminent Washington lawyer, Montgomery Blair, who was opposed by two equally prominent lawyers, Henry Geyer, then a Missouri senator, and Reverdy Johnson, a former senator and attorney general. With this all-star legal lineup, the Supreme Court's small courtroom in the Capitol's basement (it didn't move across the street to its imposing "marble temple" until 1935) was packed during arguments that stretched over six days, with an audience, the press reported, of "many distinguished jurists and members of Congress." (Lawyers are now generally limited to thirty minutes of oral argument, but the Court then allowed advocates like Daniel Webster, who argued more than two hundred cases before the Court, to speak as long as they wished.) No transcript of the arguments was made, but press accounts noted that Blair pointed to numerous state and federal laws that made no distinction between "citizens" and "free inhabitants." Only if the Court accepted this claim would Scott be entitled to bring his freedom suit in federal court, to satisfy the requirement of citizenship in diversity cases. Turning to the provision in the Missouri Compromise of 1820 barring slavery in the nation's territories, Blair argued that Congress had the power under Article IV of the Constitution to "make all needful rules and regulations respecting the territory" of the United States, and that banning slavery in those territories was "needful" to settle the sectional conflicts over slavery. Sanford's lawyers countered that Scott could be a "citizen" of both Missouri and the United States only if he were free, citing *Strader* as precedent for the claim that his residence in Illinois and Wisconsin Territory did not free him and that Missouri law controlled his status. They also argued that banning slavery in the territories was not "needful" legislation, saying it applied only to setting up interim governments, pending their later admission to the Union as states.

Even before the arguments, it would be surprising if Blair held any hope of winning the Scotts' freedom. Chief Justice Taney, who had earlier served under President Andrew Jackson, himself a slave owner, as attorney general, secretary of war, and secretary of the treasury, was born in 1777 to a slave-owning family in Maryland, although he did not own slaves himself. Taney had already made clear in his *Strader* opinion that he considered slavery outside the reach of federal legislation or courts. In addition to Taney, four other justices came from slaveholding states and were unlikely to break with him; two justices from northern states also joined him in concurrence, leaving only Justices John McLean of Ohio and Benjamin Curtis of Massachusetts in dissent.

Three months passed between the oral arguments and the Court's decision, released on March 6, 1857. During this time, all nine justices labored at writing opinions, each (perhaps thinking of posterity) penning his own; when published, they totaled 117,000 words, roughly the length of this book. Then as now, lawyers look first at the majority opinion, which becomes "the law of the case" and can be cited as precedent; concurring and dissenting opinions, although often raising points not addressed in the majority opinion (or disputing them), have no bearing on the Court's decision. In *Dred Scott v. Sandford* (a clerk's misspelling of Sanford's name was never corrected), Taney took the majority opinion for himself, as other chiefs have often done in important and contentious cases, hoping to put their personal stamp on a historic decision.

To help readers better understand the reasoning of Taney's opinion, I have excerpted its most significant portions, following them with some commentary about its logical and factual errors, about which virtually every legal scholar concurs, as well as a brief account of the heated political reactions on both sides that changed the whole course of American history. Readers with an appetite for the complete text of Taney's opinion, or for any of the six concurring and two dissenting opinions, which I have omitted, can easily find them on the internet.

* * *

Dred Scott, Plaintiff in Error, v. John Sandford, Defendant

Mr. Chief Justice TANEY delivered the opinion of the court.
There are two leading questions presented by the record:

1. Had the Circuit Court of the United States jurisdiction to hear and determine the case between these parties? And
2. If it had jurisdiction, is the judgment it has given erroneous or not?

The plaintiff in error [Dred Scott] was, with his wife and children, held as slaves by the defendant in the State of Missouri, and he brought this action in the Circuit Court of the United States for that district to assert the title of himself and his family to freedom. . . .

The defendant pleaded that the plaintiff was not a citizen of the State of Missouri, as alleged in his declaration, being a negro of African descent, whose ancestors were of pure African blood and who were brought into this country and sold as slaves. . . .

The question before us is whether the class of persons described in the plea in abatement [the reply of Sanford's lawyers] compose a portion of this people, and are constituent members of this sovereignty? We think they are not, and that they are not included, and were not intended to be included, under the word "citizens" in the Constitution, and can therefore claim none of the rights and privileges which that instrument provides for and secures to citizens of the United States. On the contrary, they were at that time considered as a subordinate and inferior class of beings who had been subjugated by the dominant race, and, whether emancipated or not, yet remained subject to their authority, and had no rights or privileges but such as those who held the power and the Government might choose to grant them. . . .

The question then arises, whether the provisions of the Constitution, in relation to the personal rights and privileges to which the citizen of a State should be entitled, embraced the negro African race, at that time in this country or who might afterwards be imported, who had then or should afterwards be made free in any State, and to put it in the power of a single State to make him a citizen of the United States and endue him with the full rights of citizenship in every other State without their consent? Does the Constitution act upon him whenever he shall be made free under the laws of a State, and raised there to the rank of a citizen, and immediately clothe him with all the privileges of a citizen in every other State, and in its own courts?

The court think the affirmative of these propositions cannot be maintained. And if it cannot, [Dred Scott] could not be a citizen of the State of Missouri within the meaning of the Constitution of the United States, and, consequently, was not entitled to sue in its courts. . . .

In the opinion of the court, the legislation and histories of the times, and the language used in the Declaration of Independence, show that neither the class of persons who had been imported as slaves nor their descendants, whether they had become free or not, were then acknowledged as a part of the people, nor intended to be included in the general words used in that memorable instrument.

It is difficult at this day to realize the state of public opinion in relation to that unfortunate race which prevailed in the civilized and enlightened portions of the world at the time of the Declaration of Independence and when the Constitution was framed and adopted. But the public history of every European nation displays it in a manner too plain to be mistaken.

They [all Black persons] had for more than a century before been regarded as beings of an inferior order, and altogether unfit to associate with the white race either in social or political relations, and so far inferior that they had no rights which the white man was bound to respect, and that the negro might justly and lawfully be reduced to slavery for his benefit. He was bought and sold, and treated as an ordinary article of merchandise and traffic whenever a profit could be made by it. This opinion was at that time fixed and universal in the civilized portion of the white race. . . .

And in no nation was this opinion more firmly fixed or more uniformly acted upon than by the English Government and English people. They not only seized them on the coast of Africa and sold them or held them in slavery for their own use, but they took them as ordinary articles of merchandise to every country where they could make a profit on them, and were far more extensively engaged in this commerce than any other nation in the world.

The opinion thus entertained and acted upon in England was naturally impressed upon the colonies they founded on this side of the Atlantic. And, accordingly, a negro of the African race was regarded by them as an article of property, and held, and bought and sold as such, in every one of the thirteen colonies which united in the Declaration of Independence and afterwards formed the Constitution of the United States. The legislation of the different colonies furnishes positive and indisputable proof of this fact. They show that a perpetual and impassable barrier was intended to be erected between the white race and the one which they had reduced to slavery, and governed as subjects with absolute and despotic power. . . .

The language of the Declaration of Independence is equally conclusive: It begins by declaring that, "We hold these truths to be self-evident: that all men are created equal; that they are endowed by their Creator with certain unalienable rights; that among them is life, liberty, and the pursuit of happiness; that to secure these rights, Governments are instituted, deriving their just powers from the consent of the governed."

The general words above quoted would seem to embrace the whole human family, and if they were used in a similar instrument at this day would be so understood. But it is too clear for dispute that the enslaved African race were not intended to be included, and formed no part of the people who framed and adopted this declaration. . . .

[T]here are two clauses in the Constitution which point directly and specifically to the negro race as a separate class of persons, and show clearly that they were not regarded as a portion of the people or citizens of the Government then formed. One of these clauses reserves to each of the thirteen States the right to import slaves until the year 1808 if it thinks proper. And the importation which it thus sanctions was unquestionably of persons of the race of which we are speaking, as the traffic in slaves in the United States had always been confined to them. And by the other provision the States pledge themselves to each other to maintain the right of property of the master by delivering up to him any slave who may have escaped from his service, and be found within their respective territories. By the first above-mentioned clause, therefore, the right to purchase and hold this property is directly sanctioned and authorized for twenty years by the people who framed the Constitution. And by the second, they pledge themselves to maintain and uphold the right of the master in the manner specified, as long as the Government they then formed should endure. And these two provisions show conclusively that neither the description of persons therein referred to nor their descendants were embraced in any of the other provisions of the Constitution, for certainly these two clauses were not intended to confer on them or their posterity the blessings of liberty, or any of the personal rights so carefully provided for the citizen.

[Dred Scott] admits that he and his wife were born slaves, but endeavors to make out his title to freedom and citizenship by showing that they were taken by their owner to certain places . . . where slavery could not by law exist, and that they thereby became free, and, upon their return to Missouri, became citizens of that State.

Now if the removal of which he speaks did not give them their freedom, then, by his own admission, he is still a slave, and whatever opinions may be entertained in favor of the citizenship of a free person of the African race, no one supposes that a slave is a citizen of the State or of the United States. If, therefore, the acts done by his owner did not make them free persons, he is still a slave, and certainly incapable of suing in the character of a citizen. . . .

In considering this part of the controversy, two questions arise: 1. Was he, together with his family, free in Missouri by reason of the stay in the territory of the United States hereinbefore mentioned [referring to what was then called the Wisconsin Territory]? And 2. If they were not, is Scott himself free by reason of his removal to Rock Island, in the State of Illinois, as stated in the above admissions?

We proceed to examine the first question. The act of Congress [the Missouri Compromise] upon which the plaintiff relies declares that slavery and involuntary servitude, except as a punishment for crime, shall be forever prohibited in all that part of the territory ceded by France, under the name of Louisiana. . . . And the difficulty which meets us at the threshold of this part of the inquiry is whether Congress was authorized to pass this law under any of the powers granted to it by the Constitution; for if the authority is not given by that instrument, it is the duty of this court to declare it void and inoperative, and incapable of conferring freedom upon anyone who is held as a slave under the laws of any one of the States. . . .

Upon these considerations, it is the opinion of the court that the act of Congress which prohibited a citizen from holding and owning property of this kind in the territory of the United States north of the line therein mentioned is not warranted by the Constitution, and is therefore void, and that neither Dred Scott himself nor any of his family were made free by being carried into this territory, even if they had been carried there by the owner with the intention of becoming a permanent resident.

Upon the whole, therefore, it is the judgment of this court that it appears by the record before us that [Dred Scott] is not a citizen of Missouri in the sense in which that word is used in the Constitution, and that the Circuit Court of the United States, for that reason, had no jurisdiction in the case, and could give no judgment in it. Its judgment for the defendant must, consequently, be reversed, and a mandate issued directing the suit to be dismissed for want of jurisdiction.

* * *

Historians and legal scholars have uniformly denounced the *Dred Scott* decision as the worst in the Court's long history. And it is, simply for the fact of callously describing all Blacks—including those free by purchase, manumission, or birth in free states—as "beings of an inferior order" and possessed of "no rights which the white man is bound to respect." These are the rankest forms of racism and a denial of the common humanity of all persons.

But it's worth pointing out the flaws in logic and fact that also permeated Taney's opinion. First, he bypassed the issue of whether state and national citizenship were the same. The Constitution provides that federal courts can decide suits between "citizens of different states," with no requirement of national citizenship. But the chief justice wanted to avoid two damaging facts; first, that the Constitution did not exclude free Blacks from either state or national citizenship; second, that several states—before and after the Constitution was ratified—allowed free Blacks to vote and exercise other political rights. In providing for the apportionment of House seats in Article I, the Framers distinguished between "free persons" and "all other persons"— their euphemism for slaves—in the three-fifths clause. The term "free persons" clearly included free Blacks, who were counted equally with Whites in apportioning House seats. Every state had free Blacks in 1787, even though most states imposed some legal disabilities on them. Taney seized on this latter fact to argue that the Framers did not mean to confer national citizenship on any Blacks. He reached this conclusion through the back door. Taney first claimed that the Framers did not consider Blacks—free or slave—as "persons," let alone as citizens. His asserted evidence for this dubious claim rested on a highly distorted reading of European and colonial history. He first conceded that "every person" who was considered a state citizen by the Framers became also "citizens of this new political body," the United States. "It becomes necessary," he continued, "to determine who were citizens of the several states when the Constitution was adopted." On this question, Taney looked for guidance not to the states that adopted Articles of Confederation but to "every European nation" of the colonial era. His shift of geographic focus reflected the fact that he found little support for his argument in the laws of the confederated states, several of which conferred political rights on free Blacks. So he looked instead to the "state of public opinion in the European nations" when the Constitution was framed and adopted. Taney could not point to any concrete evidence on this issue. He simply reflected the racial attitudes of his time and of his class of privileged White men.

Taney's claim that excluding Blacks from citizenship was the "fixed and universal opinion of the civilized portion of the white race" was flatly untrue.

In his influential *Commentaries on the Laws of England*, which the Supreme Court had often cited with respect, Sir William Blackstone wrote that "a slave or negro, the instant he lands in England, becomes a free man," with all the rights of English citizenship. Long before the *Dred Scott* opinion, Blackstone had refuted every claim Taney made about the citizenship status of Blacks in England, where slavery had been outlawed by Parliament in 1833, a fact Taney failed to acknowledge.

When Taney turned to the fourth and final question he had posed, that of Scott's alleged "reversion" to slavery, he first addressed at great length the issue of his residence in Wisconsin territory, even though Scott's two years in Illinois came earlier in time. The reason for this chronological reversal explains why Taney devoted just one page of his opinion to the Illinois question. "Our notice of this part of the case will be very brief," Taney explained, because Scott had not asked the Supreme Court to review the decision of the Missouri court. Even if he had, Taney wrote, "it is too plain for argument that the [case] must have been dismissed for want of jurisdiction in this court." And why did the Supreme Court lack jurisdiction? Because it had ruled, in deciding that the Missouri Compromise was unconstitutional and that consequently Scott's residence in Wisconsin Territory did not free him from slavery, that he was not a "citizen" of the United States. And how did that ruling affect his claim that residence in Illinois granted him freedom in Missouri? Because it barred him from raising such a claim in any court, state or federal. If this sounds like a classic catch-22 situation, it is. By ruling first on the territorial question, Taney closed the door on Scott's claim under state law, which had arisen first in time. Because the lower federal court had allowed Scott to proceed under the "diversity of citizenship" clause, it became necessary for Taney to reverse this holding before he dealt with the state law claim. Had he dealt with the issues in chronological order, Taney would have faced the more difficult task of arguing that Scott lacked standing to bring suit in state court. But these flaws in Taney's opinion had no effect on its outcome: Dred Scott, his wife, Harriet, and their daughters, Eliza and Lizzie, remained in slavery. Not only that, but Taney also stripped all free Blacks, even those born free, of their citizenship. No Black was even a "person" under the law, but simply "an article of merchandise" to be bought and sold "whenever a profit can be made by it." We recoil today at those heartless words, but for Taney and men of his class, profit from their human property was more important than any appeal to the egalitarian principle that "all men are created equal" because, in their view, no Black person was even a person.

* * *

In retrospect, it seems clear that the pro-slavery extremism of Chief Justice Taney doomed his cause to ultimate defeat. Most important, his assertion in *Dred Scott* that states which prohibited slavery nonetheless had to recognize the right of slave owners to bring their "property" into those states came close—some thought got all the way—to ruling that slavery was lawful wherever slaves resided. In that case, the charge that Taney intended to "nationalize" slavery had force, and his opinion touched off an explosive reaction on both sides of the slavery issue.

Republicans in the press and Congress denounced the ruling in heated terms: Horace Greeley's newspaper, the *New York Tribune*, hurled invective at Taney's "mean and skulking cowardice" and the "detestable hypocrisy" of his opinion. On the other side, defenders of slavery exulted. "Southern opinion on the subject of southern slavery is now the supreme law of the land," trumpeted the *Constitutionalist* of Augusta, Georgia, "and opposition to southern opinion on this subject is now opposition to the Constitution, and morally treason against the Government."

The most dramatic consequences of Taney's ruling, and the one most Americans recall from history lessons, came in the face-to-face debates between Abraham Lincoln and Stephen Douglas in 1858, when the two men campaigned across Illinois for the Senate seat Douglas then held. Douglas tried to distance himself from Taney's effort to "nationalize" slavery by advocating "popular sovereignty" on slavery in the territories, letting the voters in each territory decide the question. Ironically, six months before the *Dred Scott* ruling, Lincoln had spoken for Republicans in telling Democrats that the Supreme Court was the body charged with deciding the issue of slavery in the territories, adding, "[W]e will submit to its decisions; and if you do also, there will be an end to the matter." Shortly after the ruling, however, Lincoln changed his tune and claimed, "[T]he *Dred Scott* decision is erroneous. We know the court that made it has often overruled its own decisions, and we shall do what we can to have it overrule this. We offer no resistance to it." From a pragmatic view, of course, the Court was not going to overrule itself so long as Taney remained as its chief, and any resistance to the decision was limited to denunciatory speeches and writings.

One of the greatest ironies in American history is that Taney, in effect, handed Lincoln the presidency in 1860. Although the Illinois legislature chose Douglas over Lincoln for the Senate seat in 1858, Lincoln's performance in his debates with Douglas made him a leading candidate for the Republican presidential nomination. And Douglas, by endorsing "popular sovereignty" over slavery in the territories, lost the support of the southern Democrats who controlled that party. They were so hostile to Douglas that a rump group of pro-slavery Democrats bolted the convention that nominated him to oppose Lincoln and held their own convention, picking Vice President John Breckinridge as the second Democratic nominee. A fourth candidate was former Tennessee senator John Bell of the one-election Constitutional Union Party, which waffled on slavery. Even with four candidates in the race, the presidential campaign of 1860 had none of the drama or suspense of the Senate contest between Lincoln and Douglas. With the Democrats fatally split, Lincoln won easily even without being on the ballot in ten slave states. Although he received less than 40 percent of the popular vote, he garnered 60 percent of the electoral votes, winning eighteen northern states. Breckinridge won eleven southern states, and Bell took three border states. Douglas, even with almost 30 percent of the national vote, won only Missouri. Had Douglas been his only opponent, Lincoln would most likely have lost both the popular and electoral votes. Such are the vicissitudes of history. And Roger Taney was largely responsible for the internecine Democratic battle, as his effort to "nationalize" slavery in *Dred Scott* split the party between its "hard" and "soft" factions.

Speaking to a massive crowd at the Capitol for his inauguration, Lincoln delivered a pointed rebuke to Taney. With the chief justice sitting uncomfortably behind him, Lincoln spoke critically of the Court, asserting, "[I]f the policy of the government, upon vital questions affecting the whole people, is to be irrevocably fixed by decisions of the Supreme Court . . . the people will have ceased to be their own rulers, having to that extent practically resigned their government into the hands of that eminent tribune."

Roger Taney remained on the Court until his death in 1864, increasingly feeble but dependent on his salary to support two daughters. Few mourned his passing. One critic wrote that he "ha[d] earned the gratitude of his country by dying at last. Better late than never." Professing charity in its judgment, the *New York Times* concluded that Taney's *Dred Scott* opinion had been "an act of supreme folly" and asserted that "its shadow will ever rest on his memory." Lincoln had predicted that "an explosion" would inevitably follow Taney's opinion. Five weeks after his inauguration, on April 12, 1861, Confederate forces shelled Fort Sumter. The Civil War had begun. Dred Scott bears no responsibility for that tragedy, but Chief Justice Taney bears much.

Before we canonize Lincoln, however, it bears noting that during his debates with Douglas, he expressed views that today would sound reprehensible and a disqualification for high office:

I am not, nor ever have been, in favor of bringing about in any way the
social and political equality of the white and black races. . . . I am not,
nor ever have been, in favor of making voters or jurors of Negroes, nor
of qualifying them to hold office, nor to intermarry with white people;
and I will say in addition to this that there is a physical difference between the white and black races which I believe will forever forbid the
two races from living together on terms of social and political equality.
And inasmuch as they cannot so live, while they do remain together
there must be a position of superior and inferior, and I as much as any
other man am in favor of having the superior position assigned to the
white race.

But, just as we consider slave owners like Washington and Jefferson to have,
nonetheless, achieved great things for the nation, we should recall that
Lincoln changed his views, at least to the extent of extending to Blacks the
right to vote and hold office. It was this radical position, later adopted by the
Radical Republicans, that pushed through Congress the three constitutional
amendments that formally ended slavery, made Blacks citizens with equal
rights under the law, and gave them (only men at the time) the franchise.
In the next chapter, we'll hear arguments for and against these amendments
and examine the short-lived period of Reconstruction they made possible.
We won't discuss the war itself, except to note that slaves in the Confederate
states could hardly have supported the efforts of their masters to keep them
in bondage.

4

"Fighting for White Supremacy"

THE NEWLY FREED slaves responded to the news of their emancipation with great emotion. "After surrender, I can remember the negroes were so happy," recalled Hamp Santee, who had been enslaved in Mississippi. "They just rang bells, blowed horns and shouted like they were crazy. Then they brought a brand-new rope, and cut it up into little pieces and they gave everyone a little piece and whenever they look at the rope they should remember that they were free from bondage." To Lafayette Price of Morgan County, Alabama, the jubilation of emancipation meant "I'm free as a frog because a frog has freedom to jump where and when he please." Yet many newly freed slaves realized that this was a time of great uncertainty and danger. To W. L. Bost, freedom meant being "just like a turtle," cautiously peeking out of its shell to "understand the lay of the land." The recently freed Jenny Webb captured the essence of the problem as she told historians years later, "[W]hen the war came on to set us free, we was told that we would get 40 acres and a mule. We never did." Perhaps the most poignant response came from Harriet Tubman, who guided dozens of escaped slaves to freedom on the perilous Underground Railroad that ran from the South to slavery-free northern states and even to Canada: "I had crossed the line. I was free, but there was no one to welcome me to the land of freedom. I was a stranger in a strange land."

And who would extend a helping hand and welcome these strangers to the land of freedom? For a brief period, they were White men in Washington.

* * *

During the twelve years between 1865 and 1877, the White men who made the nation's laws faced the monumental task of "reconstructing" a Union that had come perilously close to total demolition. It was a task undertaken with a sense of urgency; the Confederacy had been defeated, but the newly freed slaves, some 4 million in number, were ill-equipped to deal with freedom. With few exceptions, they were poor, illiterate, and unskilled at any work other than plantation labor. They faced twin barriers in their struggle to escape from a century and a half of bondage: first, to gain the education and skills that would allow them to earn enough to support their families, and second, to gain a voice in the bodies—local, state, and national—that made the laws and allocated public funds for schools, roads, and "poor relief" for those who had no other way to survive.

With northern Republicans in control of both the House and the Senate, Congress took the first necessary step toward banishing slavery from the Constitution by adopting the Thirteenth Amendment, which was short and simple: "Neither slavery nor involuntary servitude, except as a punishment for crime whereof the party shall have been duly convicted, shall exist in the United States, or any place subject to their jurisdiction." Section 2 of the amendment provided that "Congress shall have power to enforce this article by appropriate legislation."

But the political struggle to abolish slavery through constitutional amendment was neither short nor simple. In fact, after the Senate approved this article in 1864, President Abraham Lincoln and Republican leaders could not secure the necessary two-thirds vote for adoption in the House. Lincoln even resorted to arm-twisting and threats to recalcitrant House members, warning John Alley of Massachusetts, "I am the President of the United States, clothed with immense power, and I expect you to secure those votes." Not until Lincoln won his second term and Radical Republicans picked up congressional seats in 1864 did the House narrowly approve the amendment, 119 to 56. The switch of three votes would have blocked the abolition of slavery once more. The final House tally on January 31, 1865, ignited wild cheering in the galleries, while congressmen "joined in the shouting" and wept openly in relief and joy. The next day, President Lincoln signed a resolution that submitted the amendment to the state legislatures for ratification.

Lincoln celebrated the congressional victory on April 11, 1865, speaking from a White House window to a throng gathered outside. He spoke at length of "the constitutional amendment recently passed by Congress, abolishing slavery throughout the nation." He praised the former Confederate state of Louisiana for being the first to ratify the amendment and for "giving the benefit of public schools equally to black and white, and empowering the legislature to confer the elective franchise upon the colored man." (He had earlier, however, privately suggested to the state's governor that Black voting be limited to "the very intelligent, and especially those who have fought gallantly in our ranks.") Tragically, these words cost Lincoln his life. Among the crowd of supporters, both Black and White, was an actor named John Wilkes Booth, who became so enraged at Lincoln's support of voting by former slaves that he vowed the president would never make another speech. Three nights later, on April 14, as Lincoln and his wife attended a play at Ford's Theater in Washington, Booth entered the president's box, which was not guarded, and shot him in the head with a pistol. Leaping from the box onto the stage, Booth shouted, "Sic semper tyrannis!" (Thus always to tyrants!) and fled the theater. He was later tracked down and shot. Lincoln died the next day, a martyr to the Constitution whose protections he had worked to extend to all Americans, White and Black, even with political reservations to avoid once again inciting the former Confederates.

Lincoln's death, so soon after the Union victory, badly damaged the reconstruction program he had labored to fashion over the preceding months. His successor, Vice President Andrew Johnson of Tennessee, was a former Democrat and slave owner who had served in both houses of Congress and as his state's governor. Despite his electoral success and his prowess as a forceful stump speaker, Johnson had few of Lincoln's political skills or forensic talents. He was crude and intemperate in speech and habits, and prone to losing his temper when confronted by hecklers. He owed his place on the Republican ticket largely to his residence in one of the border states in which Lincoln was unpopular. Johnson's unwillingness to support the reconstruction program, leading him to fire Secretary of War Edwin Stanton, who opposed Johnson's appeasement of the South—including his pardons of former Confederate officials—prompted Johnson's impeachment in 1868. He was saved from removal from office by a single vote in the Senate.

With Johnson in the White House, congressional Republicans felt a need to further protect the former slaves from presidential hostility to their plight by cementing those protections in the Constitution. Led by Representative John Bingham of Ohio, a longtime abolitionist, the House—after heated debate on both sides—adopted the Fourteenth Amendment, without doubt the most powerful guarantor of civil rights in the Constitution since its adoption in 1868. Its heart, and its teeth, are contained in its first section: "All persons born or naturalized in the United States, and subject to the jurisdiction thereof, are citizens of the United States and of the State wherein they reside. No state shall make or enforce any law which shall abridge the privileges or immunities of citizens of the United States; nor shall any State deprive

any person of life, liberty, or property, without due process of law; nor deny
to any person within its jurisdiction the equal protection of the laws." With
the twenty-eight words of its first sentence, the amendment overturned and
wiped away the blatant racism of Chief Justice Roger Taney's infamous *Dred
Scott* ruling that no Black person—free or slave—could be a citizen of the
country in which they were born and had "no rights that a white man was
bound to respect." Like the Thirteenth Amendment, Congress was authorized to enact "appropriate legislation" to enforce the new provisions.

Congressional adoption of the Fourteenth Amendment did not guarantee that it would become part of the Constitution; ratification by three-
fourths of the state legislatures was still necessary. The question was, which
states? Could the former Confederate states block the amendment? Could
their readmission to the Union be conditioned on ratification? At the time
Congress adopted the amendment, the union included thirty-six states; the
refusal of ten to ratify the amendment would create another political crisis.
Sentiment in the White South was "very unanimous against adopting the
amendment," observed an Alabama editor. To make matters worse, President
Johnson openly campaigned against ratification.

Among the former Confederate states, only Tennessee ratified the
Fourteenth Amendment. But the Radicals turned the 1866 congressional
elections into a referendum on ratification. Public sentiment in the North became almost as unanimous in support as the opposition in the South. "Rarely
in American politics," observed the *New York Times*, had elections been fought
"with so exclusive reference to a single issue." Even moderate Republicans
scrambled onto the bandwagon. "If I was ever Conservative, I am Radical
now," avowed one California congressman. The Congress that convened in
December 1866 had more than enough Radicals to override any presidential veto of its reconstruction measures. They quickly moved to depose the
all-White state governments that President Johnson had installed, replacing
them with military rule. As conditions for readmission to the Union, southern
states were required to hold conventions and write new constitutions. Each
state had to provide the ballot to all males—White and Black—and ratify the
amendment before electing members of Congress. Since Congress had denied
voting rights to most Confederate army veterans and officials, Black voters
formed a substantial majority in several states. The law provided that military
commanders would register voters and conduct elections. This was, pure and
simple, government at gunpoint. But the southern states had, in fact, invited
their own destruction by refusing to ratify the Fourteenth Amendment. After

the "reconstructed" southern legislatures voted for ratification, the amendment finally became part of the Constitution on July 9, 1868.

Protected by federal troops, Blacks voted in large numbers during the early years of Reconstruction. Turnouts ranged from 70 to 90 percent of eligible Black voters in the southern states. In elections to state conventions, Blacks not only voted but won seats in all ten occupied states, including a majority in South Carolina and Louisiana and nearly 40 percent in Florida. More than half of the 265 Black delegates to state conventions later gained election to state legislatures, and sixteen Blacks served in Congress, including two Mississippi senators, Hiram Revels and Blanche Bruce, elected by the majority-Black legislature.

However, the former Confederates who controlled southern governments resorted to violence to prevent Blacks from voting. Many of them belonged to the Ku Klux Klan, founded in 1866 as a social club in Pulaski, Tennessee. By 1870 the Klan had spread across the South and imposed a reign of terror on Blacks and their White supporters. A few examples, selected from congressional testimony on Klan violence, will illustrate this bloody record. Jack Dupree, a Black leader in Monroe County, Mississippi, known as a man who "would speak his mind," was disemboweled in front of his wife, who had just given birth to twins. In October 1870, armed Whites attacked a Republican rally in Greene County, Alabama, killing four Blacks and wounding fifty-four. That same month, after a Republican election victory in Laurens County, South Carolina, Klansmen held a "Negro chase" that ended with thirteen murders.

Confronted with wholesale slaughter across the South, Republicans in Congress decided to patch a gaping hole in the Fourteenth Amendment, which contained no protection against the intimidation of Black voters, by adopting the Fifteenth Amendment in February 1869. Like the Thirteenth Amendment abolishing slavery, this addition to the Constitution was short and simple in wording: "The right of citizens of the United States to vote shall not be denied or abridged by the United States or by any state on account of race, color, or previous condition of servitude." Like the two earlier Reconstruction amendments, the Fifteenth provided that "Congress shall have power to enforce this article by appropriate legislation." Final ratification came on February 3, 1870, a year marked by escalating violence against Blacks who dared to exercise their new electoral rights. In response, Congress utilized the powers granted by the Reconstruction amendments with three Enforcement Acts, passed in 1870 and 1871; the most important, known as the Ku Klux Klan Act, was aimed at the hooded marauders who terrorized Blacks across the South. The law provided that "if two or more persons shall band or conspire together, or go in disguise upon the public highway" with an intent to "injure, oppress, threaten, or intimidate any citizen" or to "hinder his free exercise of any right or privilege granted or secured to him by the constitution or laws of the United States," violators could be prosecuted in federal court and imprisoned for ten years.

For a short time, federal officials and courts did enforce the Klan Act against the white-hooded nightriders who terrorized Blacks, especially those who spoke out against unfair practices by White landowners who cheated their Black tenants and sharecroppers and kept them in perpetual debt. Simply voicing their complaints often provoked a nighttime visit by Klansmen on horseback, warning "uppity" Blacks to keep quiet or suffer grave consequences, from whipping to lynching. Some courageous Blacks reported this intimidation to federal officials, and some showed even more courage in testifying against Klansmen in court. One who did, a little girl, was Anna Baker, who grew up on a tenant farm near Tuscaloosa, Alabama. Her stepfather had aroused the wrath of Whites by warning other tenants to watch carefully when Whites were weighing cotton at the gins; some Black farmers couldn't read—or even see—the figures on the scales and were being short-weighted and paid less than they deserved. Decades later, Anna recounted the scary night the Klansmen showed up, demanding that her stepfather come out to face them:

> I know 'bout dem Kloo Kluxes. I had to go to court one time to testify 'bout 'em. One night after us had moved to Tuscaloosa dey come after my step-daddy. Dey was 'bout ten white mens on hosses, and dey was wearin' dere white hoods wid holes for dere eyes, but I could hear dere voices and reco'nize who dey was. Whilst my ma an' de res' went an' hid I went to de door. I warnt scared. I says, "Marster Will, aint dat you?" He say, "Sho, it's me. Whar's yo' daddy?" I tol' him dat he's gone to town. Den day head out for 'im. In de meantime my ma she had started out, too. She warned him to hide, so dey didn' git 'im. Soon after dat de Yankees hel' a trial in Tuscaloosa. Dey carried me in. A man hel' me up an' made me p'int out who it was dat come to our house. I say, "Dat's de man, ain't it Marster Will?" He coudn' say "No," 'cause he'd tol' me twas him dat night. Dey put 'em in jail for six months an' give 'em a big fine.

Although agents of the Freedmen's Bureau collected hundreds of often harrowing accounts of Klan intimidation and violence, many Blacks heeded the warnings to stay "in their place" and never reported the nightriders to federal authorities; the likely consequences of doing that far outweighed any satisfaction from testifying against them in court. Years of living in slavery had left newly freed Blacks still fearful of their former owners. Even so, most looked forward to a better life under federal protection and support as Reconstruction began.

* * *

Even before the Civil War ended, Congress responded to the great needs of southern Blacks by enacting the Freedmen's Bureau Act, designed to provide "provisions, clothing, and fuel ... for the immediate and temporary shelter and supply of destitute and suffering refugees and freedmen and their wives and children." Passed on March 3, 1865, the law established the Freedmen's Bureau (its official name was the Bureau of Refugees, Freedmen, and Abandoned Lands) as part of the War Department, administered by Union general Oliver O. Howard (historically Black Howard University in Washington, D.C., is named after him); the army was the only federal agency with the staff and resources to provide this aid, and thousands of Union troops were dispatched to southern states, not only to help with relief efforts but also to protect Blacks from hostile and increasingly violent Whites.

Perhaps the most significant program of the Bureau was setting up and staffing schools for Black children, most of whom had never set foot in a school. Along with the constant and daily struggle to house, feed, and clothe their families, the freedmen were determined to give their children something they never had as slaves: an education that would give them the tools they would need to participate as equals with Whites in the social, economic, and political systems from which slaves had been barred. The most important of these tools were reading, writing, and arithmetic. But equality with Whites in these basic skills could not be achieved quickly, given the huge gap in literacy between the races at the time slavery was abolished. The width of this gap was measured by the national census in 1870, the first in which previously enslaved Blacks were recorded by name and asked the same questions as Whites. In that year, 89 percent of Whites over fourteen indicated that they could read and write, although they were not asked how many years of schooling they had had. In stark contrast, only 20 percent of Blacks—most of them younger—claimed to be literate. Not until 1940, in fact, did the literacy rate among Blacks reach that of Whites in 1870; it took seventy years just to erase that gap, years during which Blacks were consigned to inferior, segregated schools, many of them closed for several months each year during "cotton-picking time."

Despite these barriers to education, the early years of Reconstruction gave Blacks an opportunity to provide their children with at least a basic education. Protected by federal troops, and with most former Confederates now barred from voting—an ironic twist of status—the former slaves flocked to the ballot boxes and elected delegates to conventions that rewrote the constitutions of the southern states. Several of these constitutions provided for systems of free public education, and Black children began attending school in large numbers. In Mississippi, for example, the legislature—controlled by Black members and their White Republican allies—established a school system in 1870 that enrolled 127,000 Black children the following year, 39 percent of the school-age Black population. Even under Reconstruction and Black rule, however, Mississippi's public schools were segregated, because White parents refused to pay taxes for integrated schools. Exactly a century passed before the first Black child in Mississippi attended school with Whites. But not all southern states kept Black and White children apart. The South Carolina constitution, written by Black legislators and a handful of White allies, required that all schools be racially mixed, and Black and White children attended classes together in many communities. The state also established an integrated teachers college, which trained many Black teachers. Other southern states, however, experienced serious problems with public education; even in states that funded Black schools, the lack of qualified Black teachers made it difficult to maintain academic standards.

The Reconstruction schools were largely staffed by White teachers from the North, most of whom were young women who had never been to the South and were treated with scorn and outright hostility by many Whites. One female teacher in northern Virginia, just across the Potomac River from the nation's capital, abandoned her job after being shunned by every White person in the community. "If you are mean enough to teach niggers," one told her, "you may eat and sleep with them." Male teachers were a small minority, but they became targets for threats. One teacher in Alabama received this anonymous and barely literate warning:

You have set up a nigger school in the settlement which we will not allow you to teach if you was a full blooded negro we would have nothing to say but a white skin negro is more than we can stand you can dismiss the school immediately or prepar [*sic*] yourself to travail we will give you a chance to save yourself and you had better move instanter.

Teachers who ignored the hostility and threats often lost their schools to violence. Black schools were burned and pillaged throughout the South. Seven schools were burned in Georgia in 1866; three were burned that year in Texas. A school in Orangeburg, South Carolina, was fired into; the Black school in Hardinsburg, Kentucky, was blown up on Christmas Eve in 1867. Yet despite the efforts to drive them from the South, the vast majority of the Freedmen's Bureau teachers stuck with their schools and their Black students.

By 1870, more than 9,000 teachers were instructing some 200,000 Black children, about 12 percent of the school-age population. Northern missionary groups also sent teachers into southern states, and Black churches set up schools for their children. All together, these public and private groups offered schooling to perhaps one of every five Black children in the South, which meant that four out of five Black children received no education at all during the Reconstruction period and remained illiterate, as their parents had during slavery.

Even the most sensitive and understanding teachers encountered problems that stemmed from the reality of Black life and culture in the rural South. The learning of Black children was clearly hindered by the fact that their illiterate parents could not help their children with lessons. Cut off from the written word, southern Blacks had retained the oral traditions of their African roots, which they adapted to their churches and communities, in which everyone joins in calling out verses and children's rhymes. Most teachers in Reconstruction schools reported that students in the early grades were quick to learn the alphabet, numbers, spelling of simple words, and the rote memorization of short poems and Bible passages, a reflection of this oral culture. Even in crowded classrooms, children enjoyed chanting in unison as they went through their lessons. One teacher in Virginia wrote, "[I]nstruction is necessarily mostly oral, as much time would be lost if we trained pupils singly. The little things gave us almost undivided attention, and are much stimulated by recitations in concert."

There were additional barriers to effective learning that came from outside the schoolhouse. The need for Black children to plant, hoe, and harvest crops cut weeks and even months from already short school years; many children lived miles from school and could not walk on the dirt roads the rain turned to deep mud; children got sick or injured and had no medical care; and because hostile Whites sometimes ran teachers out of town or burned schools, even when children arrived at school it was not always staffed or even standing. What is remarkable about the Reconstruction period is not that so few Black children got so little good education, but that teachers and students alike persevered in the face of such enormous odds. It is also a testament to their faith in the liberating power of education that Black parents—most of them illiterate themselves—worked hard to build schools, raise money for books and teachers, and give their children the desire to learn. One former slave, Charles Whiteside, was told by his master that he would remain in slavery "'cause you got no education, and education is what makes a man free." This remark spurred Whitehead's determination that each of his thirteen children would attend school, no matter how long and hard he would have to work. "It was all worth the labor to make them free," he said.

Nonetheless, despite the good intentions of their teachers, only a small minority of Black children received any schooling during Reconstruction. Those who did, however, rarely attended schools that went past the elementary grades, and were often taught by older children themselves. And, considering that millions of Black children were consigned to "separate and unequal" schools during the Jim Crow period and that the Supreme Court ruling in *Brown v. Board of Education* in 1954 sparked the "White flight" backlash of the 1960s and 1970s, leaving most urban Black kids in resegregated schools, it's not surprising that many of them lack the skills for all but menial, low-wage jobs. In this respect, systemic racism in education is linked to the systemic racism of the economic system and is, in fact, necessary for its functioning.

* * *

A major premise of this book is that, for most of the nation's history, White men made the laws and White men wielded the power as judges to uphold or strike down laws, depending on their reading of the Constitution. We have been through times when lawmakers enacted laws to expand and protect the rights of citizens, only to have them invalidated by conservative judges; the years of President Franklin D. Roosevelt and his New Deal program are one example, as the "Nine Old Men" on the Supreme Court tossed out the laws Congress passed to pull the country out of the Great Depression. At other times, liberal judges and justices have struck down laws passed by conservatives to cut back or eliminate the rights of citizens, especially racial and religious minorities; the Supreme Court under Chief Justice Earl Warren in the 1950s and 1960s was both praised and excoriated for its liberal rulings.

The Reconstruction years provide a sobering example of the first of these conflicts, pitting liberal (in this case, Radical) legislators against conservative (in this case, racist) Supreme Court justices. The outcome of the most significant case during this period was a disaster for recently freed Blacks in the South, stripping them of federal enforcement of their newly gained right to vote.

The Supreme Court's 1876 decision in *United States v. Cruikshank*, striking down the Enforcement Acts that were based on the Reconstruction amendments, illustrates the Court's refusal to hold White terrorists to account for the murders of hundreds of Black voters. This case began in 1873 with a massacre in the small town of Colfax, Louisiana, the county seat of Grant Parish, in the state's north-central region. (The state's parishes are comparable to other states' counties.) An election dispute between White Democrats and Black Republicans escalated into violence and turned into "the bloodiest single instance of racial carnage in the Reconstruction era," wrote Eric Foner, that period's leading historian. Black voters who feared that Whites planned to seize the parish government and evict the newly elected Republican sheriff and other parish officials, gathered at the courthouse, a thatch-roofed building that had been a horse barn, digging trenches around it and drilling with shotguns. They were assembled by the sheriff and deputized as a posse to protect the courthouse. At noon on Easter Sunday, April 13, 1873, after three weeks of sporadic gunfire, a band of 100 Whites on horseback, led by Christopher Columbus Nash, a Confederate veteran and Union prisoner of war who had been defeated in the 1872 election for Grant Parish sheriff, surrounded the courthouse and demanded that the Blacks inside leave and disperse, but none complied. Armed with rifles and a Civil War cannon, Nash's troops then blasted the courthouse; they failed to dislodge the Blacks inside, who returned the cannon and rifle fire with shotguns and some pistols. During the lopsided exchange, three of the White attackers—Stephen Parrish, James Hadnot, and Sidney Harris—were killed, although most likely by friendly fire from their compatriots, since they were shot in the back. Nash's troops then seized a Black man outside the building, handed him a burning torch and threatened him with death if he failed to set the thatched roof ablaze, which he did. With fire raging, the Blacks inside the courthouse poured out, waving a white flag of surrender. Some died in the fire; others were shot as they tried to surrender or were hunted down and shot as they sought to escape into surrounding woods. That evening, after hours of drinking, William Cruikshank and other terrorists shot fifty Black prisoners in the back of their heads; only one, Levi Nelson, survived and crawled into the woods to escape. The Whites threw the bodies of many victims into the Red River, close to the courthouse; no one knows how many bodies were washed away into watery graves. The death toll from the massacre remains in dispute; Foner wrote that "some fifty blacks" died, while a Black Louisiana legislator who visited the scene after federal troops arrived from New Orleans to protect surviving Blacks, mostly women and children, stated that "when the sun went down that night, it went down on the corpses of two hundred and eighty negroes." Whatever the true number, there is no dispute that White racists had turned the Colfax courthouse into a human slaughterhouse.

Following the massacre, Nash helped to organize a terrorist group called the White League (or White Men's League). Made up largely by Confederate veterans, chapters of the League pressured Black Republican officeholders in Louisiana to resign their posts and murdered dozens who refused these demands. Historians have estimated that, during the three years following the Colfax Massacre, at least two thousand Blacks were killed in the state by White League vigilantes and sympathizers.

(A personal story: In the late 1990s, I visited Colfax with a book about the massacre in mind, although it didn't get written for several reasons. The town then had about 1,500 people, with a two-thirds Black majority, but Whites held all town and parish offices. Since then, Colfax elected its second Black mayor. The town was bisected by a railroad track, with a long-abandoned station. Whites lived on the track's west side, in large white houses on tree-shaded lawns; Blacks lived on the east side, in small clapboard houses and house trailers. While I was there I visited the town cemetery, across from the First Baptist Church in the town's center. It was close to Easter, and four or five Black men were mowing the grass and sprucing up gravesites, supervised by a White man sitting in a municipal pickup truck. At one end of the cemetery, I noticed a twelve-foot-high granite obelisk and went over to view it. Carved into it were these words: "Erected to the memory of the heroes, Stephen Decatur Parrish, James West Hadnot, Sidney Harris, who fell in the Colfax riot fighting for white supremacy, April 13, 1873." I chatted for a while with one of the Black city workers, then asked how he felt about the monument and whether anyone in Colfax had ever proposed its removal. Pausing for a minute, and glancing a look at the supervisor, he replied, "Lots of folks don't want it here, but nobody wants to make trouble, so we get along." I also walked through the Black side of town, stopping to chat with three elderly ladies on a porch, having lemonade in the heat. They offered me a glass, and I explained why I was there and asked if anyone in town ever discussed the massacre. "No, we don't," one lady said. "But I heard my grandma tell about it when I was a girl. She said the women and children hid in the woods around the courthouse, and could see their men getting shot, and the screams of those that got burned up." Just before this writing, I called the town library, just across from the cemetery, and was told the monument to White supremacy was still standing. But Colfax is a small town, and people try to get along.)

The gunfire from the Colfax Massacre reverberated across the nation. In its wake, Foner reported, "an avalanche of heart-rending pleas for protection descended upon the South's Republican governors." But state officials did nothing to prosecute the attackers. Federal investigators, however, identified ninety-six men, who were indicted for violating the Ku Klux Klan Act of 1871. Of this group, only nine stood trial (most were hiding out in neighboring states), and six were acquitted by jurors who heard conflicting testimony about their presence at the massacre. Presented with clear evidence of the participation of three men—William Cruikshank, John Hadnot, and William Irwin—the jurors convicted them of conspiring to prevent two Black men, Levi Nelson and Alexander Tillman, from "the free exercise and enjoyment of the right to peaceably assemble" and depriving them of "life and Liberty without due process of law, rights guaranteed, by the Constitution and laws of the United States." Although Nelson had escaped from the slaughter and later testified against the three defendants, Tillman had been killed at the Colfax courthouse, but federal officials could not prosecute Cruikshank and his fellow marauders for murder because that was a state crime. Charging them with depriving Tillman of his life may seem to us like the same offense as murder, but not to the Supreme Court in 1876.

Chief Justice Morrison Waite wrote for a unanimous Court in reversing the convictions of Cruikshank and his fellow Colfax killers. An undistinguished real estate lawyer in Ohio before his appointment in 1874 by President Ulysses Grant as chief (replacing the distinguished Salmon Chase), Waite's opinion rivaled that of Chief Justice Taney in *Dred Scott* in its misreading of law and history. The Reconstruction amendments had been adopted to reverse that decision, but Waite seemed oblivious to this fact. In his *Cruikshank* opinion, Waite repeated and cited as precedent Taney's repudiated distinction between national and state citizenship. And he reached back to Chief Justice John Marshall's opinion in *Barron v. Baltimore*, decided in 1833, for the proposition that the Bill of Rights did not bind the states to their enforcement.

Waite began his opinion by searching the Ku Klux Klan Act for legal defects. Under the law, the rights "enjoyed" by Nelson and Tillman and "hindered" by the Colfax conspirators must be among those "granted or secured by the Constitution or laws of the United States." The chief justice never mentioned that more than a hundred Blacks had been murdered and could no longer "enjoy" *any* rights, or that Cruikshank had "hindered" the victims by joining in the massacre. He simply shut his eyes to these bloody facts. Among the rights that Cruikshank had denied to Nelson and Tillman was that of "peaceable assembly" at the Colfax courthouse, a right guaranteed by the First Amendment. Waite saw two problems with citing these rights as a basis for enforcing the Constitution. First, he read the amendment to require that those who assemble must gather "for the purpose of petitioning Congress for a redress of grievances." The First Amendment makes no such require- ment; the rights of assembly and petition are distinct, and the amendment speaks broadly of "the government," not just Congress. In fact, the Colfax Blacks who gathered to protect their courthouse and duly elected officials from heavily armed Whites had sent an urgent request for military protection to the state's Republican governor; in effect, a petition with a serious griev- ance. Sadly, the troops arrived too late to prevent the massacre.

The second defect Waite found in the Klan Act was that federal law, as he read the Constitution, could not protect Blacks in exercising their right to vote. He reached this conclusion by walking around the Fifteenth Amendment, which prohibits "any state" from denying "citizens of the United States" their right to vote "on account of race, color, or previous con- dition of servitude." It would be hard to ignore that Tillman, after his murder, was denied his right to vote thereafter in Louisiana elections, as Cruikshank's indictment charged. But the chief justice argued that "the right of suffrage is not a necessary attribute of national citizenship" and that the Fifteenth Amendment bound states only to protect voters against racial discrimina- tion. Waite looked closely at the indictment and found that "it is nowhere alleged in these counts that the wrong contemplated against the rights of these citizens was on account of their race or color." But he didn't look closely enough; the indictment did, in fact, charge that Cruikshank and his fellow conspirators had deprived persons "of African descent" of their constitutional rights. Were not Tillman and his fellow Black victims murdered "on account of" their race? Had they been White, they would not have been murdered. The chief justice simply ignored this obvious fact.

Having denied that the Constitution protected the Blacks who assembled in Colfax to defend their courthouse, Waite also denied that federal law could protect their "lives and liberty" from murderous conspiracies. He found this charge in the indictment "even more objectionable" than those based on rights to assemble and vote, on two grounds. First, he claimed, the power to bring prosecutions for murder "rests alone with the states." He ignored the fact that Congress had passed the Enforcement Acts because the southern states refused to protect Blacks from terrorists like Cruikshank. His opinion reached previously unscaled heights of hypocrisy in quoting the Declaration of Independence for the proposition that "the very highest duty of the States" was to protect "all persons" in their enjoyment of the "unalienable rights with which they were endowed by their Creator." Louisiana had refused to protect Nelson and Tillman or to prosecute the White murderers. But it was "no more the duty or within the power of the United States" to step in when the states failed in their duty, Waite piously stated.

The Court's opinion in *Cruikshank* slammed every legal door in the face of federal officials who tried—and ultimately failed—to protect southern Blacks against intimidation and violence. Not a single justice dissented from this ruling. By 1876, the Supreme Court—and most northern Whites—had tired of Reconstruction battles and were ready to surrender to the former Confederates. The reaction of southern Whites to Waite's opinion reflected their sense of impending victory. One prominent lawyer expressed his jubilation: "When the decision was reached and the prisoners released, there was the utmost joy in Louisiana, and with it a return of confidence which gave us best hopes for the future." Needless to say, Blacks across the South looked to the future with fear and foreboding.

Unfortunately, those fears were realized just months after the *Cruikshank* decision, in March 1876. The Supreme Court had waved the white flag of judicial surrender to politicians in both national parties, eager to abandon the increasingly unpopular Reconstruction program of providing federal military protection to Blacks in their efforts to vote in local and state elections. The resulting calamity reflected the success of campaigns of intimidation, violence, and even murders of Blacks by White terrorists of the Ku Klux Klan, the White League in Louisiana, the Red Shirts in Mississippi and South Carolina, and similar groups in all southern states. Routed in the 1874 congressional elections by voters weary of political turmoil, Radical Republicans lost nine Senate and ninety-four House seats to Democrats who vowed to remove federal "occupiers" from the South. Defeated Republicans spoke in words of resignation. "I have been a radical abolitionist from my earliest days," said House member Joseph Hawley of Connecticut, but now he felt that "social, and educational, and moral reconstruction" could "never come from any legislative halls."

Like sharks that smelled blood, Democrats looked forward in 1876 to an election contest with President Grant, whose two administrations had suffered the cuts of many scandals. Grant longed to run for a third term, but most Republicans considered him a liability, and he withdrew before the party's convention, which gave the nomination—after fractious debate and seven ballots—to Rutherford B. Hayes of Ohio, a man described by Henry Adams as a "third-rate nonentity." A graduate of Harvard Law School and a three- term governor, Hayes campaigned on a platform of civil service reform, an important issue but one that failed to excite the electorate. The party's platform completely ignored the issue of Reconstruction. Frederick Douglass, the former slave who feared a new enslavement of his people, expressed his anguish in prophetic words: "What does it all amount to, if the black man, after having been made free by the letter of your law, is unable to exercise that freedom, and, after having been freed from the slaveholder's lash, he is now to be subjected to the slaveholder's shotgun?" Douglass challenged the Republican delegates: "Do you mean to make good to us the promises in your constitution?" The answer was silence.

Sensing victory, Democrats united behind New York governor Samuel Tilden, one of the nation's richest men in a period that rewarded "Captains of Industry" with enormous wealth. Tilden gained his fortune as legal counsel to railroad and banking magnates like Jim Fisk and Jay Gould, who thanked him with stock for steering them around the shoals of bankruptcy. "He is connected with the moneyed men of the country," one supporter wrote. "That is exactly what we want."

Although Tilden won a majority of the popular vote, by some 300,000 over Hayes, Republicans claimed victory in South Carolina, Florida, and Louisiana, states controlled by Blacks and their White supporters, alleging ballot-box stuffing and (ironically) intimidation of White voters. If the nineteen electoral votes from these states, plus one disputed vote from Oregon, went to Hayes, he would prevail in the Electoral College by one vote. Without these votes, Hayes would lose to Tilden. The resolution of a great national issue rode on the outcome of this dispute.

Which candidate had the greatest number of electoral votes, Tilden or Hayes? Unable to decide the disputed claims, Congress turned the problem over to a blue-ribbon panel of fifteen: five representatives, five senators, and five Supreme Court justices. Since only two Democrats sat on the Court at that time, it was certain that the fifth justice would be a Republican. But the expected choice, Justice David Davis, was considered by many to favor Tilden. Democrats in Illinois, however, damaged their party's cause before Davis was appointed by supporting his election to the Senate, a choice made by the state legislature after the presidential election. Shortly after Davis took his Senate seat, amid charges but no definitive proof that Democratic state lawmakers had been bribed to support him, he resigned from the Court. In his place, the four remaining justices chose Joseph Bradley, a highly partisan Republican, to join them on the panel. Predictably, Bradley voted with his party colleagues to award every disputed elector to Hayes. Behind the scenes, Hayes had assured White southern Democrats that he would look with "kind consideration" of their demands that Reconstruction end. "We have been cheated, shamefully cheated," complained one Democrat. Those Republicans who supported Reconstruction knew they had lost. "I think the policy of the new administration will be to conciliate the white men of the South," one lamented. "Carpetbaggers to the rear, and niggers take care of yourself."

What became known as the "Stolen Election" of 1876 presaged a disaster for southern Blacks, who could no longer take care of themselves after federal troops, at Hayes's order, withdrew from the former Confederate states in 1877, unleashing another reign of terror against Blacks, and the takeover of state legislatures by Whites, replacing hundreds of elected Black officials. Tilden's election, of course, would certainly have resulted in the same abandonment of Reconstruction. Having lost their voices in government at all levels, Blacks had no way to block the flood of White men's laws that stripped away the rights purchased with the blood that seeped into the soil of battlefields across the still-divided nation. The shattered promise of Reconstruction gave way to the new era of Jim Crow and its imposition of "slavery without shackles."

5

"The Foul Odors of Blacks"

AS RECONSTRUCTION FALTERED and finally died of abandonment
by President Hayes, one southern editor boasted that the Fourteenth and
Fifteenth amendments "may stand forever; but we intend . . . to make them
dead letters on the statute book." The Supreme Court did the job for the un-
repentant South, as all but one justice joined the 1883 decision that imposed a
judicial death sentence on the Civil Rights Act of 1875, eight years after its congressional passage. Its most important provision had barred the proprietors of
any "place of public accommodation" from discriminating against any patron
on account of their race or color.

Under the caption *Civil Rights Cases*, the justices decided five cases from
Kansas, California, Tennessee, Missouri, and New York, states that spanned
the continent but none from the Deep South, where danger awaited any
Black with the temerity to challenge any of the Jim Crow laws. The dry legal
wording of the federal indictments in these disparate cases illustrates the humiliation that Black citizens endured every day, in the North and the South
and across the continent; these old records put human faces on cases decided
without names.

In Topeka, Kansas (the home of Linda Brown of the celebrated *Brown* case),

on the 10th day of October, in the year of our Lord one thousand eight
hundred and seventy-five, one Murray Stanley, having management
and control of a certain inn, did unlawfully deny to one Bird Gee the
full enjoyment of the accommodations of the inn by denying to Bird
Gee the privilege of partaking of a meal, to wit, of a supper, at the table
of the inn, for the reason that Bird Gee was a person of color and of
the African race, and for no other reason whatever, contrary to the act

of Congress, and against the peace and dignity of the United States of America.

The California indictment charged that

on the 4th day of January, A.D. 1876, Michael Ryan did unlawfully deny to George M. Tyler, the full enjoyment of accommodations of Maguire's Theater in the city of San Francisco, as follows, that George M. Tyler did purchase a ticket of admission, for the sum of one dollar, to the orchestra seats, and orchestra seats did possess superior advantages to any other portion of the theater, and that Michael Ryan, who was the ticket-taker of the theater, did then and there, by force of arms, deny to George M. Tyler, admission to the theater, solely for the reason that George M. Tyler was and is of the African or negro race, being what is commonly called a colored man, and not a white man.

The third case charged the Memphis & Charleston Railroad Company with discriminating against Sallie J. Robinson, stating that

on the 22nd of May, 1879, Mrs. Robinson, wishing to be carried from Grand Junction, Tennessee, to Lynchburg, Virginia, purchased tickets entitling her to be carried as a first-class passenger over the defendant's railway, and that being so entitled Mrs. Robinson got upon the defendant's train of cars at Grand Junction, Tennessee, and attempted to go into the ladies' car, being the car provided for ladies and first-class passengers, when the conductor of the train refused to admit her into the car, and that in so refusing her admission the conductor took Mrs. Robinson by the arm and jerked her roughly around, wherefore she was damaged $500, and therefore the plaintiff sues.

(This was a civil case for personal damages, not brought under the Civil Rights Act but decided with those four cases).

The fourth indictment claimed

that Samuel A. Singleton of the city and County of New York, on the twenty-second day of November, in the year of our Lord one thousand eight hundred and seventy-nine, did willfully and unlawfully with force and arms deny to one William R. Davis, junior, being then and there a citizen of the United States, the full enjoyment of the accommodations, advantages, facilities, and privileges of a theater and place of public amusement, to wit, of the theater commonly known as the Grand Opera House, said denial not being made for any reason or reasons by law applicable to citizens of every race and color and regardless of any previous condition of servitude, then and there against the peace of the United States and their dignity, and against the form of the statutes of the said United States in such case made and provided.

The final indictment, printed without dates, alleged that in St. Louis, Missouri,

one Samuel Nichols was the proprietor of a certain common inn called the Nichols House, for the accommodation of travelers and the general public, that one W. H. R. Agee was an applicant to Samuel Nichols for the accommodations of the inn as a guest therein but Nichols did deny to Agee admission as a guest in the inn, for the sole reason that Agee was a person of color and one of the Negro race.

The Supreme Court decided the *Civil Rights Cases* on October 15, 1883, with an opinion by Justice Joseph Bradley (whose deciding vote had elected Rutherford Hayes as president in 1877). His majority opinion slammed more doors in Black faces, those of restaurants, hotels, theaters, and railroads. Congressional sponsors of the Civil Rights Act had relied on the enforcement clauses of the Thirteenth and Fourteenth amendments; Bradley knocked down both laws' constitutional supports. In dealing with the Thirteenth Amendment, he offered two statements of its purpose. The amendment, he first wrote, "has only to do with slavery and its incidents." Bradley then posed a rhetorical question: Did the refusal of proprietors of "public accommodations" to admit or serve Blacks "inflict upon such persons any manner of servitude, or form of slavery, as those terms are understood in this country?" To Bradley, this question had an easy answer. "The Thirteenth Amendment has respect, not to distinctions of race, or class, or color, but to slavery."

The answer to Bradley's question was not as simple as it seemed to him. His first statement of the amendment's purpose included the prohibition not only of slavery but also of "its incidents." Bradley did not invent this term; it came from the speeches of the amendment's congressional sponsors, who defined "incidents" of slavery as laws or practices designed to keep Blacks in subjugation to Whites. Racial discrimination in public accommodations could well be considered an "incident" of slavery. Almost a century later, in 1968, the Supreme Court ruled that Congress had power under the Thirteenth Amendment to outlaw housing discrimination as an "incident" of slavery. But in 1886, Justice Bradley ignored this qualifying term in his strictly literal reading of the amendment.

Bradley treated the Fourteenth Amendment in a similar manner. He first conceded that, unlike the Thirteenth Amendment, the Fourteenth "extends its protections to races and classes, and prohibits any state legislation which has the effect of denying to any race or class, or to any individual, the equal protection of the laws." He then posed another rhetorical question: "Can the act of a mere individual, the owner of the inn, the public conveyance or place of amusement," be regulated by Congress unless "the denial of the right has some state sanction or authority?" Once again, Bradley had framed the question to provide an easy answer. Although "the laws of all the states, so far as we are aware," he wrote, required the proprietors of public accommodations to serve "all unobjectionable persons who in good faith apply for them," the Fourteenth Amendment provided no power to prohibit such "private" discrimination. In other words, Congress could deal only with "state action" that denied Blacks the equal protection of the laws. Innkeepers were not state agents; therefore, they could discriminate between patrons as they wished.

Having dismissed the claims of Bird Gee, George Tyler, Sallie Robinson, W. H. R. Agee, and William R. Davis—all U.S. citizens holding the same rights as all others—Justice Bradley concluded his opinion with a patronizing lecture to them and all other Black citizens:

> When a man has emerged from slavery, and with the aid of beneficent legislation has shaken off the inseparable concomitants of that state, there must be some stage in the progress of his elevation when he takes the rank of a mere citizen, and ceases to be a special favorite of the laws, and when his rights as a citizen, or a man, are to be protected in the ordinary modes by which other men's rights are protected.

This one sentence summed up the racial attitudes of "enlightened" Whites— like Bradley—who paid no heed to the hooded nightriders whose whips and ropes had become the "ordinary modes" of enforcing the Jim Crow laws that all southern states, and even some in the North, had adopted.

Only one justice took issue with Bradley's constitutional literalism and condescending tone. "The opinion in these cases," wrote John Marshall Harlan, "proceeds upon grounds entirely too narrow and artificial." A Kentucky native (named after the great chief justice his father had admired), Harlan came from a slave-owning family but had supported the Union during the Civil War, raising a regiment he commanded. He devoted most of his thirty-five-page dissent to Bradley's dismissal, in just four pages, of the Fourteenth Amendment claims in the cases. Congress had intended, Harlan noted, to wipe out all discrimination against Blacks and "to secure and protect rights belonging to them as free men and citizens; nothing more." He took aim at Bradley's formalistic distinction between "state action" and private discrimination. "In every material sense applicable to the practical enforcement of the Fourteenth Amendment," he wrote, "railroad corporations, keepers of inns, and managers of places of public amusement are agents or instrumentalities of the State, because they are charged with duties to the public, and are amenable, in respect of their duties and functions, to governmental regulation." On that issue, Harlan relied on the common-law principle that "when private property is devoted to a public use, it is subject to public regulation," as the Court had stated in an 1877 opinion, upholding state regulation of fees charged by owners of grain elevators. Harlan saw no legal difference between grain elevators, railroads, and restaurants: all served the public and all were subject to regulation. Bradley had conceded that owners of "public accommodations" were required to serve "all unobjectionable persons who in good faith apply for them." How, then, could those owners refuse service on the basis of race or color? Bradley's invocation of the "state action" doctrine to answer this question seemed "artificial" to Harlan.

Harlan concluded with a swipe at Bradley's patronizing lecture to Blacks. "It is," he wrote, "scarcely just to say that the colored race has been the special favorite of the laws. The statute of 1875, now adjudged to be unconstitutional, is for the benefit of citizens of every race and color." He reminded his colleagues—and the nation—that "class tyranny" could be imposed by any group that controlled power. "Today, it is the colored race which is denied, by corporations and individuals wielding public authority, rights fundamental in their freedom and citizenship," Harlan wrote. "At some future time, it may be that some other race will fall under the ban of race discrimination." He was prescient. Eight years after this decision, in 1882, Congress passed the Chinese Exclusion Act, responding to pressure from White nativists to bar the admission of "coolies" who were supposedly taking jobs from deserving Americans. And in 1942, President Franklin D. Roosevelt authorized military officials to round up and imprison all Japanese Americans on the West Coast, two-thirds of them native-born citizens; the Supreme Court upheld this mass incarceration, relying in part on claims that members of this racial group could not be "assimilated" as "an integral part of the white population." The parallel lines of racism and xenophobia behind these legal attacks on minorities ran straight through White America's refusal, from colonial settlement until now, to consider those of darker skin colors as fit to share the rights enjoyed by "real Americans."

* * *

For most southern Blacks after their emancipation from slavery, the right to enjoy "public accommodations" on an equal basis with Whites was less important than their right to vote, protected by the Fifteenth Amendment. With federal troops monitoring voter registration and guarding polling places, Blacks in every former Confederate state had elected Black candidates to local, state, and federal offices. However, even before Reconstruction ended with the withdrawal of Union troops from the South in 1877, White southerners began organizing and plotting their return to power. Just as South Carolina had begun the Civil War with secession in 1860, and the shelling of Fort Sumter the next year, the Palmetto State became the center of White resistance to Black voting and participation in government. In 1873, two former Confederate generals, Martin Gary and Matthew C. Butler, proposed that White men form paramilitary organizations, known as "rifle clubs," and use force and intimidation to drive Blacks from power. Members of these groups became known as Red Shirts, after their garb. Benjamin Tillman, a wealthy planter, was an enthusiastic recruiter for a group called the Sweetwater Saber Club, whose members assaulted and intimidated Blacks who registered to vote.

The election in 1876 for South Carolina governor marked perhaps the most vicious and murderous campaign by Red Shirts to drive Blacks from office and completely take over the state government. The incumbent governor, Daniel H. Chamberlain, was a moderate Republican who sought reelection, supported by Blacks and even some White Democrats. To carry the banner of White supremacy, Martin Gary recruited Wade Hampton III, a Confederate war hero who returned to his native state to run for governor as a Democrat. The resulting campaign turned into a bloodbath, with scores of Blacks and White Republicans murdered by Red Shirt gangs.

The most notorious episode of violence became known as the Hamburg Massacre, for the small, largely Black town on the Savannah River boundary with Georgia. Black militiamen had been drilling and marching in a Fourth of July celebration when a buggy driven by White farmers tried to ride through their ranks, leading both sides to file criminal charges against the other. A court hearing was set for July 8, but the Black militiamen, wary of the influx of armed Red Shirts into the town, refused to attend. Matthew Butler and Ben Tillman demanded that the Blacks apologize to the farmers and surrender their arms. Barricaded in their drill room above a local store, the Blacks refused this demand, knowing they were outnumbered and not trusting the Red Shirts to let them peacefully leave. Shots broke out, and a White man was killed. The Red Shirts then stormed the building and captured about thirty militiamen. Five were murdered on the spot, including a Black constable who had arrested several Whites for various offenses. Another two Blacks who attempted to flee were shot and killed. Tillman and his Red Shirt compatriots even held a celebratory meal after the massacre; he later boasted that "the leading white men" of the area had agreed "to seize the first opportunity that the Negroes might offer them to provoke a riot and teach the Negroes a lesson" by "killing as many of them as was justifiable." Although ninety-four White men, including Tillman, were indicted for the killings by a coroner's jury, none was prosecuted. Later in the election campaign, "rifle club" members murdered another thirty Black militiamen; others were saved by the arrival of federal troops. Tillman also directed Red Shirts who murdered Simon Coker, a Black state senator who had come to Hamburg to investigate reports of violence, shooting him as he knelt in prayer. After Black voters had been thoroughly intimidated from voting, Wade Hampton was declared the victor in the gubernatorial election by a narrow margin over Chamberlain. Years later, at a reunion of Red Shirts, Tillman spoke of the Hamburg Massacre: "The purpose of our visit to Hamburg was to strike terror, and when the negroes who had fled [into the nearby swamps] returned to the town, the ghastly sight which met their gaze of seven dead negroes lying stark and stiff, certainly had its effect. . . . [Their lives] had been offered up as a sacrifice to the fanatical teachings and fiendish hate of those who sought to substitute the rule of the African for that of the Caucasian in South Carolina."

Tillman became a hero to South Carolina Whites, who elected him governor in 1890; in his inaugural address, he lauded "the triumph of democracy and white supremacy over mongrelism and anarchy, of civilization over barbarism." After two terms as governor, Tillman was elected to the U.S. Senate in 1895 by his state's legislature, serving until his death in 1918. In one Senate speech, he defended the disenfranchisement of Blacks who had voted until 1895:

Then we had a constitutional convention which took the matter up calmly, deliberately, and avowedly with the purpose of disenfranchising as many of them as we could under the Fourteenth and Fifteenth amendments. We adopted the educational qualification [literacy test] as the only means left to us. The Negro is as contented and as prosperous and as well protected in South Carolina today as in any state of the Union south of the Potomac. He is not meddling with politics, for he found that the more he meddled with them the worse off he got. As to his "rights," we of the South have never recognized the right of the Negro to govern white men and we never will. . . . I would to God that the last one of them was in Africa and that none of them had ever been brought to our shores.

During his entire political career, as South Carolina's governor and then in Congress as his state's senator, "Pitchfork Ben" Tillman (he got the nickname, which he enjoyed, after threatening to use that implement on President Grover Cleveland, calling him a "bag of beef" over some dispute) epitomized the racist politicians who vowed to "redeem" the South from the "boot heel" of Reconstruction. Tillman's incendiary rhetoric has rarely been matched by any Dixiecrat, then or since. A few examples will suffice to give readers a sense of the unvarnished racism that still persists in American politics, although largely through code words and "dog whistles" aimed at fearful White voters. After President Theodore Roosevelt enraged southern bigots in 1901 by inviting the most prominent Black of that time, Booker T. Washington, to dine with him at the White House, Tillman responded with vitriol: "The action of President Roosevelt in entertaining that nigger will necessitate our killing a thousand niggers in the South before they learn their place again." Mississippi senator James K. Vardaman joined Tillman, complaining that the White House was now "so saturated with the odor of nigger that the rats had taken refuge in the stable."

With racism as their banner and murder as their ultimate weapon, Tillman and his compatriots in other southern states paved the way for Democratic domination of the "Solid South" until the success of Richard Nixon's "Southern Strategy" in the 1960s and 1970s of tarring Democrats as captives of Black politicians; it would be hard to imagine a greater reversal of political fortunes. Tillman put his strategy in these terms:

Republicanism means equality, while the Democratic Party means that the white man is supreme. That is why we southerners are all Democrats. . . . If we had our say, [Blacks] could never vote. I believe that God made the white man out of better clay than that which the

Negro was made from. . . . We reorganized the Democratic Party with one plank and only one plank, namely, that this is a white man's country and the white man must govern it.

* * *

Although South Carolina holds the dubious distinction of employing the most violence to wrest control of its government from Black voters and officials in the debris of Reconstruction and to enshrine White supremacy in its constitution, other former Confederate states used similar tactics to achieve these goals. Mississippi held a convention in 1890 to replace the post-Emancipation constitution that had been adopted by a majority-Black convention, after most former Confederates were stripped of their voting rights as punishment for their treasonous rebellion against the Union.

Although blacks made up 58 percent of Mississippi's population and had elected two Blacks to the U.S. Senate, only one Black won election to the 1890 convention. During the preceding decade, a campaign of intimidation and violence had almost eliminated Black voters, leaving Whites eager to regain control of the state's government. White Democrats in Mississippi even resorted to murder to prevent White Republicans from securing election to the convention; F. M. B. "Marsh" Cook of Jasper County, who supported the right of Blacks to vote and hold office, was ambushed on a country road and his body riddled with twenty-seven bullets by six White men, enraged by his apostasy from the virtual religion of White supremacy.

The convention president, Solomon Calhoon, a judge from Hinds County and a lieutenant colonel in the Confederate army, stated its goal bluntly: "Let's tell the truth if it bursts the bottom of the Universe. . . . We came here to exclude the Negro; nothing short of this will answer." Calhoon did not temper his racist contempt for Blacks, asserting that they had "no advancement, no invention, no history, no literature, no governmental polity. We see only ignorance, slavery, cannibalism, no respect for women, no respect for anything." Another delegate, a Bolivar County planter named George P. Melchoir, was equally blunt in stating his purpose: "It is the manifest intention of this constitution to secure to the state of Mississippi 'white supremacy.'" A delegate from Adams County named Will T. Martin challenged the convention's members, asking, "What are you here for, if not to maintain white supremacy." The Democratic Party adopted the slogan "This is a White Man's country: Let the White Man rule!"

Adopted and ratified by White voters, the new constitution embodied the Jim Crow regime that spanned the entire South. One clause provided, "Separate schools shall be maintained for students of the white and colored race," undoing the bar on school segregation in the previous constitution. Other provisions were designed to keep Blacks from exercising the franchise they had been guaranteed by the Fifteenth Amendment. One stated, "A uniform poll tax of two dollars, to be in aid of the common schools, and for no other purpose, is hereby imposed on every male inhabitant of this state between the ages of twenty-one and sixty." Poll taxes, of course, were imposed on Whites as well as Blacks, and many poor Whites could not afford them and were effectively disenfranchised.

The Mississippi convention also inserted a literacy test in the new constitution: "Every elector shall . . . be able to read any section of the constitution of this State; or he shall be able to understand the same when read to him, or give a reasonable interpretation thereof." The job of deciding what constituted a "reasonable interpretation" of a constitutional provision was given to county registrars—all White—who could administer the literacy test as they pleased. When Blacks applied to register as voters, the registrars would select complicated technical passages to read or interpret, informing all prospective Black voters they had failed, regardless of how well they did. By contrast, the clerks would pass illiterate Whites by picking simple sentences in the state constitution for them to explain. (A story I recall, perhaps apocryphal, is that a Black college professor in Mississippi visited his county courthouse to register. The White clerk handed him a sheet with a lengthy, highly technical provision of the state constitution, which he recited without a single error. The clerk frowned, then handed him an even more convoluted provision to read, again receiving a flawless answer. Frustrated, the clerk then ordered the professor to interpret a section whose title the clerk could not even pronounce. "What does this mean?" he demanded. Sensing the futility of this exercise, the professor glanced at the sheet in his hand. "It means this nigger ain't gonna vote," he replied.)

Mississippi also enacted a "grandfather clause" in its constitution that permitted registering anyone whose grandfather was qualified to vote before the Civil War. Obviously, this benefited only White citizens. This barrier to Black voting, along with poll taxes and literacy tests, had its intended effects: Mississippi cut the percentage of Black men registered to vote from over 90 during Reconstruction to less than 6 in 1892.

With Blacks driven from office and purged from the voting rolls, Mississippi Whites turned to the legal system and its all-White judiciary to rebuff any challenge to their total dominance of the state government. In an 1896 ruling, the Mississippi Supreme Court delivered a legal opinion regarding the justification and reasoning the Democrats had used for the adoption of the 1890 constitution in *Ratliff v. Beale.* The court's opinion reeked of unvarnished and unapologetic racism. Referring to the terrorist violence that had swept Blacks from elective office, the justices lauded the

> uprising, under which the white race, inferior in number, but superior in spirit, in governmental instinct, and intelligence, was restored to power. The federal constitution prohibited the adoption of any laws under which a discrimination should be made by reason of race, color, or previous condition of servitude. . . . Within the field of permissible action under the limitations imposed by the federal constitution, the convention swept the circle of expedience to obstruct the exercise of the franchise by the negro race. By reason of its previous condition of servitude and dependence, this race had acquired or accentuated certain peculiarities of habit, of temperament, and of character, which clearly distinguished it as a race from that of the whites—a patient, docile people, but careless, landless, and migratory within narrow limits, without forethought, and its criminal members given rather to furtive offenses than to the robust crimes of the whites.

J. B. Chrisman, a judge from Lincoln County, praised the new constitution as a badge of honor for White men: "My God! My God! Is there to be no higher ambition for the young white men of the South than that of keeping the Negro down?"

* * *

After the Supreme Court's 1883 decision in the *Civil Rights Cases* had gutted the "public accommodations" provision of the 1875 Civil Rights Act, all-White southern lawmakers enacted hundreds of Jim Crow laws, mandating the separation of Whites and Blacks in virtually every place that people go and every activity in which they engage. It was inevitable that one of these Jim Crow laws would eventually reach the Supreme Court, challenging their violation of the Fourteenth Amendment's guarantee of "equal protection of the laws" for Whites and Blacks alike. The case that forced the Court to decide this issue began on June 7, 1892, when Homer Adolph Plessy entered the New Orleans station of the East Louisiana Railway and bought a

first-class ticket to Covington, Louisiana, a trip of about fifty miles around
Lake Pontchartrain. Plessy had no particular business in Covington; what he
wanted—and expected—was to be arrested for violating the 1890 Louisiana
state law requiring that "no person or persons shall be permitted to occupy
seats in coaches, other than the ones assigned to them on account of the race
they belong to." The law required that railroads provide "equal but separate"
facilities for those of different races; however, it did not define "race" and left
to conductors the job of assigning passengers to the proper cars.

Plessy and his backers had, in fact, arranged his arrest before he bought
his ticket, although perhaps not the way it was carried out. According to the
Supreme Court's later statement of facts, Plessy "entered a passenger train,
and took possession of a vacant seat in a coach where passengers of the white
race were accommodated." The conductor then ordered him "to vacate said
coach" and move to one "for persons not of the white race." When Plessy
refused to move, "he was, with the aid of a police officer, forcibly ejected
from said coach and hurried off to imprisonment in the parish jail of New
Orleans." His stay in jail was brief; he was released after arraignment in the
local recorder's court. (The "police officer" who arrested Plessy was actually
a private detective hired by his supporters for that purpose, who might have
overplayed his role.)

Why did the Separate Cars Act challengers choose Homer Plessy to buy
a railway ticket for a trip he did not intend to take? The answer lies in his ancestry. As his name suggests, he had French forebears, as did many residents of
New Orleans, stemming back to France's ownership of what became known as
the Louisiana Purchase after its sale to the United States in 1803. In the racial
gumbo of New Orleans, those mixed-race people were known as Creoles or
"free persons of color" (*les gens de couleur libre* in the French they spoke), and
occupied positions of influence in the city. Like many Creoles, Plessy could
"pass" for White, although under Louisiana law, he (and all Creoles) was
considered Black and thus would be barred from sitting in a "White" coach,
but only if a conductor knew of his "legal" race. As his lawyers later stated,
"the mixture of colored blood was not discernable in him." This explains why
Plessy most likely informed the conductor of this fact; otherwise, he would
have been allowed to remain in the "White" car.

As an aside, most accounts of Plessy's life and case have described him as an
"octoroon," a person with one Black and seven White great-grandparents. I'm
not sure how that designation began, and lingered in later writings, but some
genealogical research and census records reveal that he was in fact a "mulatto,"

a person with one White and one Black parent, or in Plessy's case, two mu-latto parents. His father, Joseph, was listed as "mulatto" in the 1850 census, when he was seventeen. Joseph's father and Homer's grandfather, François Germain duPlessis, was born in France and later moved to Haiti, fleeing to New Orleans after the Black revolution ousted the French colonists in 1804. Finding work as a carpenter, he married Joseph's mother, Catherine Mathieu, a "free woman of color." Plessy's mother, Rosa Debergue, was herself mulatto, the daughter of mulatto parents Michel Debergue and Josephine Blanco. I was surprised to learn from Louisiana state records that Michel Debergue, a "free person of color," came from a slave-owning family; the 1810 census listed eight slaves as property, two adult males, two adult females, and four children, most probably two families. These slaves were listed without names in the census, but other records show Michel buying and selling slaves named Congo, Marinette, and Aspazie. In fact, as state records show, hundreds of "free persons of color" in Louisiana owned slaves, mostly for household work. It's difficult to quantify Homer Plessy's racial percentages, but most likely he was about one-third White. On both the 1900 and 1910 census forms, Plessy (who died in 1925) and his wife, Louise Bordenave, were listed as "black." But, to be a bit facetious, they somehow changed color by the 1920 census, which listed both as "white."

I mention all this, not that it would have affected Plessy's case and its out-come, but to make the point that racial classifications, including those in the census, are subjective and arbitrary, often reliant on the enumerator's guess-work or what residents tell them. In Louisiana, every person was designated under state law as "white" or "black," with nothing in between. Legally, every Creole should have been counted as Black, no matter how remote their Black ancestry, but it's likely that many light-skin Creoles were listed as White on census forms.

Creoles in New Orleans chafed under the Jim Crow laws and organized a campaign in 1890 to challenge them. Plessy, then a twenty-seven-year-old shoemaker, was a friend of Rodolphe Desdunes, a leader of the American Citizens' Equal Rights Association in New Orleans and a prominent figure in the Creole community. Along with a prominent Creole lawyer, Louis Martinet, Desdunes helped to organize the Citizen's Committee to Test the Constitutionality of the Separate Car Law and recruited the nation's leading civil rights lawyer to handle the court battle. Albion Tourgée of New York was a former Union army officer who moved to North Carolina during Reconstruction; he helped to write its Radical constitution and served as a state judge for six years. After the White "Redeemers" took control in 1877, Tourgée returned to New York and became, in his biographer's words, "the most vocal, militant, persistent, and widely heard advocate of racial equality in the United States, black or white."

Plessy's challenge to his arrest came before Judge John H. Ferguson in the Criminal District Court of New Orleans on October 28, 1892. Representing Plessy at the hearing was his local counsel, James C. Walker, a White veteran of the Confederate army but a "good, upright, conscientious man," Martinet assured Tourgée, who prepared a brief for the hearing. Citing the Thirteenth and Fourteenth amendments, Tourgée claimed the law imposed a "badge of servitude" on Plessy and deprived him of the "privileges and immunities" of citizenship. On the state's behalf, Lionel Adams defended the law as a "reasonable" exercise of the state's "police powers" to protect public health, safety, welfare, and morals. In a bluntly racist statement, Adams claimed that "the foul odors of blacks in close quarters" made the law reasonable as a protection of presumably odorless Whites. The record does not show that he presented any evidence for this claim, nor does it mention that most Blacks lived in homes without bathtubs or even running water and labored for long hours in hot, humid weather.

Judge Ferguson issued his ruling on November 18, 1892. In a brief opinion, he denied Plessy's constitutional challenge, citing Supreme Court decisions holding that the protections of the Thirteenth and Fourteenth amendments did not extend to state laws that had a "reasonable" basis for racial discrimination. After this decision, Tourgée and Walker appealed to the Louisiana Supreme Court. Chief Justice Francis T. Nicholls, despite the fact that he had signed the Jim Crow law as governor in 1890, issued a "writ of prohibition" that ordered Judge Ferguson to "show cause" why his ruling should not be reversed. But after hearing oral argument a second time, the court upheld Ferguson's ruling on January 2, 1893. Three days later, Justice Nicholls issued a "writ of error" to the U.S. Supreme Court, setting the stage for a final decision on the Louisiana law, a decision that would likely determine the fate of Jim Crow laws in all southern states. Plessy's case had completed its journey through the Louisiana courts in less than eight months, but then sat on a siding in the Supreme Court clerk's office for another three years. The lengthy delay stemmed largely from the Court's swollen docket, as the justices were then required to decide almost every appeal from state court rulings; they decided 392 cases in 1895, most with brief or summary rulings. (Not until 1925 did Congress give the Court the power to exercise its "discretion" in deciding which cases to hear.)

In his brief to the Supreme Court, Albion Tourgée threw caution to the wind and challenged the justices to look racism in the face. "Suppose a member of this court, nay, suppose every member of it," he wrote,

should wake tomorrow with black skin and curly hair—the two obvious and controlling indications of race—and in traveling through that portion of the country where the "Jim Crow Car" abounds, should be ordered into it by the conductor. It is easy to imagine what would be the result, the indignation, the protest, the assertion of pure Caucasian ancestry. But the conductor, the Autocrat of Caste, armed with the power of the state conferred by this statute, will listen neither to denial nor protest.

His philippic continued:

What humiliation, what rage would then fill the judicial mind! How would the resources of language not be taxed in objurgation! Why would this sentiment prevail in your minds? Simply because you would then feel and know that such assortment of citizens on the line of race was a discrimination intended to humiliate and degrade the former subject and dependent class—an attempt to perpetuate the caste distinctions on which slavery rested.

In concluding his brief, Tourgée added a sentence that wound up, slightly changed, in the solitary dissent: "Justice is pictured blind and her daughter, the Law, ought at least to be color-blind."

The Supreme Court heard oral argument in *Plessy v. Ferguson* on April 13, 1896; no transcript was made and news accounts were skimpy, but Tourgée had prepared lengthy notes for his argument, stressing the "badge of servitude" the law placed on Blacks and its lack of a clear racial distinction between Whites and Blacks. Five weeks later, on May 18, the Court handed down its decision. Seven justices voted to uphold the Jim Crow law, while only John Marshall Harlan dissented. (Justice David Brewer had been absent during argument and did not vote, although he could have.) Justice Henry B. Brown, a Michigan lawyer who specialized in cases involving Great Lakes shipping, wrote for the majority; his most noteworthy opinion in fifteen years on the Court was certainly his worst. The list of Brown's deficiencies is long: he virtually ignored the constitutional issues raised by Plessy's lawyers; he relied heavily on cases that had little or no authority as precedent; and he based his decision on thinly veiled racism, dressed up in polite language.

Brown first addressed the Thirteenth Amendment claim that the Jim Crow law imposed a "badge of servitude" on Homer Plessy and all Blacks. In just three paragraphs, he brushed aside this claim as "too clear for argument." That amendment abolished "the ownership of mankind as a chattel" and did nothing more, Brown asserted. Turning to the Fourteenth Amendment and its guarantee of equal protection for all citizens, regardless of race, Brown admitted its intent to prohibit state-imposed racial discrimination and laws "imposing upon the colored race onerous disabilities and burdens," which was precisely what Louisiana did to Homer Plessy. Brown used an old lawyer's trick to escape this dilemma: semantic evasion. The Jim Crow law did not "discriminate" on racial grounds, he claimed; it simply recognized a "distinction between the races which must always exist so long as white men are distinguished from the other race by color." And why was that "distinction" a valid reason to "discriminate" between races? Brown left this crucial question unanswered. Also left out of his opinion was any mention of the supposed "foul odors" of Blacks as a ground for discrimination and the obvious racism behind all Jim Crow laws. In determining the "reasonable" basis for these laws, Brown granted a "large discretion" to the state legislature, asserting that lawmakers were at liberty to act "with reference to the established usages, customs and traditions of the people, and with a view to the promotion of their comfort, and the preservation of the public peace and good order." The people Brown had in mind, to whose "customs and traditions" he deferred and whose "comfort" he wished to protect, were those White people in Louisiana who did not want to share railway cars with Blacks. In other words, the racists of Louisiana. However, Brown sought to salve his capitulation to these racists by quoting the requirement of the Separate Railway Cars law that the coaches be "equal but separate."

It might be possible to provide railway cars that were equal in accommodation for Blacks and Whites; it proved virtually impossible to provide separate schools for Blacks and Whites that were remotely equal in funding, buildings, and teacher credentials. It took another fifty-eight years, until the Court ruled in *Brown v. Board of Education* that public school segregation was unconstitutional, holding that separate schools—regardless of their quality—could never be equal because they imposed the "stigma" of inferiority on Black kids. The Court's unanimous ruling in *Brown* was a complete refutation of Justice Brown's claim that the "customs and traditions" of White people justified educational racism. But for those fifty-eight years, and beyond, Black children in the South (and parts of the North) were robbed of decent educations by White men in black robes.

Justice Brown concluded with a patronizing lecture to Homer Plessy and all persons, no matter how fair their skin, the law considered Black, although with no definition of race. "We consider the underlying fallacy of the plaintiff's argument," he wrote, "to consist in the assumption that the enforced separation of the two races stamps the colored race with a badge of inferiority. If this be so, it is not by reason of anything found in the act, but solely because the colored race chooses to put that construction upon it." Condescension took the place of constitutional analysis in Brown's opinion.

Brown's majority opinion covered twelve pages in the Court's reports; Justice Harlan's dissent matched it precisely in length. Point by point, case by case, Harlan answered with a devastating rebuttal. He turned first, as had Brown, to the Thirteenth Amendment. "It not only struck down the institution of slavery," he wrote, "but it prevents the imposition of any burdens or disabilities that constitute badges of slavery or servitude. It decreed universal civil freedom in this country. This court has so adjudged." Despite the intent of those who framed that amendment, Harlan recognized that it proved "inadequate to the protection of the rights of those who had been held in slavery," which led to adoption of the Fourteenth and Fifteenth amendments. Between them, the Civil War amendments "removed the race line from our government systems." It was no longer allowed for "any public authority to know the race of those entitled to be protected in the enjoyment" of constitutional rights.

A major thrust of Harlan's dissent was that Brown had erred in distinguishing between "political" and "social" rights, limiting the former to jury duty and removing the latter from constitutional protection. Harlan used the broader term "civil rights" to include protection from discrimination in all places subject to state regulation, reaching back almost five decades in citing a Supreme Court ruling that a railroad company held "a sort of public office, and has public duties to perform," which must be done without discrimination. But Harlan did not rest his dissent on precedent; he cited just ten cases, against more than forty in Brown's opinion. He relied on one simple point: the Civil War amendments were designed to prohibit states from discriminating against Blacks in their enjoyment of the civil rights that all citizens held. Borrowing from Tourgée's brief, Harlan put this point into a sentence that has become famous, perhaps the most quoted in Supreme Court history: "Our constitution is color-blind, and neither knows nor tolerates classes among citizens." But those who quote the "color-blind" sentence invariably fail to quote the sentences that preceded it in Harlan's opinion: "The white race deems itself to be the dominant race in this country," he wrote. "And so it is, in prestige, in achievements, in education, in wealth and power. So, I doubt not, it will continue to be for all time, if it remains true to its great heritage and holds fast to the principles of constitutional liberty." Harlan stated in these sentences the reality of race in 1896. Whites held the reins of power, which they used to whip Blacks into submission and to harshly punish those who resisted the Jim Crow system.

As a footnote to the *Plessy* decision, it's telling that it was barely mentioned in press accounts of the Court's fifty-three decisions that day. Three of these—dealing with the laws of contract, inheritance, and copyright—were reported on the front page of the *New York Times*. The editors relegated the *Plessy* decision to a third-page column on railroad news, between cases on train routes and improvement bonds. And the Court's leading historian, Charles Warren, did not even mention *Plessy* in his massive work, published three decades later. One reason for this dismissal, I think, is that the Court's supposed new doctrine, upholding Jim Crow segregation in public facilities, did nothing more than reaffirm long-standing "customs" of White people. That was hardly newsworthy at this time in American history.

Viewed in the broader context of the status of Blacks in the century's last years, it bears notice that seventy-five Blacks were lynched the year of the *Plessy* ruling. One of those victims, Sidney Randolph, was accused of the brutal ax murder of a seven-year-old White girl, Sadie Buxton, as she slept in her home in Gaithersburg, Maryland, just twenty miles from the nation's capital. Police found no physical evidence linking Randolph to the murder, and Sadie's mother, also wounded in the assault, was unable to identify Randolph or even the race of the assailant. Nonetheless, a mob seized Randolph from the Montgomery County Jail on the Fourth of July and led him to a nearby chestnut tree, a noose around his neck. Randolph's last words, recorded by a *Washington Star* reporter, could have been those of hundreds of falsely accused lynch-mob victims. "I know I'se goin' ter be hung," he told his executioners. "I'se a nigger, 'thout a cent ner a fren', but I don't know nothin' 'bout hittin' dem people." Then they hung him. Citing the lack of "a scintilla of evidence" against him, the Washington *Times* concluded that "Randolph was made the vicarious sacrifice for another man's crime." The *Plessy* decision placed the stamp of judicial approval on Jim Crow segregation; the lynching of Sidney Randolph and thousands more victims of racist terror, hardly ever prosecuted and even praised by public officials, reflects the role of extralegal "law enforcement" as an integral part of the system devoted to social control, in which Blacks were most often helpless to challenge the Jim Crow regime of racial subjugation and White supremacy.

* * *

As the nineteenth century neared a close, Blacks in the former Confederacy no longer wore the shackles of slavery. But, with few exceptions, they endured conditions that—in the words of historian David Oshinsky—were even "worse than slavery." Legally free to live and work where they pleased, most lacked the skills and resources to leave the plantations on which they had labored without compensation. Instead, many remained on the land of their former masters, now as sharecroppers or tenant farmers.

Sharecroppers, as the name suggests, agreed to turn over a "share" of their crops to White landowners—usually a third or half—in return for "loans" of seed, tools, horses and mules, and supplies from stores that extended credit at exorbitant rates. After delivering their "shares" to landowners, at prices they had no power to dispute, and paying off the credit extended by merchants whose prices they also had to accept, most "croppers" wound up each year in debt, never able to put aside enough cash to leave the plantation and purchase any land of their own. A Black sharecropper in Alabama put it this way: "The colored folks stayed with the old boss man and farmed on the plantations. They were still slaves, but they were free slaves." Tenant farmers, who rented land in return for a share of the crops they farmed, generally owned their livestock and tools and could end a crop year with a modest profit. But hardly any croppers or tenants could escape from "debt slavery," condemned to a perpetual life of poverty. At the end of the nineteenth century, only 15 percent of Black farmers in the South owned the land they farmed. Making things worse, declining prices for cotton during the last two decades of that century—plummeting from $1.26 a pound during the Civil War to only $0.06 in the 1890s—took an even greater toll on Blacks, who were forced to work harder and longer just to stay alive.

Put into numbers, the plight of southern Blacks as the century ended was dire. Out of 8 million Blacks counted in the 1900 federal census, about 12 percent of the national population, 90 percent lived in the former Confederacy, almost all as sharecroppers or tenant farmers. Only 45 percent of Black adults were literate, compared to 95 percent of Whites. Not a single White institution of higher learning in the South admitted Blacks. Not a single White church allowed Blacks to worship with its congregants. And only a tiny number of southern Blacks owned a substantial business. Every single institution in southern society was owned or operated by Whites, who had no interest in admitting Blacks into their ranks. For those Blacks who refused to stay "in their place," the ultimate punishment of lynching proved a powerful deterrent to wrongdoing, real or alleged. During the last decade of that century, at least 1,100 Blacks were lynched, more than two every week. Given all of these barriers to a decent life for them and their families, it's no wonder that millions of southern Blacks looked to the North for an escape from "slavery without shackles," as runaway slaves had escaped from real shackles by taking the Underground Railroad to northern freedom. In the next chapter, we'll witness the mass exodus of the Great Migration and examine the conditions that made life in the urban North barely more tolerable for most Blacks than they had endured in the rural South.

6

"Negroes Plan to Kill All Whites"

The problem of the Twentieth Century is the problem of the color-line.

THIS ONE SENTENCE, written in 1903 by W. E. B. Du Bois, the country's leading Black intellectual and social scientist, is perhaps the most prophetic of anything said about American society in that entire century. I chose it to introduce this chapter because Du Bois, by ancestry and education, was ideally suited to look critically at a society riven by race; in a way, he was both an insider and an outsider in the world in which he grew up and which he observed.

Du Bois (whose initials stand for William Edward Burghardt) was born in 1868 to parents who were each a mélange of races and ethnicities: Black and White, with forebears who had been slaves on southern plantations, and others who had come from France and the Netherlands. Raised in the relatively tolerant and bucolic town of Great Barrington in western Massachusetts, Du Bois attended its public schools and then, with funds donated by White benefactors, earned a bachelor's degree at historically Black Fisk University in Nashville, Tennessee, where he first experienced the Jim Crow system and the White racism from which it grew. Returning to Massachusetts, he enrolled at Harvard College, obtaining another bachelor's degree in history in 1890; Harvard wouldn't let him transfer credits from Fisk, an elitist and racist dismissal of "Black" education. Despite having to start over as an undergraduate, Du Bois continued at Harvard—his mentor was William James, the noted philosopher—and in 1895 became the first African American to obtain a doctorate from the nation's first college; his dissertation in sociology was entitled "Suppression of the African Slave Trade in the United States of America, 1638–1871."

After a series of short teaching posts at several colleges, in 1897 Du Bois was offered a professorship in history and economics at historically Black Atlanta University in Georgia, where he wrote many scholarly works in sociology;

his best known is *The Philadelphia Negro*, based on his fieldwork during a research fellowship at the University of Pennsylvania. In that book, Du Bois documented the many problems of the city's Black residents, among them crime, poverty, poor education, and family disruption. What distinguished this book was the direct link Du Bois drew between these disabilities and their roots in slavery, portraying what we now label "systemic racism." That was not a popular stance among critics who attributed these social problems to "bad choices" by Blacks who failed to take advantage of free public education, a position we now call "blaming the victim." Du Bois challenged this dominant view with statistics and analysis showing that "bad choices" by individual Blacks stemmed from "bad conditions" in all the institutions—especially schools and colleges—in which Blacks held very few positions of power and influence. In that respect, Du Bois was one of the earliest scholars whose pathbreaking studies and trenchant analysis served as models for later generations of scholars and social critics who explore the history and consequences of systemic racism, as this book—by a longtime admirer of Du Bois and his work—attempts to do.

Another reason for quoting Du Bois as a prophet of America's conflicts over race during the previous century is that, in addition to his scholarly work, he became an activist—as one of the founders of the NAACP in 1909 and a Socialist Party member—in fighting racism. That resolve stemmed in part from his shock and revulsion at the lynching of Sam Hose near Atlanta in 1899. Charged with murdering his White employer with an ax—Hose claimed he acted in self-defense after being threatened with death and facing a pistol—and falsely rumored to have raped his employer's wife, Hose was seized by a mob from jail and taken to a field, where some two thousand Whites gathered to watch the lynching. His captors first cut off Hose's ears, fingers, and genitals, then chained him to a tree, doused him with kerosene, and burned him alive as the crowd, reported a journalist who witnessed the spectacle, watched "with unfeigned satisfaction" as Hose's body writhed and twisted. That gruesome episode convinced Du Bois that "one could not be a calm, cool, and detached scientist while Negroes were lynched, murdered, and starved." In confronting White racism, he wrote, "the cure wasn't simply telling people the truth, it was inducing them to act on the truth." More than a century earlier, Du Bois had expressed the anger and activism of today's Black Lives Matter movement.

In words that presaged those of later Black activists and intellectuals, people like James Baldwin and Ta-Nehisi Coates, Du Bois reflected, in his

best-known book, *The Souls of Black Folk*, on the dilemma he faced as a person
with roots in two races and two cultures:

> Between me and the other world there is ever an unasked ques-
> tion: How does it feel to be a problem? One ever feels his two-ness;
> an American, a Negro; two thoughts, two unreconciled strivings; two
> warring ideals in one dark body, whose dogged strength alone keeps it
> from being torn asunder.

Speaking of himself in the third person, Du Bois continued:

> He would not Africanize America, for America has too much to teach
> the world and Africa. He would not bleach his Negro soul in a flood
> of white Americanism, for he knows that Negro blood has a message
> for the world. He simply wishes to make it possible for a man to be
> both a Negro and an American, without being cursed and spit upon
> by his fellows, without having the doors of opportunity closed roughly
> in his face.

* * *

My point in beginning this chapter with homage to Du Bois is that his
unique perspective—as a person of mixed race, a perceptive social scientist, and a man living in both the North and the South—helps us to
better understand the conflicting pressures of being a "Negro" in a society dominated by those who have appropriated the term "American" for
themselves. Would it be possible to be both Black and American in a society, at the beginning of the twentieth century, in which Blacks had so
recently been enslaved, robbed of an education beyond basic literacy, or
given none at all, and subjected to Jim Crow laws that kept them apart
from Whites who would not even share a water fountain or railway coach
with them?

In 1900, 90 percent of Blacks lived in the eleven formerly Confederate
states. Almost all lived in pine shacks on cotton plantations or small farms,
and the vast majority had no skills other than agricultural work. More than
half (55 percent) of Black adults were illiterate, compared to 5 percent of
Whites; most Blacks over forty had never attended school, even during the
Reconstruction era, when only one-fifth of Black children had any schooling,

which ended for most before the eighth grade. By all measures, the conditions of life for southern Blacks were little better than slavery.

What kept most southern Blacks in rural poverty throughout the nineteenth century was the lack of any viable alternative or, more accurately, any means of escape from generations of poverty. That changed, however, during the first three decades of the twentieth century, with the simultaneous decline of the cotton economy (from both the depredation of boll weevils and mechanization that sharply reduced the need for stoop labor) and the rapid growth of manufacturing in northern states, creating the need for unskilled or semiskilled factory labor, but labor that paid more in wages than sharecropping. These two factors, the push and pull of changing economies, combined to produce what historians now call the First Great Migration. Between 1900 and 1930, some 1.5 million rural Blacks boarded railroad coaches that took them to northern cities, and to radically different lives. (These migrants left behind, we should note, about 7 million Blacks who remained in a Jim Crow society, most in perpetual debt as sharecroppers or tenant farmers.)

Two-thirds of this first wave of Black migrants settled in eight cities: Baltimore (then still southern in Jim Crow attitudes and customs), Philadelphia, New York, Pittsburgh, Cleveland, St. Louis, Chicago, and Detroit. Each of these cities had different industries with needs for cheap labor: clothing manufacture in New York sweatshops, steel mills in Pittsburgh, meatpacking in Chicago, and automobiles in Detroit. Significantly, during those years, each of those cities had a White majority and White control of municipal government; none took any meaningful steps to help their new Black residents adjust to urban life, find decent housing, or gain steady employment in all but menial jobs, such as janitors or sanitation workers. (It's worth noting that all of these cities now have Black populations, ranging from 23 percent in Pittsburgh to 83 percent in Detroit, and each has elected at least one Black mayor. It's also notable that each is centered in a metropolitan area, as defined by the U.S. Census Bureau, that is predominantly White, largely the result of "White flight" from cities to suburbs, a phenomenon we'll discuss in later chapters.)

One fact rarely discussed by historians is that the Blacks who moved into northern cities during these decades were outnumbered, two to one, by 3 million White southerners—many of them, like the Black migrants, impoverished tenant farmers—who brought with them the Jim Crow attitudes they held toward Blacks and who developed an equal hostility toward other migrant groups who spoke strange languages and practiced strange customs and religions. During the years from 1900 to 1930, "native" White Americans reacted with animosity toward some 15 million immigrants—few of whom spoke English, most of them Catholic or Jewish—from Italy, Greece, Poland, Russia, and other countries mired in serfdom and poverty; another 12 million had earlier arrived between 1880 and 1900. After the Russian Revolution in 1917, a "Red Scare" swept the country, prompting federal officials to round up and imprison or deport thousands of real and suspected "Bolshevists" and anarchists, with active support from members of a revived Ku Klux Klan that gained some 2 or 3 million recruits in northern states from Pennsylvania to Oregon. At its peak, the Klan held twin parades in 1925 and 1926, the first with thirty thousand and the second with fifteen thousand robed and hooded Klansmen (and women and children) who waved American flags and marched along Pennsylvania Avenue in the nation's capital, filling streets from the Capitol building to the White House. (I've been told that my paternal grandfather, an accountant in the western Pennsylvania town of Beaver, was a Klan member in the 1920s; I haven't found any records of his membership, but he fit the profile of northern Klan members, many of them small businessmen and skilled workers, and I know he was hostile to Catholics, Jews, and Blacks.) These were decades of conflict and violence the country had not experienced since the Civil War. And Blacks in northern cities were the most visible and defenseless targets of racist and nativist hostility.

* * *

It would be impossible in one book to list and chronicle every incident of racial violence between 1900 and 1930: during this period, there were more than seven hundred lynchings, roughly one every five days, most in the South but dozens in northern states. In addition, two of these years, 1919 and 1921, were marked by massacres in which Whites killed at least two hundred Blacks in each paroxysm of hatred. Other forms of hostility and harassment, such as mobilizing Whites to drive Blacks from "Whites only" neighborhoods, occurred in hundreds of cities and towns across the country. Few of the Whites who took part in these racist events were arrested and charged with crimes like assault, and even fewer were convicted by juries that were mostly all-White.

Before we look at the most deadly of these outbursts, it's worth looking first at the one person whose leadership (or lack thereof) can affect and influence a substantial segment of the public, for good or bad: the occupant of the Oval Office in the White House. Presidents can't cure every social ill by themselves, or intervene in every disruptive event, but they can—if motivated by character and concern—set a tone to which most people will respond. In this respect, Woodrow Wilson lacked both the character and the concern that was sorely needed during a period of political and racial turmoil. Wilson presided over the federal government during eight tumultuous years of the century's first three decades, from 1913 to 1921. Elected as a Democrat, Wilson's two terms were bookended by two Republicans, William Howard Taft and Warren G. Harding. Unlike those men, whose records on racial issues were relatively tolerant for that time, Wilson was an unabashed southern racist, of the "genteel" variety common among the Virginia gentry in his home state, but equally believing, like Klan members, in the inherent inferiority of Blacks. He came to the White House with a reputation as a scholar of congressional politics and having served as president of his alma mater, Princeton University, for eight years, followed by a two-year term as New Jersey's governor.

Compared to the Republican presidents who preceded and succeeded him, Wilson also had a reputation as a "progressive" politician, sensitive to the needs of struggling workers and families and opposing the financial corruption of giant corporations and banks. Nonetheless, he had long held racist views of Blacks, to whom he was condescending and dismissive. Although he made pro forma statements deploring lynching, he didn't use his office to prevent or punish those who took part in or condoned these crimes. One example of Wilson's indifference toward Blacks was his go-ahead to cabinet secretaries and agency directors who sought permission to segregate their employees in their workplaces. Postmaster General Albert Burleson, a Texas racist, told Wilson that Black and White employees shared water glasses, towels, and washrooms, which offended him. Wilson agreed, although urging Burleson to have "the matter adjusted in a way to make the least friction." Taking their cue, other officials mandated similar segregation in their agencies. One federal official in Alabama fired all his Black employees, saying, "There are no government positions for Negroes in the South. A Negro's place is in the corn field." Reports about these practices upset W. E. B. Du Bois, who had supported Wilson's election; writing an open letter to Wilson in 1913, Du Bois told of "one colored clerk who could not actually be segregated on account of the nature of his work [and who] consequently had a cage built around him to separate him from his white companions of many years." There's no record that Wilson responded to Du Bois.

Perhaps the most telling example of Wilson's racist views occurred in 1915, when he invited film director D. W. Griffith to screen his cinematic paean to the "Lost Cause" of slavery, *The Birth of a Nation,* for the president and guests at the White House. Thomas Dixon, whose novel *The Clansman: A Historical Romance of the Ku Klux Klan* was the model for Griffith's film, had been a classmate of Wilson and was an honored guest at the screening. The film, of course, was silent, but dialogue was printed on cards for viewers. Among the cards flashed on the screen were three with quotes from Wilson himself. Referring to Reconstruction, one read, "The white men were roused by a mere instinct of self-preservation . . . until at last there had sprung into existence a great Ku Klux Klan, a veritable empire of the South, to protect the Southern country." In the original of that quote, Wilson had also written that White southerners were determined "to rid themselves, by fair means or foul, of the intolerable burden of governments sustained by the votes of ignorant negroes and conducted in the interest of adventurers." Another card in the film excoriated White Reconstruction officials (Wilson's "adventurers") as seeking the "veritable overthrow of civilization in the South . . . in their determination to put the white South under the heel of the black South." *The Birth of a Nation* became the first Hollywood blockbuster, its glorification of the Klan drawing millions of viewers who were exposed to Wilson's racist views. More important, Wilson did not speak out forcefully to condemn the White racists who turned the summer of 1919 into a "Red Summer" of blood shed by Blacks in murderous attacks across the country. Whether Wilson could have deterred this violence by using his presidential podium to decry it has no answer, but his ingrained racism made that unlikely.

* * *

Between the spring and autumn of 1919, "race riots" erupted in at least thirty-eight cities and towns across the country. Each had a different spark for the White attacks on Blacks—rumors of Black men raping White women the most incendiary—but with underlying factors common to all. The most significant were the economic slump that followed the end of World War I in November 1918, during which jobs became scarce and competition for them often pitted White against Black workers, and the return from European battlefields of more than 3 million White troops, many of whom discovered that Blacks had been recruited to fill the jobs, especially in relatively well-paid factory work, such as steel mills and automobile plants, that White soldiers had relinquished to serve in the armed forces.

Also returning from service were some 380,000 Black troops; virtually all had been relegated to all-Black support units commanded by White officers, many of them southerners with Jim Crow attitudes. With the Red

Scare against radicals underway, President Wilson predicted darkly, "[T]he American Negro returning from abroad would be our greatest medium in conveying Bolshevism to America." Du Bois, then editor of the NAACP magazine *The Crisis*, viewed the returning Black troops not as potential Bolsheviks but as recruits to the nascent civil rights movement. In one article, he voiced the feelings of returning Black troops:

> We return from the slavery of uniform which the world's madness demanded us to don to the freedom of civil garb. We stand again to look America squarely in the face and call a spade a spade. We sing: This country of ours, despite all its better souls have done and dreamed, is yet a shameful land.

In another, he struck a militant tone: "By the God of Heaven, we are cowards and jackasses if now that the war is over, we do not marshal every ounce of our brain and brawn to fight a sterner, longer, more unbending battle against the forces of hell in our own land."

Those "forces of hell" took shape in mobs of Whites who took out their fears and grievances in bloody rampages against Blacks. The first eruption in a big city swept across the nation's capital from July 19 to 23, beginning with the rumored arrest of a Black man for raping a White woman, although no such arrest had occurred. On hearing these rumors, groups of recently discharged White sailors, fueled by a days-long drunken spree, swarmed through the city, beating any Blacks they encountered, dragging Black passengers off streetcars, and torching Black-owned homes and shops. When the city's White police refused to intervene, Blacks—many of them military veterans—fought back with guns, posting snipers on rooftops to guard their neighborhoods. After the second night of violence, the *Washington Post* reported, "In the negro district along U Street from Seventh to Fourteenth streets, the negroes began early in the evening to take vengeance for the assaults on their race in the downtown district the night before." Only after fifteen people had been killed, ten White and five Black, did President Wilson mobilize the National Guard to restore order; the Washington "riot" was one of few in which more Whites died than Blacks.

With order restored at gunpoint, federal troops withdrew from Washington on July 25, 1919. Just two days later, a larger and deadlier outbreak of mob violence turned Chicago into a literal war zone. It began when a seventeen-year-old Black grocery store worker, Eugene Williams, decided to escape the 95-degree heat and humidity by floating on a homemade raft along a crowded Lake Michigan beach, with three teenage friends. But when the raft crossed an invisible and informal line separating White and Black swimmers, a twenty-four-year-old White bakery worker named George Stauber began yelling slurs and hurling rocks at the young Black "trespassers." One large rock hit Williams in the head, knocking him off the raft and into the lake. He drowned before anyone could rescue him. (His death certificate listed its cause as "drowned during a race riot.") A White police officer refused to arrest Stauber, although people on the beach pointed him out as the rock thrower. After Williams's body had been removed from the water, an angry crowd of about a thousand Blacks gathered to protest the refusal of police to arrest and charge Stauber for the assault; he was later charged with manslaughter, but was acquitted and returned to his bakery job.

The Black protest against Williams's murder prompted dozens of armed White men to drive through Black neighborhoods, firing randomly at Blacks on the streets. Other White mobs stormed through the largely Black South Side of Chicago, torching whole blocks of homes and businesses. The violence ebbed and flowed for thirteen days, until several thousand National Guard troops finally occupied the city and restored order; a later Commission on Race Relations report listed the toll: 38 fatalities (23 Blacks and 15 Whites), 527 injuries, and 1,000 Black families left homeless from the White-led arson. But Chicago remained a racial powder keg, with sporadic explosions of violence, many sparked by Whites who resisted the steady influx of Blacks into "Whites only" neighborhoods, as growing numbers of Blacks looked for housing outside the crowded ghettos into which Whites had kept them confined.

At this point, a step outside this historical narrative is instructive. Looking at Chicago today, a century after the Red Summer erupted in White terror, the city is even more segregated in housing and schools and still plagued by violence, with Black children too often the innocent victims of drive-by shootings and gang turf wars. In June 2020, for example, seven Black children under eighteen were fatally shot over a two-week period; the youngest victim was twenty-month-old Sincere Gaston, shot while he was riding in a car with his mother. Ironically, his father, Thomas, was a former gang member who left the "street life" to work for an antiviolence group called CRED, for Creating Real Economic Destiny. The immense task of ending violence and creating decent jobs for Black and Brown young people (each group now makes up 30 percent of Chicago's population) is one that faces every city in America, with no prospect of easy solutions for the systemic racism from which inequality stems and persists. These problems, of course, are hardly limited to

Chicago; in various forms, they have led to protests and soul-searching in virtually every city and town across the country, a stock-taking both painful and necessary.

* * *

"NEGROES PLAN TO KILL ALL WHITES." This inflammatory headline in the *Arkansas Gazette*, the state's leading newspaper, published in Little Rock but read statewide, spurred more than a thousand White men to descend on the small town of Elaine, in the Delta region along the Mississippi River, on October 1, 1919. This hastily assembled mob, with recruits from across Arkansas and others from Mississippi and Tennessee, launched a killing spree that ended with the deaths of at least two hundred Black men, women, and children. What became known as the Elaine Massacre was the last and by far the most deadly attack on Blacks during the Red Summer that stretched from spring into the fall of 1919.

Unlike earlier "race riots" in Washington, D.C., and Chicago, the "nigger hunt" in Phillips County, Arkansas, began as a conflict between Black sharecroppers and tenant farmers and White plantation owners over complaints that Blacks were being systematically cheated at the White-run cotton gins and company stores at which they were forced to buy food and supplies. Also unlike the big-city attacks on Blacks, those killed in and around Elaine had remained in the rural South as many other Blacks left their farms and joined the Great Migration to northern cities.

For cotton farmers, 1919 promised to be a profitable year, as record crops and rising cotton prices gave hope to those mired in seemingly perpetual "debt slavery." But the widespread cheating at the gins and stores threatened to wipe out the hoped-for profits of croppers and tenants. In response, many of them joined a union called the Progressive Farmers and Household Union of America, whose constitution ended with this slogan: "WE BATTLE FOR THE RIGHTS OF OUR RACE: IN UNION IS STRENGTH." Many of the union members had recently returned from military service and had stockpiled rifles and ammunition to defend themselves against possible White attacks. On the night of September 30, about two hundred union members and their families had gathered at the Black Hoop Spur Church, about three miles from Elaine, a market town with about four hundred residents, 90 percent of them Black; most Whites in Phillips County lived in the county seat of Helena, with some eight thousand residents. Rumors of a strike by union members to withhold cotton until they received fair prices had upset Whites;

Charles Young, the publisher of the weekly *Helena World*, spread word that "the niggers was fixin' to uprise" after the postmaster showed him a copy of a militant Black newspaper from New York, urging sharecroppers to revolt: "Strike! Southern white capitalists know the Negro can bring down the white bourbon South to its knees by one strike at the source of production."

The Blacks at the Hoop Spur Church that night were debating whether to call a strike when armed guards saw a group of White men approaching, shining a flashlight in the dark. Fearing an attack, the guards opened fire, killing a White man and wounding a White deputy sheriff. By the next morning, a White posse, deputized by the sheriff, "began to hunt Negroes" across the county, killing dozens. The following day, six hundred federal troops, dispatched by Secretary of War Newton Baker, arrived with twelve machine guns and orders to "kill any negro who refuses to surrender immediately." One soldier later boasted that "they were shooting them down like rabbits." Other soldiers captured an elderly Black man; when he became "extremely insolent," they doused him with kerosene and burned him alive. By the end of the "nigger hunt," some two hundred Blacks—perhaps more, as many bodies lay rotting in fields or were tossed into the Mississippi River— had been killed, including sixteen men who were hanged from a bridge and twenty-eight whose bodies were "thrown into a pit and burned," as a White schoolteacher later testified.

Having crushed the never-called strike, White officials exacted revenge on surviving Blacks by indicting 122 men and women on charges from murder to nightriding. An all-White jury inside the Phillips County courthouse, while hundreds of Whites gathered outside, many brandishing guns and menacing the proceedings, convicted and sentenced to death twelve Black men for the murders of three White men, although two had been killed by fellow Whites in a hail of gunfire. Despite the claim of the army commander that only two Blacks had been killed, reports of the massacre prompted Black leaders of the NAACP to press for new trials of the convicted men, on grounds that the threatening courthouse mob had intimidated the jurors and deprived the defendants of their due process right to a fair trial.

After two years of legal back-and-forth in state and federal courts, the death sentences were appealed to the U.S. Supreme Court in 1922 in the case of *Moore v. Dempsey*. (Frank Moore was one of the condemned Blacks, and E. H. Dempsey was the White Arkansas state penitentiary warden who "held the body" of Moore and his fellow defendants; wardens were generally the defendants in habeas corpus cases, a judicial writ commanding them to "bring the body before us.") On February 19, 1923, a six-justice majority ruled that the defendants had been denied a fair trial, ordering the case back to the federal district court in Arkansas for a further hearing to gather facts and call witnesses on whether the state trial had been fatally infected by a threatening White mob. Despite the lack of a final Supreme Court ruling in the case, the justices broke new legal ground by holding that state court convictions could be appealed to federal courts through writs of habeas corpus, alleging due process violations.

In his majority opinion, Justice Oliver Wendell Holmes Jr. referred to the mob atmosphere and described the state trial in these words:

> The Court and neighborhood were thronged with an adverse crowd that threatened the most dangerous consequences to anyone inter- fering with the desired result. The [appointed White lawyer for the defendants] did not venture to demand delay or a change of venue, to challenge a juryman or to ask for separate trials. He had no pre- liminary consultation with the accused, called no witnesses for the de- fense, although they could have been produced, and did not put the defendants on the stand. The trial lasted about three-quarters of an hour, and in less than five minutes, the jury brought in a verdict of guilty of murder in the first degree. According to the allegations and affidavits [of the Black defendants], there never was a chance for the petitioners to be acquitted; no juryman could have voted for an ac- quittal and continued to live in Phillips County, and if any prisoner by any chance had been acquitted by a jury, he could not have escaped the mob.

Quoting from an earlier Supreme Court decision in a Georgia case, Holmes stated that "if the State, supplying no corrective process, carries into execution a judgment of death or imprisonment based upon a verdict . . . produced by mob domination, the State deprives the accused of his life or liberty without due process of law."

Following the Supreme Court ruling, the Arkansas governor, Thomas McRae, knowing that a federal court hearing would reveal the brutal tor- ture of the defendants and the murder of many others, commuted the death sentences and made the Black men—after four years in prison, and only two days from execution—eligible for parole, which was granted on January 13, 1925. This delayed justice, however, came only after at least two hundred Blacks, falsely accused of plotting the mass murder of Whites, themselves became victims of mass murder by Whites—including U.S. Army troops—who reveled in "shooting them down like rabbits."

The Red Summer of 1919 ended with the Elaine Massacre, but White attacks on Blacks continued over the next decade, including 378 recorded lynchings of Blacks, more than three each month. But the most deadly, and notorious, of these violent attacks was another horrific massacre, this one in Tulsa, Oklahoma. A booming oil town, Tulsa then had a population of seventy-five thousand, including about ten thousand Black residents, most of them living in the Greenwood neighborhood, also known as the "Black Wall Street" for the prosperous Black-owned businesses that thrived during these years. Relations between Blacks and Whites in Tulsa had been relatively peaceful, although the city and state still enforced Jim Crow laws and customs.

That all changed on May 30, 1921, when police arrested Dick Rowland, a nineteen-year-old Black shoeshine man, for allegedly assaulting Sarah Page, a seventeen-year-old White elevator operator in the nearby Drexel Building, which housed offices and shops on Main Street in downtown Tulsa. Supposedly, Rowland had entered the building to use the "Colored" restroom on the top floor, a courtesy the nearby shine-parlor owner had arranged with the building manager. Rowland got on the elevator Page was operating and (according to later accounts) tripped, grabbing her arm to avoid falling, which prompted her to scream; a White store clerk heard the screams and called the police to report an assault on Page and having seen Rowland, whom he recognized, flee the building. Rowland was quickly apprehended and taken to the jail in the county courthouse. (Unfortunately too late to prevent the carnage that followed, Page informed the county attorney that she did not wish to testify against Rowland, and the charges against him were dismissed; there were also later reports that the two young people had a romantic relationship that both, understandably, wanted to conceal. Whether their brief encounter that day was an accident or an assault made no difference in what soon happened.)

What soon happened was that the city's afternoon paper, the *Tulsa Tribune*, published a hastily written editorial titled "To Lynch Negro Tonight," although it cited no sources for this claim. Nonetheless, by 7:30 that night, hundreds of Whites had gathered at the courthouse, demanding the sheriff hand over Rowland, which he refused to do. With the mob still milling around the courthouse at 9:00, a group of about twenty-five armed Black men, many of them recent veterans, arrived from the Greenwood neighborhood and offered to help the sheriff defend Rowland; when he declined, they returned to Greenwood. An hour later, rumors that Whites were storming the courthouse prompted a larger group of armed Black men, about seventy-five, to return and again offer to guard the courthouse. The sheriff again declined, and the Blacks turned to leave for Greenwood, when a White man tried to grab the rifle of a Black veteran; during this scuffle, a shot was fired, although no one was hit.

Enraged by their failure to seize Rowland for what surely would have been his lynching, and by the sudden gunfire, Whites stormed from the courthouse and descended on Greenwood, joined by hundreds more armed Whites who, according to later reports, were deputized on the spot by police and instructed to "get a gun and get a nigger." All through that night, Whites roamed Greenwood, shooting any Blacks on the streets and systematically looting and torching Black-owned buildings and homes. Local National Guard troops were mobilized but spent the night protecting White areas from a rumored Black invasion. By the time additional Guard units arrived from Oklahoma City, Greenwood had been reduced to smoldering rubble and six thousand Blacks were left homeless, many spending the following months living in tents while rebuilding began in Greenwood. A complete tally of those killed during the White invasion was impossible, as many bodies had been dumped in mass graves and covered with blood-soaked soil; the best estimates are that two hundred to three hundred Blacks perished in the Tulsa Massacre. (Beginning in July 2020, archaeologists and forensic analysts undertook a search for human remains in suspected mass grave sites, guided by ground-penetrating radar that showed "anomalies" in several areas; at this writing, their efforts have not been reported.)

* * *

This chapter began with the prediction of W. E. B. Du Bois in 1903: "The problem of the Twentieth Century is the problem of the color-line." During the first three decades of that century, that "problem" affected the nation's Black population in ways that most Whites did not share. For those Blacks who rebelled, in ways both large and small, against the system of White supremacy, the consequences could be deadly, as we have seen in this account of lynchings and massacres. But even those Blacks who escaped with their lives from this systematic terror paid a price in poverty, poor or no education, exclusion from skilled, well-paid jobs, and—in the northern cities that became the terminus of the Great Migration—segregation into ghettos with boundaries patrolled by hostile Whites.

At this point, we will look closely at the experience during this period of Blacks who migrated to one of these cities, to explore in some detail the factors that have, since that period, kept many Blacks from breaking out of inner-city segregation and the disabilities it has imposed on them. This new focus, which will form parts of subsequent chapters as well, is meant to provoke thought about the persistence of racial inequality and, hopefully, about possible solutions to what has become the problem of the twenty-first century.

The city I have chosen for this closer look is Detroit, Michigan. Let me briefly explain my reasons for this choice. First, among the nation's fifty largest cities, Detroit has the greatest concentration of Black residents; as of 2020, some 83 percent, with just 9 percent White. Back in 1930, the proportions were almost precisely reversed: 92 percent White and 8 percent Black. What happened in those intervening decades makes Detroit an exemplary case study in racial inequality. Other major cities, of course, have also experienced a major shift in racial composition, although less pronounced than in Detroit. But, in my view, looking at the "most Black" major city (although now just one-third of its population peak in 1950) will help in understanding the factors that have combined to produce our current national struggle to deal with the damaging effects of deep-rooted and long-standing institutional and systemic racism. To deny or disparage those causes and effects is, in effect, to hinder the search for solutions that will enable us to create a more equitable and inclusive society. If we can't find solutions for Detroit, we can't find them for the nation as a whole.

* * *

Founded by French traders who built a fort in 1701 to protect the soldiers, farmers, and merchants against both British and Indian attack, Detroit soon became the most important French city between Montreal and New Orleans. In 1763, France ceded its territories east of the Mississippi River to Great Britain after its defeat in the Seven Years War. Twenty years later, after the British defeat in the American Revolution, the Treaty of Paris expanded the United States to include nearly all land east of the Mississippi and south of Canada; Michigan became a state in 1837 and Detroit its largest city, with an 1840 population of just 8,909, of whom only 193 were Black.

During the rest of the nineteenth century, Detroit's population almost doubled every decade, to 286,000 in 1900. But only 1.4 percent in that year were Black; in fact, the Black proportion of the city's residents fell by half from that in 1860. Again, Detroit's population almost doubled in each of the next three decades, reaching 1.6 million in 1930. But the Black population grew by more than six times during these years, to 120,000, though still only 8 percent of the White total. The story of these two racial groups, crowded into one compact city, will show us the unbroken link between Detroit in 1900 and today, the persistence of racial inequality, and its roots in the rural South.

The Motor City was fueled by the production of cheap, durable cars and the paving of streets in many cities and towns, giving Americans a means of transportation that did not need grain for fuel and stalls for housing. And no one was more responsible for the explosive growth of the auto industry than Henry Ford, who launched the Ford Motor Company in a converted garage on Mack Avenue in Detroit in 1903, turning out just a few cars a day by teams of two or three workers. But Ford invented and implemented the assembly-line method of production, in which workers did the same job (installing bumpers, for example) as each chassis moved down the line, allowing hundreds of cars to be assembled every day. In 1908, Ford introduced the Model T, which sold millions over twenty years, until it was replaced by the Model A, which sold more millions.

What makes Henry Ford a major figure in the growth in the number of southern Blacks in Detroit was that he not only hired many Black workers, who needed little training to perform repetitive jobs on assembly lines, but he paid them the same wages as Whites, the famous "five dollars a day" beginning in 1908, earning the loyalty of his employees. Ford also promoted Blacks who showed promise into supervisory and managerial positions; some White workers harassed their Black fellow workers, and some even quit their jobs, but Ford did not back down. Historians debate whether this was altruism on Ford's part or simply a way to attract and retain an efficient and loyal workforce; given his notorious anti-Semitism, the latter seems more likely. Either way, southern Blacks who migrated to Detroit earned vastly more and had steadier jobs than sharecroppers. Ford even sent recruiters to Mississippi and other southern states, offering "freedom tickets" on trains to Detroit.

Although working in the auto and related parts industries made Detroit a magnet for southern Blacks, they also faced hostility from two very different groups. Beginning in the 1880s, immigrants from Poland flocked to Detroit; they were the first to lay railroad track and pave streets and then to work in the auto plants, not only Ford's but also those of the Dodge brothers, John and Horace, and Walter Chrysler, whose plants turned out more expensive models than Ford's. Detroit soon had the second-largest Polish community in the country, after Chicago, growing from 13,000 in 1904 to 115,000 in 1930, in a city with 120,000 Black residents. Most Polish immigrants, like Blacks, came from farms and had little education, although most learned English fairly rapidly, the older immigrants speaking Polish at home and in their communities. Like other immigrant groups, including Irish and Italian, Poles tended to cluster in ethnic neighborhoods within walking distance of their churches, schools, and shops.

The city of Hamtramck, surrounded on three sides by Detroit and incorporated in 1922, became almost entirely Polish; in 1920, two-thirds of its fifty thousand residents were born in Poland, and almost all the rest had Polish-born parents. The significance of Detroit's Polish population to this account of racial inequality is that Polish immigrants, few if any having ever seen a Black person in Poland, were susceptible to the racism with which most native-born Americans viewed Blacks; older Blacks recall being warned by their parents not to stray into Hamtramck, to avoid being chased out by Polish kids.

If Poles (and other European immigrants) responded to the influx of Blacks to Detroit with suspicion and hostility, born of ignorance and lack of prior contact, another immigrant group displayed even more hostility, erupting into violence in several bloody "riots" that were actually lynch mobs. These were the southern-born rural Whites who migrated to northern cities in greater numbers than Blacks, pushed by the decline in cotton production and other agricultural products and pulled by the prospect of better-paying, more steady jobs. This aspect of the First Great Migration has been largely ignored and overlooked by historians who focus on Black migration, but in fact more than twice as many Whites left the South during the first three decades of the twentieth century; 27 percent of all southern migrants were Black, but 69 percent were White. In 1930, Detroit had 120,000 Black residents, almost all of the adults born in the South, but they were outnumbered two to one by the 273,000 White southerners, most of them also unskilled and poorly educated. Unlike Poles, who first encountered Blacks in Detroit, White southerners brought with them a long history of racism and Jim Crow attitudes; many of them had probably witnessed lynchings, and virtually all considered Blacks inferior and dangerous.

During the first three decades of the twentieth century, organizers of the Populist and Socialist parties had tried, with some success, to convince poor White farmers to join biracial coalitions with their Black counterparts. But these efforts foundered and disbanded after the White power elite crushed them with intimidation (threatening their members with eviction from their farms) and often with threats of violence against organizers. The great majority of poor southern Whites, however, had never joined these coalitions; those who migrated to Detroit and other northern cities had been raised to believe in White supremacy and Black inferiority and succeeded for decades in keeping Blacks out of "White" neighborhoods. There were even banners on buildings that read, "This Is a White Man's Neighborhood. Keep It That Way!"

The story of Ossian Sweet reflects the violence that Whites in Detroit would use to keep Blacks out of their neighborhoods. But it is only one of hundreds of similar stories in cities across the country, most of which went unreported and ignored by police and other officials. What makes the ordeal of Ossian Sweet remarkable and remembered, at least by older Blacks in Detroit, is that even a well-educated, community-minded professional is not welcome in a White neighborhood if he is Black, and only because he is Black. A brief account of the story of Ossian Sweet should remind us that racism takes no account of a person's character, accomplishments, and service to less fortunate people, if that person is Black. This story says much about Detroit, but also about cities across the country in which most Black people, and almost all poor Black people, remain segregated in run-down and deteriorating housing, in neighborhoods that lack basic municipal services, and whose children are crowded into segregated schools that leave them without the skills required by an economy based on advanced technology and proficiency in written and verbal communication.

Ossian Sweet was born in 1895, in the small farming town of Bartow, Florida, one of ten children of a former slave who worked in the fields. At the age of five, Ossian watched in horror, hiding in bushes, as a White mob burned a Black teenager to death, then picked pieces of his charred flesh as souvenirs. After leaving Florida at the age of thirteen, Ossian was fortunate in being able to work his way, stoking furnaces and washing dishes, through preparatory school and then college at all-Black Wilberforce University in Ohio, and then through medical school at all-Black Howard University in Washington, D.C.

Sweet moved to Detroit in 1921, living with his wife and infant daughter in the impoverished Black Bottom neighborhood. Unable to find a position at any of the "White" hospitals in Detroit, he set up a practice in a local pharmacy, treating poor Whites and Blacks alike. In 1924, after a year of medical training in Vienna and Paris, he returned to Detroit and gained a position at Dunbar Hospital, the first for Blacks in Detroit. Saving money and seeking better housing for his family, he bought a modest two-story house on Garland Avenue, in an all-White, working-class neighborhood, and moved in on September 8, 1925. The next night, a menacing crowd gathered outside, shouting racist slurs, but a police presence dispersed them. Fearing violence,

Sweet recruited two younger brothers and seven colleagues and friends to protect him and his wife. A larger crowd showed up the following night, throwing stones at the house, breaking an upstairs window. Several of Sweet's defenders had brought guns, and as more stones and bricks hit the house, a shot was fired from the upstairs window. That shot wounded one White man and killed another. The police, who had been standing by without dispersing the crowd, quickly entered the house and arrested all eleven people inside, including Sweet's wife, Gladys. All those arrested were charged with murder and held in jail without bail until their trial.

The mass arrests and murder charges galvanized the Black community, not only in Detroit but across the country, prompting the general secretary of the NAACP, James Weldon Johnson, to recruit the famed—and, to some, infamous—criminal lawyer Clarence Darrow to represent the defendants. Their trial began on October 30, before Municipal Judge Frank Murphy, later the mayor of Detroit, governor of Michigan, and liberal Supreme Court justice, named by President Franklin Roosevelt. Judge Murphy had dismissed charges against three defendants; the remaining eight faced an all-White jury. Darrow argued that whoever fired the fatal shot—which was never determined—did so in self-defense, to protect himself and the others from a violent mob. After lengthy deliberations, the jurors told Judge Murphy they were unable to reach a verdict, although the majority had voted for acquittal. Murphy declared a mistrial, and the retrial began on April 19, 1926, before another all-White jury. Darrow had moved to have each remaining defendant tried separately; Sweet's youngest brother, Henry, was the first to be tried. Darrow's self-defense argument convinced the jury to acquit Henry, and the prosecuting attorney moved to dismiss the charges against the remaining seven defendants, including Sweet. Sadly, the remainder of his life was marked with tragedies. His wife, Gladys, his two-year-old daughter, Iva, and his youngest brother, Henry, all died of tuberculosis after long illnesses. Depressed and almost penniless, Ossian Sweet ended his life at sixty-five with a gunshot to his head.

What was hailed as a victory for Sweet and those charged with the murder of a White man did little to open Detroit's White neighborhoods to Blacks, even those able to find realtors who would show them properties and banks willing to finance mortgages. Many realtors, in fact, engaged in what was called "block-busting," posting fliers in White neighborhoods warning homeowners that Blacks were moving in, then buying houses at fire-sale prices from Whites who fled to other parts of Detroit or its suburbs, then selling those houses to Blacks at inflated prices. In many cases, White neighborhoods turned Black almost overnight. Banks also practiced "redlining," for the lines on maps designating neighborhoods in which they would not underwrite mortgages for Blacks. These two schemes, along with restrictive covenants that prohibited the sale or rental of property to Blacks (and often Jews and sometimes Asians as well), were employed across the country and operated to solidify the residential segregation that now characterizes most low-income areas of America's large cities. Once enclosed in urban ghettos and saddled with poor education and few skills, the majority of Blacks found it difficult—and for many impossible—to escape the walls of hostility that surrounded them. Whether those walls could be toppled during the Great Depression of the 1930s and the wartime and postwar years of the 1940s was a question that faced millions of Blacks across the country. The answer was far from certain.

7

"Intimate Social Contact with Negro Men"

They say white folks up north are having a depression, out of work, can't feed their children, lose their home. I feel sorry for them, I surely do. The good Lord don't want anybody to go hungry, no place to sleep. But you ask what things are like for folks around here. Lordy, the colored folks in this county been in a depression forever. Hard times is what we always had. Some times are better, some worse, but always hard. But we take care of each other, that's what we always do. Most colored folks got gardens, got chickens, got hogs, got a mule and a wagon. Folks that need help, neighbors help them out. They might not have much, but what they got, they share. So nobody round here goes hungry. I hope things get better up north, but folks here know what hard times is like. Help each other, and trust in the Lord.

THESE WERE THE words of McKinley Brown, speaking in 1931 with a writer for the publication of a northern relief agency, hoping its donors would contribute funds to help southern Blacks weather the Great Depression. Brown owned a crossroads grocery store in Lowndes County, Alabama, heavily Black both then and now, part of the Black Belt that stretched across the Deep South. He told the writer he extended credit to people who couldn't pay for food and supplies, not expecting repayment, and bartered with others in exchange for vegetables, eggs, and home-butchered pork. Lowndes County had lost 40 percent of its population between 1900 and 1930, from thirty-six thousand to twenty-three thousand, part of the Great Migration to the North. Those who left were mostly young, including children, leaving behind the elderly and those who felt tied to their land through ancestry and habituation to its routines of planting, tending, and harvesting their crops. For many of them, the hardship "up north" had little effect on their lives of hard work and the satisfactions of church and community.

But there was also, during these hard years, the ever-present danger of violent retaliation for Blacks who—even accidentally—failed to stay "in their place" in dealings with Whites. A few months after McKinley Brown spoke with the writer, this headline appeared in newspapers across the country: "Negro Boy Is Killed by Mob in Alabama." With the dateline of Hayneville, Alabama, August 5, 1931, the article read:

> A 16-year-old Negro boy, accused of an attempted attack on an 11-year-old white girl, was lynched by a posse of citizens in the Sandy Ridge community near here Wednesday. According to Sheriff Meadows of Lowndes County, the Negro accosted the girl on the way to a grocery. She fought him and escaped home. When the sheriff arrived, he said he found the Negro's body with 32 bullet holes in it, tied to the trunk of a tree. No arrests have been made.

The article didn't name the young lynching victim. According to the 1930 federal census, Henry Oneal Quinn, born in 1914, was the third of fourteen children of Johnny and Mary Jane Quinn, sharecroppers in the small town of Sandy Ridge, near the Lowndes County seat of Hayneville. (Later reports referred to him as Neal Quinn; he was nine days shy of his seventeenth birthday when he was lynched.) Sheriff William F. Meadows, the most powerful White man in Lowndes County, must have known some of the White men who riddled Neal Quinn's body with bullets, but they all escaped arrest and trial for the lynching. At a perfunctory grand jury inquest, Sheriff Meadows testified his investigation was hampered by "censor," which I presume means "nobody would talk." Such were the ways in the Alabama of the 1930s. (One of the "Blackest" Alabama counties at 75 percent, Lowndes did not elect its first Black sheriff until 1970, after the Voting Rights Act of 1965 spurred Blacks to register across the South, against fierce White resistance that included the shotgun murder in Hayneville in August 1965 of Jonathan Daniels, a White Episcopal seminarian, by Tom Coleman, a Lowndes County sheriff's deputy who was acquitted of manslaughter charges by an all-White jury. Such were the ways of Alabama in the 1960s and 1970s.)

* * *

The 1930 census showed that 79 percent of the country's Black population still lived in the states of the former Confederacy; the Great Migration of 1.5 million rural Blacks to the urban North had slowed as jobs became scarce after the stock market crash in October 1929 sent stock prices plummeting almost 90 percent by July 1932, before a long, slow recovery during the rest of that decade. Industrial production fell by half during that period, and the unemployment rate, just 3.2 percent in 1929, reached an all-time high of 25 percent in 1933, with millions more absorbing wage cuts to keep their jobs. The human toll during the Great Depression could be measured in dry statistics of lost jobs and homes but is best seen in the poignant photography of Dorothea Lange, Lewis Hine, and Walker Evens of Dust Bowl Whites whose farms had blown away; of Blacks in the cotton fields, bags for the prickly bolls trailing behind them; of children toiling in textile mills and as coal-dust-covered "breaker boys" in mines.

The first three years of the Great Depression were hard on both Whites and Blacks, as the administration of President Herbert Hoover and the Republican-led Congress failed to grasp the enormity of the economic catastrophe. With the federal government unwilling to enact and implement meaningful relief programs, Hoover, an engineer by training, stepped away from any responsibility for the economic and social wreckage: "Economic depression cannot be cured by legislative action or executive pronouncement. Economic wounds must be healed by the action of the cells of the economic body—the producers and consumers themselves." But with the production of goods down by more than half and the income of consumers equally cut by unemployment and wage cuts, the economic "body" could not be healed by palliatives and reassuring words. Speaking as the country slid further into depression, Hoover adopted an upbeat tone, assuring worried Americans, "[W]e shall soon, with the help of God, be in sight of the day when poverty shall be banished from this nation." God, who had said that "the poor ye shall always have with you," added that "whenever you want, you can do good for them." But God did not put food on the tables of the millions of newly poor, let alone the already poor, or construct homes for the displaced and despairing.

* * *

Would FDR's election also usher in a "Black New Deal" to help those whose needs were even greater than Whites'? Jim Crow laws kept all but a handful of southern Blacks from voting, laws imposed by White Democrats and still enforced by intimidation and violence. Those Blacks who could vote, in both North and South, had traditionally backed the Republicans as the party of Lincoln, the Great Emancipator whose portrait hung on the walls of many Black homes, often alongside one of Jesus. Public opinion polls had not yet been invented (the Gallup polls began in 1936), but one study showed that only 21 percent of Blacks in Chicago had voted for Roosevelt, whose party was still infected with racism; that percentage soared to 76 in 1936, as the realignment of the two parties became a permanent feature of national politics. But the Democrats, during and after FDR's terms in office, were split between northern progressives and southern Dixiecrats who were entrenched in Congress, holding Roosevelt hostage to their demand that Jim Crow laws remain beyond congressional repeal. Most of the Dixiecrats, however, supported FDR's relief program as benefiting their White constituents.

The Republican electoral debacle in Roosevelt's first term left the party of Lincoln with no power to block congressional legislation: the 1932 elections sent 313 Democrats to the House and 58 to the Senate; only 117 House and 37 Senate Republicans survived that year. The 1934 midterm elections accelerated the GOP decline: 322 House Democrats and 69 in the Senate vastly outnumbered 103 House Republicans and 25 Senators. With these majorities, Congress moved quickly after Roosevelt's inauguration in March 1933 to enact the "Hundred Days" programs he had promised voters in his campaign.

In his inaugural address to a throng that spilled from the Capitol portico, the new president struck a tone of both sacrifice and hope in words that did not shy from grim reality:

> So, first of all, let me assert my firm belief that the only thing we have to fear is fear itself—nameless, unreasoning, unjustified terror which paralyzes needed efforts to convert retreat into advance. In every dark hour of our national life a leadership of frankness and a vigor has met with that understanding and support of the people themselves which is essential to victory. And I am convinced that you will again give that support to leadership in these critical days.

With leadership from the White House, Congress established and funded new agencies designed to put unemployed workers into federal jobs and to aid their struggling families. These "alphabet agencies" included the Civilian Conservation Corps (CCC), putting young people to work cutting trails and building campgrounds in national parks and forests; the Federal Emergency Relief Administration, which spent $500 million (about $7 billion now) on soup kitchens, shelters, and nursery schools for homeless and hungry people; the Agricultural Adjustment Administration to help farmers keep their farms by raising crop prices; and the National Recovery Administration, with provisions to improve working conditions, outlaw child labor, and set minimum wages (beginning at 25 cents an hour). Republicans railed against this "creeping socialism" to no avail; they were essentially bystanders in Congress, repudiated by the voters who blamed them—and their big-business and Wall Street allies—for the financial ruin of capitalism gone wild in the Roaring Twenties.

Black Americans responded to Roosevelt's election and his New Deal program with a mixture of hope and fear: hope that they would share equally with Whites in getting jobs and relief, but also fear that the Dixiecrats who ruled the Jim Crow states might shut them out of these programs. Hope was expressed by Mary McLeod Bethune, the noted Black educator, who said the New Deal represented "the first time in their history" that Blacks felt the "expectancy of sympathetic understanding" of their plight. Other Black leaders, however, voiced fears that New Deal relief programs would replicate the Jim Crow segregation in federal agencies that President Wilson had encouraged and that persisted under his three Republican successors.

As it turned out, both the hopes and the fears of Black leaders and their followers were realized in part, with advances and setbacks as good intentions met harsh realities. Under the auspices of Eleanor Roosevelt, an informal group known as the "Black Cabinet" pulled together Black officials in federal agencies to voice their concerns and press for equal treatment for Blacks in New Deal programs. Headed by Bethune, who directed the Office of Negro Affairs in the National Youth Administration and had access to the White House through her friendship with the First Lady, the forty-five members of the Black Cabinet included William Hastie, assistant solicitor of the Interior Department (later named by FDR as the first Black federal judge), and Robert Weaver, who served in the Federal Housing Authority (later named by President Lyndon Johnson as the first Black cabinet member, heading the Department of Housing and Urban Development). The major goal of these advisors was to ensure the allocation of at least 10 percent of relief funds and jobs to Blacks (their proportion then in the national population). They achieved some success: the CCC enlisted more than 350,000 young Black men, about 11 percent of its workforce; the National Youth Administration assisted more than 300,000 young Blacks and hired more Black supervisors than any other New Deal agency; the government's literacy program taught over 1 million illiterate Blacks to read and write. However, many New Deal programs, especially in the South, practiced segregation in deference to "local customs," including the CCC work camps and housing programs that increased the already existing separation of Blacks and Whites in cities both North and South. Their grudging acceptance of these Jim Crow practices was the price the Black Cabinet paid for a place at the table in the White House and desperately needed relief for jobless, homeless, and hungry Blacks. Perhaps the most significant achievement of this group was the tripling of Black professionals—lawyers, engineers, librarians, and other skilled and educated employees and officials—in federal agencies.

Aside from their material needs of food, clothing, and housing, the greatest need of Blacks in the 1930s was the institution that could give them the skills to find decent jobs and support their families. Education was the key to unlocking doors that had long been closed. During that decade, the literacy rate among Blacks rose to 84 percent (from just 45 percent in 1900), and almost as many Black children between age five and nineteen were enrolled in school as Whites, although fewer Black children continued past the eighth grade; between them, the Deep South states had only a dozen Jim Crow high schools for Blacks. For those Blacks who completed high school, the public colleges and universities in the former Confederacy remained segregated, so Blacks attended Agricultural and Mechanical universities in most southern states; as the name suggests, their curricula centered on training farmers and teaching skilled trades. These Jim Crow schools offered little for prospective doctors, lawyers, or scientists. Most private colleges in northern states were lily-white, educating the children of the White upper class for careers in law, business, medicine, and other well-paid professions. Among the few all-Black private colleges were Lincoln University near Oxford, Pennsylvania (undergraduate alma mater of Thurgood Marshall in 1930), Fisk University in Nashville (where W. E. B. Du Bois earned his first degree in 1888), and Atlanta University (where Du Bois later taught). All but a handful of Black physicians in the 1930s had attended just two all-Black medical schools: Howard University in D.C. and Meharry Medical School in Nashville. Several private northern universities, including Harvard and Columbia, admitted small numbers of Black students to their law schools, as did state universities, but the largest number of Black lawyers (including Marshall) were graduates of Howard University's law school, known by some as the "Black Harvard." It's telling that both the American Medical Association and the American Bar Association excluded Blacks from membership through the 1940s, denying them many privileges enjoyed by White doctors and lawyers.

* * *

We tend to believe that public school segregation was first declared unconstitutional by the Supreme Court in *Brown v. Board of Education of Topeka, Kansas* in May 1954. That is true for public elementary and high schools, although desegregation of those schools was fiercely resisted in both the South and the North, and most big-city schools have been effectively resegregated by decades of White flight to the suburbs that encircle these cities. But in fact, the legal building blocks on which the *Brown* decision was constructed were first laid in a series of lawsuits that began in 1936 in Baltimore, Maryland. How these cases were carefully planned and litigated is a story little known but worth telling, a story that marks the first sharp turn by a legal system that had consistently rebuffed challenges to school segregation, as far back as 1850, when a Black parent in Boston, Benjamin Roberts, sued to enroll his daughter, Sarah, in a White primary school that was closer to her home than the segregated school for Blacks to which she was assigned (much like Oliver Brown's suit a century later for his daughter Linda). In *Roberts v. City of Boston*, Lemuel Shaw, chief justice of the Massachusetts Supreme Judicial Court, wrote that judges should defer to the "reasonable" judgments of Boston school officials who decided that the interests of students of both races "will best be promoted by maintaining the separate primary schools for colored and for white children." Answering the argument that racial prejudice lay behind the school board's policy, Shaw wrote, "This prejudice, if it exists, is not created by law, and probably cannot be changed by law." Notably, this decision came from the abolitionist capital of that time, not from any states in the antebellum South, where no schools enrolled Black children, all of them slaves and legally barred from education.

Almost everyone recognizes Thurgood Marshall as the lawyer who argued and won the *Brown* case and later served as the first Black Supreme Court justice. (He did not, in fact, argue *Brown* but one of the combined school cases from South Carolina in the Supreme Court.) He has been lauded for the brilliant legal strategy that culminated in *Brown*, having won several earlier cases that each pulled a brick from the shaky edifice of Jim Crow education, forecasting its eventual collapse. Hardly anyone recognizes Nathan Margold, the lawyer who drafted the original proposal for legal attacks on school segregation. And even fewer have read the document called the Margold Report.

A Harvard Law School graduate and protégé of Professor Felix Frankfurter, Margold was hired by the NAACP in 1930 to prepare a report on possible strategies for a long-range legal assault on Jim Crow schooling. His

214-page report, completed in 1931, included piles of statistics documenting the gross inequalities of White and Black schools in the South. Margold took the Supreme Court's "separate but equal" ruling in *Plessy v. Ferguson* as his starting point, recognizing that it was a precedent that could be used either to force Jim Crow states to provide truly equal schools—an impossible task for cash-strapped districts—or as a barrier to confront directly, urging its reversal by the courts. Margold outlined the arguments for and against each possible approach. He first advised the NAACP leaders that "it would be a great mistake to fritter away our limited funds on sporadic attempts to force the making of equal divisions of school funds in the few instances where such attempts might be expected to succeed." This approach would force civil rights lawyers to file separate lawsuits suits in each southern school district, recruit plaintiffs in each district who had the courage and fortitude to face hostility from Whites and delays in courts, and perform the laborious task of digging out the evidence of school funding disparities in each case. Even if they succeeded, lawsuits to equalize facilities would require judges to act as school superintendents, checking the quality of textbooks, playgrounds, and restrooms in the separate schools. But with this strategy, Margold wrote, "we should be leaving untouched the very essence of the existing evils" of segregation. "On the other hand," he urged, "if we boldly challenge the constitutional validity of segregation if and when accompanied irremediably by discrimination, we can strike directly at the most prolific sources of discrimination."

Although completed in 1931, the Margold Report remained in a file cabinet until 1933, when Marshall joined the NAACP legal staff. Born in Baltimore in 1908, son of a waiter at a tony yacht club and great-grandson of slaves, Marshall graduated from Lincoln University in Pennsylvania in 1930 and planned a career in law; he considered applying to the University of Maryland's all-White law school but decided against it, certain of rejection because of his race. He then entered Howard University's law school, graduating in 1933; the Depression took a toll on his classmates, only six of thirty-six in his class making it through. After starting a struggling law practice in Baltimore, he volunteered his services to the NAACP branch in Baltimore (the country's largest at the time); he moved to New York in 1936, working at NAACP headquarters on a variety of cases, including a murder trial in Virginia; he later said he won a victory in sparing his Black client from electrocution.

Before he left Baltimore, Marshall dug out the Margold Report and read it carefully. A pragmatist by nature and training, he felt that Margold's option of a direct attack on school segregation, with *Plessy* standing in the way, should be the end, not the beginning, of the legal campaign. But first he had a score to settle with his home-state law school, whose "No Negroes Need Apply" sign had turned him back from even submitting an application. He got his revenge by recruiting a young Black man, Donald Murray, as a client. A graduate of Amherst College in Massachusetts, Murray had applied to but was rejected by the University of Maryland's law school. On Murray's behalf, Marshall sued the university's president, Raymond Pearson, in state court, arguing that the state's decision to operate only one law school, restricted to Whites, violated the Equal Protection clause of the Fourteenth Amendment. Ironically, *Plessy* gave Marshall support, since Maryland's one law school for Whites was not "separate" from one for Blacks, which did not exist. Marshall noted that *Plessy* applied only to facilities—whether railway coaches or schools—provided to both Whites and Blacks and supposedly "equal" in quality. Ruling in 1936, the Maryland high court agreed, ordering Murray's admission to the all-White law school after state lawyers conceded there was no plan to establish a separate school for Murray and other would-be Black lawyers. Marshall was pleased with the outcome, but the ruling applied only to Maryland and had no precedential weight in other states.

Two years later, Marshall won another victory, this time in the U.S. Supreme Court. His client in this case was Lloyd Gaines, a graduate of Lincoln University in St. Louis, an all-Black state school; his application to the University of Missouri's law school in the state capital of Columbia was rejected because of his race. However, university officials cited a recently enacted state law that offered to pay the tuition and expenses of Blacks at the integrated law schools in the adjoining states of Iowa, Illinois, Nebraska, and Kansas. This outsourcing scheme did not satisfy Gaines, and neither did it satisfy the Supreme Court. After listening to Marshall's argument in his appeal from Missouri state courts, Chief Justice Charles Evans Hughes wrote for six colleagues in *Gaines v. Canada* (Silas Canada was the university's registrar) in ordering state officials to either establish a law school for Blacks that was "substantially equal" in quality to the White school or to admit Gaines to the "Whites only" school. The justices were certainly offended (and perhaps amused) at the state's effort to head off their ruling by purchasing a former cosmetology school in St. Louis and christening it Lincoln University School of Law, with three part-time instructors and hand-me-down law books in a one-room library. This ploy drew predictable scorn from the justices, but their "choose-one" order nonetheless left intact, if wounded, the "separate but equal" doctrine of *Plessy*. How long it would survive further judicial cuts was unclear, but Marshall was satisfied by the "half a loaf" decision. Abandoning the never-opened "Lincoln Law School," Missouri's all-White school offered to enroll Gaines, but in a strange and never-solved puzzle he had literally disappeared, leaving only rumors of his whereabouts or death.

As it turned out, Marshall's long-term assault on Jim Crow schooling took a back seat as the nation entered World War II and NAACP lawyers became occupied with cases of discrimination against Black workers in wartime jobs.

* * *

The Great Depression ended slowly and fitfully. From a high of 25 percent in 1931, unemployment for all workers declined—after a brief recovery in 1936 and 1937—to 14 percent in the latter year, then shot up during a second economic downturn to 19 percent in 1938. Employment statistics by race weren't tallied until 1950, but with jobless rates for Blacks consistently double those for Whites, it's fair to assume that about 40 percent of Blacks were unemployed in 1938. Much of that disparity reflected the much lower educational status of Blacks, itself a reflection of Jim Crow schooling in the South, putting well-paid jobs out of reach for Blacks, who were also "last hired and first fired" in most shops and factories. The 1940 census put the Black-White disparity into numbers: among males between eighteen and forty-four years old, the prime working years for men (there were no figures for women), 43 percent of Whites had completed eight years or fewer of schooling; the rate for Blacks was 80 percent, an almost two-to-one gap. While 44 percent of Whites in that age group had at least some high school, and 21 percent earning diplomas, the figures for Blacks were 17 and 12 percent, respectively. At the college level, 13 percent of Whites and just 3 percent of Blacks had completed at least one year.

So, with just one in five Black males having stayed in school past the eighth grade, compared to almost three in five Whites, the vast majority of Black men wound up in low-paid, low-skill jobs with virtually no chance of moving up the economic ladder. Both educational and economic institutions in American society—staffed and controlled by White men—worked in tandem, the first consigning Black children to Jim Crow schools in the South and equally segregated schools in northern cities, the second relegating Black workers to jobs that most White workers shunned but that were essential to the functioning of many service and manufacturing businesses. Many generations of Black families, although unaware of the term, became victims of systemic racism. Despite their hopes that President Roosevelt's promise of a New Deal for struggling and suffering Americans would help pull them out of poverty, Blacks wound up the 1930s still far behind Whites, some complaining they had been handed a "Raw Deal" by White politicians, whose White constituents had no desire to help those for whom slavery and Jim Crow laws were not a distant memory but still a festering wound to their dignity and livelihoods.

* * *

The decade of the 1940s began with ongoing wars in Europe and China, and ended in June 1950 with a Chinese-backed war on the Korean peninsula. The United States did not enter these wars until after hostilities began, but responded with troops, munitions, tanks, planes, and warships to the Japanese attack on Pearl Harbor in December 1941 and the threatened Nazi takeover of Europe and Britain, and later to the imminent collapse of South Korea in September 1950. In between these years, Americans endured wartime dislocations and disruptions, and—after the end of the U.S.-Soviet alliance to defeat Nazi Germany and Japan in 1945—a growing and dangerous Cold War against our former ally, now threatening to swallow Eastern Europe into its expanding Soviet Empire.

Although the United States was spared any active hostilities on its mainland, protected on both shores by oceans, there was also, during this momentous decade, a series of battles in cities and towns across the country that cost lives and destroyed homes: battles over race, instigated by Whites and designed to keep Blacks "in their place" and out of White neighborhoods and White jobs. Even after World War II ended, Blacks who had fought to defeat Nazi brutality and bigotry came home to find that—even when dressed in their service uniforms—they became targets of racist brutality and bigotry and were still denied the bedrock rights to vote and to use public facilities on an equal basis with Whites in the Jim Crow states, in which more than two-thirds of Blacks still lived.

The First Great Migration brought some 1.5 million Blacks from South to North between 1900 and 1930; during the decade of the 1930s, the number of migrants fell sharply, as northern jobs dried up during the Great Depression, reducing the lure to find better work in northern cities. However, the Second Great Migration lasted from 1940 through the 1960s, three decades in which some 5 million Blacks left the South, most heading north but a substantial number moving west, to cities like Los Angeles and Seattle, where wartime production of ships and planes had created several million jobs for which workers had been recruited from all over the country. Some 1.5 million Black

migrants moved north and west during the 1940s alone, as many as in the
First Great Migration, with 80 percent settling in cities. With existing Black
neighborhoods in most cities already crowded and with no open space for
new home or apartment construction, this influx brought with it strains on
housing. In addition, those Blacks who found work in newly converted defense plants and factories were mostly relegated to the lowest-skilled and
lowest-paid jobs and were often harassed—from racist epithets to hanging
nooses in lockers—by White workers, with little intervention from foremen
and supervisors.

It was the combination of these conditions—crowded housing, job discrimination, and official tolerance of harassment—that prompted the first
organized campaign to ensure equal treatment for Blacks in the wartime
economy. Although many Black leaders participated in this campaign, one
assumed the most visible role, lending his organizing skills and powerful voice
to what became a precursor of the Black civil rights movement of the 1950s
and 1960s.

A. Philip Randolph ("A" for Asa, although he was called "Phil" by everyone
he met) was born in 1889, the son of a seamstress and a tailor who was also an
African Methodist Episcopal minister. He grew up in Jacksonville, Florida, in
a thriving Black community, and attended the only academic high school for
Blacks in Florida, where he excelled in public speaking and graduated as class
valedictorian in 1907. One of his memories of that period was of the night his
mother sat in their front room, a loaded shotgun in her lap, while his father
took a pistol and went to the county jail, joining other Black men to prevent a White mob from lynching a Black prisoner; fortunately, the lynching
did not happen and Randolph's father returned unharmed. Randolph did
not attend college after high school, instead working at odd jobs until he
moved to New York City in 1911, where he took social science courses at the
City College of New York. He had read and was powerfully affected by Du
Bois's essays in *The Souls of Black Folk* and their message of collective action
to combat racism. His work in Harlem, helping to provide job training for
young Blacks, brought him into contact with union organizers and Socialist
Party members. He joined the Party and in 1917 founded a radical monthly
magazine, the *Messenger*, which urged Blacks to join unions and opposed the
military draft in World War I; Randolph's writing drew a backhanded com-
pliment from the Justice Department, which labeled the *Messenger* "the most
able and the most dangerous of all the Negro publications."

After several years of organizing unions of New York elevator operators
and Virginia shipyard and dock workers, Randolph began a long career as

president of the Brotherhood of Sleeping Car Porters, which he founded in 1925; most porters—all of them Black—worked for the Pullman Company, which responded to union organizing and strike threats by firing union members and making counterthreats to replace strikers with strikebreakers, known as "scabs." The Brotherhood of Sleeping Car Porters barely survived the Great Depression (it was down to 658 members in 1933) but was revived by congressional passage in 1934 of amendments to the Railway Labor Act, which added protection for union organizing. With union members now protected from retaliation for their organizing efforts, Randolph negotiated with the Pullman Company for $2 million in pay increases, overtime pay, and shorter work hours.

Even before the United States joined the war in December 1941, Randolph pushed for protection of Black defense workers against discrimination in hiring and workplace segregation. Along with his lieutenant, Bayard Rustin (later a key aide to Martin Luther King Jr. and primary organizer of the August 1963 March on Washington) and pacifist leader A. J. Muste, Randolph announced in early 1941 plans to bring fifty thousand Black workers to Washington for a march from the Capitol to the White House on July 1, demanding federal action to outlaw segregation in federally funded defense work. Eager to avoid disruption of production, FDR headed off the march by issuing Executive Order 8802 in June, which banned racial and ethnic discrimination in defense facilities and also set up a Fair Employment Practice Committee to ensure compliance with the order. This victory, although not as far-reaching as Randolph had urged, gained widespread publicity and propelled him into a prominent role in the labor and civil rights movements; during his long career, he joined Marshall and King in a triumvirate of legal, religious, and labor advocates and activists. Randolph, in fact, was the titular leader of the March for Jobs and Freedom at the Lincoln Memorial in August 1963; his powerful speech (which I heard from the bottom of the memorial's steps) was overshadowed by King's "I Have a Dream" call to action, but many younger Black and White activists looked to Randolph for experience and inspiration.

* * *

The nationwide wave of White attacks on Blacks during the Red Summer of 1919—engulfing Washington, Chicago, and other cities and culminating in the massacre of some two hundred Blacks in rural Phillips County, Arkansas—had spared Detroit. At the beginning of the 1940s Blacks numbered 150,000 in that city, just 9 percent of the population of 1.6 million, making Detroit the nation's fourth-largest city. By the end of that decade, an influx of 150,000 southern Blacks had pushed the population to 1.8 million and the Black percentage to 16, one of every six residents in a city with overcrowded Black neighborhoods.

As Blacks seeking housing began pushing into hostile White neighborhoods, Detroit officials obtained federal funds to construct two public housing projects, one for Whites and one for Blacks; the Federal Housing Administration adopted a policy of segregation, fearful of racial turmoil if the projects were integrated. However, the Black project was located in a largely White neighborhood and was named for Sojourner Truth, who escaped from slavery in 1826 and became the most prominent Black woman in the abolitionist and early women's movements. Enraged Whites protested so loudly that officials decided to reserve the Sojourner Truth Homes for Whites, which brought more protests from Detroit mayor Edward Jeffries and civil rights groups. Changing their minds again, officials reversed course and announced that Black families would begin moving in on February 28, 1942. The first arrivals were met with a large crowd of angry Whites, who pelted the newcomers with curses and rocks. Violence broke out, egged on by members of the National Workers League, a Nazi front group allied with the Ku Klux Klan, with hundreds of members and supporters in the region. The melee resulted in forty injuries and the arrests of 217 Blacks and three Whites; fearing more violence, authorities called off the planned Black move-in. Not until late April, as White protests continued, did 1,100 state and city police and 1,600 National Guard troops restore order and protect the first six Black families who braved White hostility to their presence. Eventually, 218 Black families lived in the Sojourner Truth Homes, but racial tension still crackled in Detroit.

During the hot summer of 1943, conditions were ripe for more outbreaks of racial violence across the country, particularly where Blacks and Whites competed for well-paying defense jobs. The first major eruption took place in the Gulf Coast city of Beaumont, Texas, where shipyards employed more than ten thousand workers, about a third of them Black; racial slurs and harassment sparked frequent fist fights and set the city on edge. On June 15, 1943, a White woman claimed she had been raped by a Black man, and police arrested and jailed several suspects. As news of the alleged rape spread, some four thousand Whites marched on the jail, although police kept order. When the woman was unable to identify any of the jailed Black men as her assailant, White mobs swarmed through Black neighborhoods, burning a hundred homes and terrorizing residents; during the fighting, two men—one Black, one White—were killed and fifty more injured. Officials declared martial law and imposed a curfew, which lasted until June 20.

Even before the turmoil in Beaumont subsided, a larger—and deadlier—outbreak of racial violence erupted in Detroit. Tension was already high in June 1943 after the Packard Motor Car Company promoted three Blacks to work alongside Whites on the assembly line; in response, twenty-five thousand Whites walked off their jobs at Packard in a wildcat strike, temporarily halting war production, although company officials stuck with the Black promotions. It took just one spark on the hot night of June 20 to ignite a conflagration that was not extinguished until 34 had died (24 of them Black), 433 were injured, and 1,800 had been arrested, along with hundreds of burned homes, cars, and businesses.

That Sunday evening, several thousand Detroit residents of both races were coming back into the city after picnics and playgrounds on Belle Isle, an island in the Detroit River, across from the Canadian city of Windsor, Ontario. The footbridge across the river was crowded, and fights broke out between young Blacks and Whites; no one knows what or who started the fights, but they soon spread into the city, fueled by rumors that a mob of Whites had thrown a Black mother and her baby into the river. Although the rumors were false, groups of young Blacks responded by looting White-owned businesses. Likewise, groups of Whites, mostly young men, swarmed into the largest and poorest Black neighborhood (ironically called Paradise Valley), pulling Blacks off streetcars and beating them and looting Black-owned shops. The violence became deadly as Whites drove through Black areas, shooting people, and as Blacks returned fire while guarding their homes and businesses. Only after three days and nights of violence did some six thousand federal troops—ordered into Detroit by President Roosevelt—impose a curfew and restore order.

Leaders on both sides blamed the other for the riot: Mayor Jeffries claimed that "Negro hoodlums started it" and praised the "magnificent" work of the city's police, almost all White. Thurgood Marshall, by then the NAACP's legal director, charged that Detroit police had refused to intervene while Whites burned cars and beat Blacks: "This weak-kneed policy of the police commissioner coupled with the anti-Negro attitude of many members of the force helped to make a riot inevitable." Whichever racial group instigated the violence, Detroit's Black population suffered the lion's share of the resulting death and destruction.

* * *

Unlike World War I, which was followed by economic hardship for many Americans and by the Red Scare against radicals and the Red Summer of White attacks on Blacks in 1919, the end of World War II in August 1945 was greeted with jubilation and economic good times for most Americans. Among the 16 million troops who served during the war, a bit over 1 million were Black, of whom only 125,000 took part in combat, the rest being relegated to homeland duty or support troops abroad. With few exceptions, Black soldiers, sailors, and airmen were forced into segregated units with White officers in command, many with Jim Crow attitudes and harsh treatment of troops who objected to their second-class status. Many shared the questions posed by James G. Thompson, a Black soldier from Wichita, Kansas, in a letter to the *Pittsburgh Courier*, a widely read Black newspaper: "Being an American of dark complexion and some 26 years, these questions flash through my mind: 'Should I sacrifice my life to live half American?' 'Will things be better for the next generation in the peace to follow?' 'Is the kind of America I know worth defending?'"

Those Black veterans who returned to the Jim Crow South discovered that little had changed since their enlistment and service. Wearing a uniform, even one adorned with hard-won medals for valor, did not impress Whites who still judged people solely by color. One young Black man on his way home to South Carolina after his discharge at Camp Gordon in Georgia discovered that wearing his uniform was no protection against racist violence.

Isaac Woodard Jr. had enlisted in the army in 1942 and served in a segregated labor battalion in the Pacific theater as a longshoreman, rising to the rank of sergeant. He earned a battle star by unloading ships in New Guinea while Japanese troops were shelling the dock, and later was awarded a Good Conduct medal before his honorable discharge. He left Camp Gordon on a Greyhound bus, which pulled into a rest stop near Augusta, Georgia. When he asked the driver for time to visit the "Colored" restroom, it was grudgingly given after an argument. When the bus next stopped in the small town of Batesburg, South Carolina, he remained in his seat while the driver went into the station, returning with police officers who dragged Woodard from the bus, beating him with billy clubs. Chief Lynwood Shull put Woodard in the local jail, charging him with "disorderly conduct." During his night in the jail cell, Chief Shull again beat Woodard with his club, leaving him permanently blind from blows to his eyes. Taken to a hospital in nearby Aiken, Woodard languished there for three weeks without treatment for his wounds, until his family reported him missing. (They had not known when Woodard had been discharged at Camp Gordon.) Although Woodard identified Sheriff Shull as his assailant, South Carolina officials refused to charge him for the assault. Only after the NAACP's executive secretary Walter White raised the issue directly with President Harry Truman in September 1946, after widespread news reports of Woodard's blinding by the sheriff, did Truman direct Attorney General Tom Clark to open an investigation, which led to Shull's indictment by a federal grand jury for violating Woodard's civil rights, and a trial before an all-White jury. During the trial, Woodard testified that Shull asked him if he'd been honorably discharged. When he answered yes, Shull hit him in the head and said, "Don't say 'yes' to me, say 'yes, sir.'" Shull's lawyer directed racial slurs at Woodard and threatened the jurors, "[I]f you rule against Shull, then let South Carolina secede again." After just fifteen minutes of deliberation, the jurors acquitted the sheriff, who had admitted on the stand that he had struck Woodard repeatedly in his eyes; the courtroom reportedly burst into cheers when the verdict was read.

Although horrifying in its brutality, Woodard's ordeal was only one of many incidents in which Black veterans, coming home after contributing to the war against Nazi bigotry and brutality, found themselves still subjected to Jim Crow laws. Many of these veterans later took leadership roles in civil rights struggles for voting rights and equal schooling for their children. It's likely that Truman's revulsion at Woodard's blinding opened the president's eyes to the unequal treatment of Blacks in the military and helped persuade him—while facing a difficult reelection campaign—to issue Executive Order 9981 on July 26, 1948, formally barring racial segregation in the armed forces. Truman was also pushed to act on this issue by civil rights leaders, most prominently A. Philip Randolph, who had earlier pushed Roosevelt to issue an order banning discrimination in defense industries.

Announcing his order in a radio address from the steps of the Lincoln Memorial as a symbolic backdrop, Truman went beyond any previous president, including his immediate predecessor, in reaching out to Black Americans: "It is my deep conviction that we have reached a turning point in our country's efforts to guarantee freedom and equality to all our citizens. Recent events in the United States and abroad have made us realize that it is more important today than ever before to ensure that all Americans enjoy these rights. When I say all Americans—I mean all Americans."

* * *

World War II had interrupted the NAACP campaign against segregated education, which had won a "separate and unequal" case in *Gaines v. Canada* in 1938. With the war over, Thurgood Marshall returned to court in 1946 with suits against segregated graduate programs in Oklahoma and Texas. In the first case, Ada Lois Sipuel had been turned away from the University of Oklahoma's law school but was promised that state legislators would create a Black law school with "substantially equal" facilities. The lawmakers' foot-dragging prompted Marshall to ask the Supreme Court to put a match to their toes. Faced with the ruling in 1948 that cited the *Gaines* decision for precedent and ordered the state to provide Sipuel with a legal education "as soon as it does for white applicants," university officials roped off a section of the state capitol building and called it a law school, although the pretend school had no library and no faculty of its own. Sipuel refused to be a pretend student, and Marshall returned to the Supreme Court later in 1948 in *Sipuel v. Oklahoma Board of Regents* to argue, for the first time, that segregation was flatly unconstitutional. Even if states provided Blacks with better schools than Whites, he said, separating them by race imposed a "badge of inferiority" on Blacks. But the justices shied away from this divisive issue during a presidential election year and sent the case back to state court for hearings on whether the pretend law school was equal to its real, all-White school. After the voters returned Truman to the White House with a strong civil rights program, Oklahoma officials wearied of legal battles and admitted Sipuel to its real law school.

Another law school case began in 1946 but did not reach the Supreme Court until 1950, along with a second challenge to segregated graduate education in Oklahoma. The first case involved the University of Texas's law school, which denied admission to Heman Sweatt, a Black postal worker. After NAACP lawyers filed suit, state judges ordered the university to give Sweatt a legal education "substantially equivalent" to that provided Whites. The law school dean offered plans for an all-Black school that would occupy four basement rooms in an Austin office building, with no library and three part-time instructors. When White Texas judges agreed that four rooms for Blacks matched in quality the massive building in which 850 White students attended classes, Marshall filed an appeal with the Supreme Court. In the second Oklahoma case, the state university admitted George McLaurin to its graduate education program shortly after Sipuel became the first Black law student on the campus. McLaurin, however, was forced to listen to lectures outside the classroom, sitting in a hallway seat marked "Reserved for colored." He could study at a "colored" desk in the library's mezzanine but not in the reading room, and he could eat at a "colored" table in the cafeteria, but only after White students finished their meals. NAACP lawyers challenged these demeaning conditions as "badges of slavery" imposed on McLaurin, but they lost the first two rounds in lower federal courts.

The *Sweatt* and *McLaurin* cases reached the Supreme Court for argument in April 1950. The NAACP's briefs in both cases offered the justices a choice: they could order Texas and Oklahoma to provide equal facilities for Black students in graduate programs, which would require either full integration or massive spending on schools that were separate but truly equal in quality; or they could overturn *Plessy* and rule that racial segregation violated the Constitution. The Court's decisions would help NAACP lawyers determine their strategy in school cases from the Deep South. Perhaps the time was near for the final assault on Jim Crow education.

Marshall argued for Sweatt, and his young NAACP assistant counsel, Robert L. Carter, argued for McLaurin. Both lawyers urged the Court to abandon the *Plessy* doctrine of "separate but equal." Marshall pointed out the physical inequality of the separate Texas law schools, but he focused on the issue of racial segregation. "They can build an exact duplicate but if it is segregated, it is unequal," he insisted. The attorneys general of eleven former Confederate states filed an amicus brief that dropped any pretense of legal argument. Southern Whites, they warned the justices, do not "want their womenfolk in intimate social contact with Negro men." Enforcing this taboo required segregation at every educational level, from kindergarten to graduate school.

The justices declined Marshall's appeal to overrule *Plessy*, and they ignored the southern appeal to sexual fears. In decisions handed down on June 5, 1950, Chief Justice Carl Vinson wrote for a unanimous Court in both cases. His opinion in *Sweatt v. Painter* accepted Marshall's invitation to look closely at the separate Texas law schools. After comparing their facilities, Vinson found it "difficult to believe that one who had a free choice between these law schools would consider the question close." The answer depended not only on factors like books and buildings, he added, but also on "those qualities which are incapable of measurement but which make for greatness in a law school." The Black school could not match the "reputation of the faculty" and "influence of the alumni" that added to the "rich traditions and prestige" of the White school. The Court ordered that Heman Sweatt "be admitted to the University of Texas law school without delay."

George McLaurin had already been admitted to the University of Oklahoma graduate education school. The only question in his case, Vinson wrote in *McLaurin v. Oklahoma State Regents*, was his separation from other students in the classroom, library, and cafeteria. "Such restrictions impair and inhibit his ability to study, to engage in discussions and exchange views with other students, and in general, to learn his profession." McLaurin "must receive the same treatment at the hands of the state as students of other races," the Court instructed his instructors. The "Colored" signs came down, and McLaurin finally taught the university a lesson.

* * *

These legal victories, in cases that spanned the late 1940s and into the 1950s, were the fruits of Thurgood Marshall's strategy of "encirclement," much like a military strategy of attacking your enemy's weakest spots. The weakest spots in Jim Crow education were the border states—Maryland, Missouri, Oklahoma, and Texas were first on Marshall's battle plan—where resistance to integration was not entrenched and where Black graduate students wouldn't arouse the hostility that seating little White girls next to little Black boys was almost certain to provoke. The ultimate target, of course, were those Deep South states that segregated children from kindergarten to college. As we move into the 1950s, the prosperous, optimistic, comfortable years of Dwight Eisenhower and Howdy Doody, it's worth noting that, as the decade began, the average White family earned $3,445 and the average Black family earned $1,869 (about $20,000 and $11,000 in today's dollars). As the economy expanded, would Blacks be able to make up at least a part of that long-term disparity? Or would they always start so far behind they could never catch up? And how would laws, made and interpreted by White men, aid or hinder those efforts? Those are questions to which 15 million Black Americans sought answers at the century's halfway mark.

8

"I Thanked God Right Then and There"

THIS CHAPTER WILL introduce readers to the Black parents and their children who first challenged Jim Crow schooling in the five cases that were unanimously decided—four in one opinion, the fifth in a separate opinion—by the Supreme Court in May 1954 under the caption *Brown v. Board of Education of Topeka, Kansas.* Everyone knows about the *Brown* case, and many recognize Linda Brown as the eight-year-old Black girl whose father, Oliver, sued on her behalf after Linda was turned away from the all-White Sumner grade school in Topeka, just six blocks from her home, and sent to the all-Black Monroe school, a half-hour bus ride away. But few people know that Oliver and Linda Brown were joined at the Supreme Court by Black parents and their children whose segregated schools were located in South Carolina, Virginia, Washington, D.C., and Delaware. We will take a journey from the Deep South to the Midwest heartland to help us understand how the institutions of education and law each responded to these legal challenges to almost a century of separate and unequal schooling for Black children. These two institutions wield enormous influence in determining how America's children will be prepared for jobs in an ever-changing economy, and for their roles in civic affairs. Who brings these cases and who decides them at various times in the nation's history reveals much about our society's commitment to the founding ideal of equality for all citizens.

We begin our journey in the small town of Summerton, South Carolina, ten miles south of Manning, the seat of Clarendon County, midway between Charleston and the state capital of Columbia. The 1950 census showed a county population of 32,215, with Summerton at 1,419 and Manning at 2,775. Eighty percent of county residents lived in rural areas, mostly on tenant farms, and 70 percent were Black. The average Black adult had just 4.2 years of schooling, and two-thirds of Black families had incomes of less than $1,000 a year. In short, Blacks in Clarendon County were poorly educated, earned barely enough to feed and clothe their families, and held no public office, despite their numerical majority. In 1950, the county school board spent $179 for each White student but only $43 for each Black child. In these respects, Clarendon was much like every Black-majority county in the Deep South.

What set Clarendon County and the town of Summerton apart from others like them was a visit to the Columbia office of Harold Boulware, the state's only Black civil rights lawyer, by Thurgood Marshall in March 1949. Boulware had been advising two Summerton parents, Levi Pearson and Rev. J. A. DeLaine, about a possible legal attack on the county's fourfold disparity in funding White and Black schools, and the all-White school board's refusal to provide school buses for Black children, many of them forced to walk miles over dirt roads to schools in converted sharecroppers' cabins, while White kids passed them by in shiny yellow buses. Boulware was hopeful that federal judges, confronted with facts about the county's grossly unequal schools, would apply the "separate but equal" doctrine of the *Plessy* case to public schooling and order the Clarendon board to begin steps toward equalizing the separate schools. Even if federal judges in South Carolina, who owed their black robes to segregationist White politicians, ruled against an equalization lawsuit, judges at the higher rungs of the federal judicial system—the Fourth Circuit Court of Appeals in Richmond, Virginia, or the top rung at the Supreme Court—would give the Black Clarendon children what *Plessy* clearly mandated, holding county officials responsible for providing "substantially equal" schools for Black and White children in every area: buildings, teachers, books, and buses.

Marshall arrived at Boulware's office with a challenge to Pearson and DeLaine, who met him there. He would assist Boulware in filing an equalization suit, Marshall told them, on condition that the two men find twenty parents willing to serve as plaintiffs, to spread the risk of retaliation by Whites who held economic power over Blacks: landowners of sharecropping farms, business owners who employed Blacks, and bankers who provided loans to Black farmers for equipment and supplies. Marshall was realistic about these risks, which Blacks faced every time they challenged White power. Losing a farm or a job would be devastation for "uppity" Blacks. Equally well aware of these risks, Pearson (who had two children in Clarendon schools) and DeLaine (who also taught in Clarendon schools) nonetheless agreed to Marshall's challenge.

It would take another eight months before the two men returned to Boulware's office in November with a list of twenty Black parents for whom a good education for their children outweighed the possibility—perhaps a probability—of losing jobs or farms. The complaint Boulware filed in federal court in Charleston listed the plaintiffs in alphabetical order; first on the suit's caption was Harry Briggs, a U.S. Navy veteran with five children. Briggs pumped gas and fixed cars at H. C. Carrigan's Sinclair station in Summerton, while his wife, Eliza, worked as a maid at a local motel. The town's twelve-term mayor, Carrigan, expressed a rosy view of race relations between White farm owners and their Black sharecroppers. "Colored have made wonderful progress down here," he assured a northern visitor. "I have several farms, and they all have Negroes on them. I sharecrop with them, and they are all as happy as can be." David McClary, who owned the largest feed and livestock business in Summerton, agreed. "We got a good bunch of nigras here," he boasted.

The White reaction to the suit that Boulware filed in December 1949 was swift and unforgiving. Mayor Carrigan fired Harry Briggs on Christmas Eve, handing him a carton of cigarettes as severance pay; the motel at which Eliza Briggs cleaned rooms fired her too. (Unable to make a living on a small farm, Harry Briggs packed up his children and belongings and moved to New York, where his lack of education kept him in a string of menial jobs; he finally returned to Summerton two decades later, although his name stayed on the lawsuit.) Other plaintiffs suffered reprisals as well: Bo Stukes lost his garage job; James Brown was fired by a trucking company; and John McDonald, a combat veteran of Iwo Jima and Okinawa, lost his credit for farm equipment.

Marshall was pleased that his suit was assigned to federal district judge J. Waties Waring. The eighth-generation scion of a prominent Charleston family and a member of the city's social elite, Waring had shed his earlier support for segregation (he had once served as campaign manager for South Carolina's stridently racist senator Ellison "Cotton Ed" Smith) and had ruled for Black plaintiffs in several cases. He later said that "the cancer of segregation will never be cured by the sedative of gradualism." At the first hearing in *Briggs v. Elliot* (Roderick Elliot was chairman of the Clarendon school board), Waring surprised Marshall with his own challenge, virtually demanding that he amend his complaint, which sought equal funding for White and Black schools. "It's very easy to decide the case on that issue," he told Marshall and the school board's lawyers. The complaint, he suggested in a tone Marshall took as a directive, should charge that South Carolina's segregation laws "are unconstitutional, and that'll raise the issue for all time as to whether a state can segregate by race in its schools."

Marshall accepted Waring's challenge with some misgivings; federal law provided that suits alleging state laws violated the Constitution would be heard and decided by panels of three judges, one from a federal court of appeals. Marshall was certain of Judge Waring's vote, but the two judges named to sit with him were both known for segregationist views. John J. Parker of the Fourth Circuit bench in Richmond had run for governor of North Carolina in 1920. "The participation of Negroes in politics," he told White voters, "is a source of evil and danger to both races." And District Judge George B. Timmerman, the third panel member, made no bones of his belief that God had made Whites the superior race.

At the hearing before the three-judge panel, chaired by Judge Parker, Marshall and his associate counsel, Robert Carter, pressed the Clarendon school superintendent, L. B. McCord, to explain why the county gave each White student more than four dollars for each dollar spent to educate Black children. "It is not, I don't think, because of the color" of the children, McCord replied, suggesting it was cheaper to run the Black schools, most of them in wooden shacks, than the White schools in brick buildings. McCord's refusal to admit that the Black schools were inferior in quality rankled Marshall, who asked the superintendent why the county schools were segregated. "You would have to ask the children why," McCord responded. "None of them have ever asked me to go to one school or the other." The next witness, Roderick Elliott, proved as obtuse as McCord had been adept at dodging questions. After twenty-five years as school board chairman, Elliott could not identify the district's boundaries or name the schools whose affairs he supervised.

Carter then called Matthew Whitehead, a Howard University education professor, who had visited several of the county schools, both White and Black. He told the judges that none of the Black schools he visited had blackboards, maps, globes, an auditorium, or music room, facilities all the White schools had. Whitehead described the outdoor toilet facilities at the Black grade schools in words that brought their stench into the courtroom. He recounted his visit to the Black high school and the "disgust" he felt "to see 694 students serviced by two toilets for boys and two toilet seats for girls," with "no running water, no urinals," and no sinks for washing hands.

In a written opinion after the hearing, Judge Parker, joined by Judge Timmerman, hewed closely to the precedent laid down by the *Plessy* case. He quoted the board's lawyer as conceding the Black schools "are not substantially equal to those afforded for white pupils," but he credited the state's promise to build new schools and upgrade existing ones so that "Negro children will be afforded educational facilities and opportunities in all respects equal to those afforded white children." This was a promise that set no time-line for construction or detailed plans for implementation, but it satisfied Parker and Timmerman. "We think," Parker wrote, "that segregation of the races in the public schools, so long as equality of rights is preserved, is a matter of legislative policy for the several states, with which the federal courts are powerless to interfere."

After this judicial capitulation to South Carolina lawmakers, who showed no real concern for Black children, Judge Waring wrote a lengthy dissent, chiding his colleagues for "judicial evasion" of the central question in the case, the Fourteenth Amendment's guarantee of "equal protection of the laws" for every citizen, including Black children, the most needful of equal education and powerless to achieve it through the political process. Waring was blunt, almost caustic in what became his farewell address to Charleston society. He predicted:

> [T]hese very infant plaintiffs now pupils in Clarendon County will probably be bringing suits for their children and grandchildren decades or rather generations hence in an effort to get for their descendants what are today denied to them. If they are entitled to any rights as American citizens, they are entitled to have these rights now and not in the future.

Waring concluded with a reference to Marshall's legal attacks on segregated graduate and professional education:

> There is absolutely no reasonable explanation for racial prejudice. It is all caused by unreasoning emotional reactions and these are gained in early childhood. Let the little child's mind be poisoned by prejudice of this kind and it is practically impossible to ever remove these impressions however many years he may have of teaching by philosophers, religious leaders or patriotic citizens. If segregation is wrong then the place to stop it is in the first grade and not in graduate colleges.

For this apostasy from the dogma of segregation, Waring and his wife were ostracized by the social elite of Charleston; they even found a burning cross on their lawn. Fed up, they moved to New York City. The judge only returned to Charleston in 1968 for burial in his family's plot, at a service attended by a handful of Whites and two hundred Blacks, many from Clarendon County, coming to pay their respects. "He's dead," James Gibson told a reporter, "but living in the minds of the people here still." But in the year of Waring's death, fourteen years after the Supreme Court ruled public school segregation unconstitutional, Clarendon schools remained segregated, proving the prescience of his prediction that future generations of Black parents and children would be forced to continue the legal battle against Jim Crow schools. It took more lawsuits to finally force the recalcitrant county to comply with a federal desegregation order.

Ironically, Summerton now has a state-of-the-art high school, Scott's Branch, with a student body that is 98 percent Black; all but a handful of White parents send their high school children to Clarendon Hall, a former "seg school" in a dilapidated wooden building, now with a token handful of Black students. (I visited both schools in 2001 and met with Black and White students at Scott's Branch High to talk about their education; one told me that several White kids at Clarendon Hall had confessed they would rather attend Scott's Branch, but their parents wouldn't let them.)

After a second hearing to examine the state's plans for "equalizing" the county's separate schools, with Judge Waring having been replaced on the panel by Fourth Circuit Judge Armistead Dobie, another segregationist, Judge Parker wrote an opinion—this time unanimous—lauding the state's yet unfulfilled promises. "There can be no doubt," Parker wrote, "that as a result of the program in which defendants are engaged the educational facilities and opportunities afforded Negroes within the district will, by the beginning of the next school year in 1952, be made equal to those afforded white persons." Speaking for all three judges, Parker concluded, "[W]e think that the law requiring segregation is valid," a holding that offered Marshall a direct appeal to the Supreme Court. By the time he filed that appeal on May 10, 1952, judges in four other cases that challenged school segregation had issued decisions that would join the *Briggs* case in the Court.

We have spent considerable time in Summerton and Clarendon County for three reasons: first, Boulware's invitation to Marshall to meet with Pearson and DeLaine offered Marshall his first chance to challenge school segregation in the Deep South; second, the disparity between the county's White and Black schools, both in funding and quality, was among the sharpest of any southern district; and third, Marshall was impressed by the courage of the county's Black parents to risk retaliation—which came quickly—for taking the county to court. Because of these factors, our visits to the other four cities and towns where these cases began will be shorter, although each has a story worth learning about a time when most White people felt comfortable in their communities, paying little or no attention to the growing insistence of Black parents that their children deserved an education that would help them climb out of generations—centuries, in fact—of poverty and discrimination.

* * *

Prince Edward County is near the top of Virginia's southern tier of counties, a rural area known as the Southside, and lies about sixty miles southwest of Richmond. Its county seat and only sizable town, Farmville, had a population of some five thousand in 1950. The countryside is mostly pine forest, with hundreds of small farms on cleared land. The major crop back then was tobacco, but most of the plots were just a few acres, and few of the county's farmers, Black or White, grew rich from their backbreaking labor. "It's right hard to grow," recalled Mary Croner, a matriarch of the Black community. "You got to plow it, plant it, sucker it, top it, and worm it, and there weren't any spraying then. We sold it over in Farmville, mostly for cigars and chewin.'" The 1950 census showed that Blacks made up 45 percent of the county's residents, and that more than 80 percent of them lived on farms. The average Black family in 1950 got by on $852 a year, and almost one-third had incomes under $500. Needless to say, the county's Black residents were woefully deficient in education. Those who were twenty-five or older had completed an average of 5.5 years of schooling, and more than two-thirds had not gone past the sixth grade.

Also needless to say, the county's schools for Blacks were woefully deficient in every way; the all-Black Moton High lacked the gymnasium, cafeteria, and science labs that Farmville High provided White students. Moton was so overcrowded that many students had classes in hastily constructed pine shacks with tar-paper covering. These conditions upset Barbara Rose Johns, a strong-willed Moton High junior, who recalled a talk with her music teacher.

> I told her how sick and tired I was of the inadequate buildings and facilities and how I wished to hell—I wasn't this profane in speaking to her, but that's how I felt—something could be done about it. After hearing me out, she asked simply, "Why don't *you* do something about it?" Soon the little wheels began turning in my mind. I decided to use the student council.

Barbara presented her audacious plan to her fellow students, who agreed to join her in the first strike by Black students in the former Confederacy.

Shouldering picket signs they constructed in the school's carpentry shop, the group marched from Moton to the Farmville courthouse, with placards that read "WE WANT A NEW SCHOOL—OR NONE AT ALL" and "WE ARE TIRED OF TAR-PAPER SHACKS—WE WANT A NEW SCHOOL." The picketers met with the school board chairman, Maurice Large, stating their demand for a new school. He told them, "[G]o back to school; nobody will talk to you about it until you do."

Later that day, the students met with the Rev. L. Francis Griffin, the young firebrand pastor of the county's largest Black church. Griffin, who had served during World War II in a tank battalion commanded by Gen. George Patton, urged them to contact Spottswood Robinson III, who headed the NAACP legal office in Richmond. After visiting Farmville and hearing their story, Robinson agreed to file a suit on their behalf, on the condition that it would directly challenge school segregation in Virginia; he had recently met with Marshall, who told him about the Clarendon County case and urged a similar attack on segregation. Robinson filed *Davis v. Prince Edward County* in January 1951; he listed Dorothy Davis, a fifteen-year-old Moton student, as the lead plaintiff, since Barbara Johns's parents, fearful for her safety after she had become the face of the protest, sent her to stay with relatives in Montgomery, Alabama.

The case against the Prince Edward school board came to trial before another three-judge panel, on February 25, 1952. Both sides called expert witnesses who testified for an entire week on conditions in the county's schools, with testimony that filled more than a thousand pages of trial transcript. A week after the hearing ended, Judge Albert Bryan issued a unanimous opinion of just three pages, with no reference to the trial testimony. Finding school segregation a "reasonable" exercise of the board's powers, Bryan found the reason in "the ways of life in Virginia" and a practice that "has for generations been a part of the mores of her people. To have separate schools has been their use and wont," using an archaic term for "custom" or "habit." With this expected decision, Robinson filed an appeal with the Supreme Court, joining the *Briggs* case on its docket.

* * *

Just across the Potomac River from Virginia, the nation's capital proudly features impressive memorials to Thomas Jefferson and Abraham Lincoln, one a slave owner, the other the Great Emancipator. In 1950, Washington's public schools followed Jefferson's lead in segregating its public schools; his most favored project, the University of Virginia, remained segregated until admitting one Black graduate student in 1950. This practice upset Gardner Bishop, a Black barber and the father of thirteen-year-old Judine. In 1947, Judine was turned away from the Whites-only Eliot Junior High School, the nearest school to her home. The Eliot school had a capacity of 918 students, but only 765 were enrolled that year. Judine had been assigned to the Black school, Browne Junior High, which was designed to hold 783 students but had an enrollment of 1,638. Faced with more than twice the number of students over the school's capacity, the D.C. board of education had put Browne students on double shifts and had refused to move any Black students into the empty seats at the Eliot school.

Gardner Bishop refused to put up with overcrowded, run-down Jim Crow schools for his children. He had attended a speech by Charles Houston, the dean of Howard Law School and mentor of Thurgood Marshall. At that time, Congress—which supervised the District like a plantation and controlled its budget—was considering a bill to appropriate funds to construct several new schools for Black students. Bishop was struck by Houston's argument that new schools for Black children, no matter how well equipped and staffed, could not erase the stigma of segregation. Bishop sought out Houston, and the two men became close friends, working together in planning a legal attack on the District's separate schools. But Houston had serious heart problems and was often hospitalized. In April 1950, he knew he was dying and called Bishop to his bedside. "He told me that it looked as if he wasn't ever going to practice again," Bishop recalled, "and that the important thing was for us to carry on the fight." Houston told Bishop to contact James Nabrit, a Howard law professor. "I explained it all to him," Bishop said of his meeting with Nabrit, "including Charlie's wish that he should take over the lawsuits and continue the fight." Nabrit agreed to represent the Consolidated Parents group that Bishop headed, with the understanding that any lawsuit against the D.C. school board would directly challenge the constitutionality of segregation.

One new school, completed just before classes began in the fall of 1950, was John Philip Sousa Junior High in southeast Washington, intended for White students. Sousa had a spacious auditorium, a double gymnasium, a playground with seven basketball courts and a softball field, and several empty classrooms. On September 11, 1950, the first day of the new school year, Gardner Bishop escorted eleven Black children into the building and guided them to the principal's office. The principal refused to enroll the children, sending them to the all-Black schools to which the board of education had assigned them.

One of the junior high students who had been turned away from Sousa was Spottswood T. Bolling, a twelve-year-old whose widowed mother worked for the federal government as a bookbinder at $57 a week, more than twice the average wage for a Black woman in Washington at that time. Spottswood had been assigned to Shaw Junior High for the seventh grade. Shaw was located in a run-down and overcrowded building in northwest Washington; the school had no playground and its science room had just one Bunsen burner for several hundred students. Early in 1951, Nabrit filed a lawsuit in federal court with Spottswood Bolling as the lead plaintiff and C. Melvin Sharpe, president of the District board of education, as the first defendant. Nabrit left out of his complaint any mention of unequal school facilities or curriculum. He also left out any reference to the Fourteenth Amendment, looking elsewhere in the Constitution for support. This was necessary because the Supreme Court had ruled that the Fourteenth Amendment's guarantee of "equal protection" applied only to states, not to the congressionally governed District of Columbia. Nabrit relied instead on the Fifth Amendment, which—like the Fourteenth—provided that "no person" could be deprived of "life, liberty, or property, without due process of law." That "liberty" included the right to be free from racial discrimination, Nabrit argued.

The *Bolling* case had its first hearing before Judge Walter Bastian in April 1951; shortly after this, he dismissed the case without an opinion, issuing a three-page order stating that because Nabrit had not alleged any inequality between the Sousa and Shaw junior highs, there was no need for a hearing. Bastian's order added that judicial precedent foreclosed any attack on the constitutionality of segregation in District schools. Nabrit, who expected this ruling, began preparing an appeal to the federal Court of Appeals for the District, which handled many cases involving federal agencies, including the District's board of education. He was surprised to receive a phone call from the Supreme Court's clerk in October 1952, informing him the Court wanted to add the *Bolling* case to its docket for argument on December 9, along with four other cases that challenged school segregation, bypassing the appellate court. Nabrit was pleased but a bit concerned that he now had just six weeks before he faced the justices.

* * *

Many people don't think of Delaware as a southern state, but it lies just below Pennsylvania on the southern side of the Mason-Dixon line; although it was a Union state during the Civil War, Delaware had allowed slavery until it was abolished by the Thirteenth Amendment in 1865. In most respects, the state was southern in "custom" and attitude. Blacks made up 14 percent of the state's population in 1950, with incomes and education well below those of Whites; Black adults averaged just 7.2 years of schooling, more than three years behind Whites, while the average yearly income of Blacks was slightly more than $1,000, barely one-third of White families' earnings.

Delaware also, as of 1950, segregated its public schools by law. This practice angered two Black mothers who lived in two small towns just below the Pennsylvania border, close to the state's only big city, Wilmington. Sarah Bulah's six-year-old daughter, Shirley, went to first grade in the one-room school for Black children in Hockessin, a rural district that provided a school bus for the White children in its elementary school. The bus went right past Shirley's home but would not pick her up, so her mother had to drive her two miles each way to the Black school. Bulah resented this burden and wrote a letter to the state Department of Public Instruction, asking that the bus stop for Shirley and take her to school. The reply from the state school superintendent was curt and blunt, informing her, "[S]ince the State Constitution requires separate educational facilities for colored and white children, your children may not ride on a bus serving a white school." Shirley could not even sit in the back of the bus.

In Claymont, a suburban town northeast of Wilmington on the Delaware River, Ethel Belton was upset that her teenage daughter, Ethel Louise, could not attend Claymont High, just a mile from her home, but was forced to ride on a bus for two hours each day to attend all-Black Howard High in downtown Wilmington. Surrounded by factories and run-down tenements, the old school housed more than 1,300 students; the only four-year high school for Blacks in Delaware, Howard lacked most of the facilities enjoyed by the White students at Claymont High, which occupied a fourteen-acre campus with baseball diamonds and football fields and offered courses in Spanish, economics, and trigonometry, none of which Howard students could take.

Both mothers, who didn't know each other, reached out to Louis Redding, the state's only Black lawyer who handled civil rights cases; a graduate of Harvard Law School, he agreed to help the two women and decided to file separate lawsuits against the two school districts in which they lived. "He said he wouldn't help me get a Jim Crow bus to take my girl to any Jim Crow school," Sarah Bulah recalled, "but if I was interested in sendin' her to an integrated school, why, then maybe he'd help. Well, I thanked God right then and there." Naming the members of the State Board of Education as defendants, with Francis Gebhart the first, Redding filed *Bulah v. Gebhart* and *Belton v. Gebhart* in federal court, asking for a three-judge panel to hear the challenges to state law. Much to Redding's surprise, the Delaware attorney general asked the federal judges to transfer the cases to the state's Chancery Court, which handled civil matters.

Redding was pleased by this move, for it put the two cases before the vice chancellor, Collins Seitz, who had already ruled, in a case brought by Redding, that the Delaware College for Negroes in the state capital of Dover was far inferior to the all-White University of Delaware in Newark, ordering the university's immediate integration, which began in 1949 without incident, the first in the nation to desegregate its undergraduate programs by judicial order. When the Claymont and Hockessin cases came before Seitz for hearing, Redding—assisted by Jack Greenberg, a young NAACP lawyer dispatched by Marshall—called fourteen witnesses, a veritable Who's Who of American social science, all of whom testified that segregated schools, no matter how equal in quality, imposed a "stigma" and feelings of inferiority on Black children. The witness whose testimony seemed to impress Seitz the most was Frederic Wertham, a noted psychiatrist at Bellevue Hospital in New York City. Wertham had brought thirteen children—eight Black and five White—to New York from Delaware, and interviewed each five times. The children of both races did not hide their feelings about segregated schools and each other. One Black boy made a profound statement: "If I have to go to segregated schools all the time, I won't know how to react to different people in life." One White girl reported what her classmates said about Black children: "They should work and we should play." Wertham summarized his findings for Chancellor Seitz: "Most of the children we have examined interpret segregation in one way and only one way—and that is they interpret it as punishment. There is no doubt about that." Redding confronted the state's primary witness, George Miller, the state school superintendent, who claimed the state was working to make the Black schools equal to those for Whites; Redding asked Miller if they were still unequal. "Well, I would have to say yes," Miller conceded.

After the hearing concluded, Chancellor Seitz conducted his own fact-finding tour, visiting Claymont High and Howard High and the two elementary schools in Hockessin. In his written opinion, issued on April 1, 1952, Seitz compared the course offerings, teacher qualifications, and facilities at the respective schools, finding, "[I]n our Delaware society, State-imposed segregation in education itself results in the Negro children, as a class, receiving educational opportunities which are substantially inferior to those available to white children similarly situated." The only remedy for Shirley Bulah and

Ethel Louise Belton, he concluded, was "admission to the school with superior facilities." In that ruling, Seitz did something no other judge had done: he ordered state officials to admit Black children to White public schools. "This is the first real victory in our campaign to destroy segregation of American pupils in elementary and high schools," Marshall crowed in a press statement. However, Seitz put a hold on his order, pending the state's appeal to the Delaware Supreme Court; after it upheld Seitz's order, the Delaware cases—the only ones ruling against Jim Crow schooling—joined the other four school cases on the Supreme Court's docket, as the state's lawyers appealed once again from a ruling by the state's own judge.

(A personal story: Between 1950 and 1954, my family lived in New Castle, a charming small town on the Delaware River, six miles south of Wilmington, the seat of New Castle County. I attended the fifth and sixth grades in elementary school, then the seventh and eighth at Carrie Downey Junior High, in an imposing brick building. All my classmates were White, although New Castle had a small Black community in a hamlet called Buttonwood, about a mile from where I lived. Years later I returned to New Castle for a visit and stopped in Buttonwood, which had made a museum of its one-room wooden school for its Black kids. It's a sad commentary on American education and society that while I attended segregated schools in New Castle, I never once asked myself, *Where are the Black kids from Buttonwood?* We lived then in two separate—and very unequal—societies, one with privileges for its favored members, the other denied those privileges by "custom" and law. We still do.)

* * *

Many people, I'm sure, think of public school segregation as confined to the states of the former Confederacy. In fact, as we've seen, even Boston, the capital of the abolitionist movement, separated White and Black children, a policy upheld by the Massachusetts Supreme Court in 1850. Many people also, I'm sure, call the Supreme Court case that struck down school segregation either "Brown" or perhaps "Brown versus Board of Education," but without finishing the full caption as "Board of Education of Topeka, Kansas." The Sunflower State is far north and west of the Mason-Dixon line, not a state one would expect to have segregated even a few of its schools. The state legislature had voted in 1879 to allow "first-class" cities with more than fifteen thousand residents to segregate their elementary schools, but all high schools—except for one in Kansas City, across from Missouri—and the state university were always integrated. And of the first-class cities, only the state's capital of Topeka segregated its grade schools, with four schools for Black children.

In 1950, Topeka had a population of eighty thousand, with about six thousand Black residents. But much of the city was off-limits to Blacks, including hotels, restaurants, movie theaters, and even the swimming pool in Gage Park, the site of a well-kept zoo and a well-tended rose garden. Black children were allowed to swim in the Gage pool just once a year, when the park directors invited Topeka's Blacks to hold a picnic. And although Topeka High School was integrated, it fielded two basketball teams, the Trojans for Whites and the Ramblers for Blacks, with separate squads of cheerleaders and pep clubs. Few children in the segregated grade schools complained about the inferior conditions in them; those who did were told to keep quiet by Harrison Caldwell, a Black teacher who enforced the internal segregation at Topeka High and also ran the grade schools under superintendent Kenneth McFarland. One Black student at Topeka High in the 1940s recalled that Caldwell "would tell [them] not to rock the boat and how to be as little offensive to whites as possible—to be clean and study hard and accept the status quo—and things were getting better."

Things didn't get better enough to satisfy the most outspoken Black leader in Topeka, McKinley Burnett, president of the city's NAACP chapter, whose job at the Forbes Air Force Base protected him from retaliation for his civil rights activism. Burnett began a campaign in 1948 to end grade school segregation, speaking at school board meetings about the schools' deficiencies. One board member got so angry when Burnett said that Blacks paid taxes just like Whites and deserved the same rights that he jumped from his seat and shouted, "Let's go outside and settle this matter right now." Burnett calmly replied, "I don't settle these matters that way. I settle them by legal means." Burnett carried through on his threat, sending a letter to NAACP headquarters in New York, asking for help in preparing a lawsuit against the Topeka school board and venting his anger at the board's open hostility toward him. "Words cannot express the humiliation and disrespect in this matter," he wrote.

Burnett's letter reached Marshall, who assigned Carter to help draft a complaint. Carter visited Topeka and enlisted the help of four of Topeka's five Black lawyers, three of them members of one family, Elisha Scott and his sons John and Charles, both of them World War II veterans who had chafed under the Jim Crow army. With Carter's guidance, the lawyers drafted a complaint, while Burnett searched for Black parents of grade-school children who were willing to join as plaintiffs. He found twenty; most were

NAACP members, and all but one were women. The lone male in this group was Oliver Brown, who was not a member but had once given the invocation at an NAACP meeting. Brown was thirty-two, a Topeka native and graduate of Topeka High, who worked at the Santa Fe Railway yards and was also an ordained minister. (Interestingly, the 1920 federal census listed him and both of his parents as "Mulatto," although I've found no record of their White ancestry.) Mamie Williams, who taught Oliver in his segregated grade school, recalled her former pupil: "He was an average student and a good citizen—he was not a fighter in his manner." But he reacted with the same anger as Burnett when he took his eight-year-old daughter, Linda, to enroll in the third grade at Sumner Elementary, just six blocks from her home. Ironically, the school was named after a famous abolitionist, Charles Sumner, but was reserved for White kids only. Linda later recalled that when they reached the school, she sat on a chair in the foyer while her father went into the principal's office. She heard loud voices, then her father came out and walked her home without saying a word of what had happened. Linda knew he was upset, although she didn't know what he planned to do about it. But Oliver knew Burnett through his ministry, and he joined the lawsuit as one of twenty plaintiffs. When Carter and the four Topeka lawyers filed their complaint in federal court, Oliver Brown's name was first on the caption. (Linda and I were on a panel some years ago, and she told me that the other plaintiffs, all women, felt a man's name should go first; otherwise, Darlene Brown—no relation—would have been the lead plaintiff. Such are the vagaries of history.)

After the complaint's filing on February 28, 1951, the hearing before the three-judge panel began on June 22. Heading the panel was Judge Walter Huxman, a former Kansas governor and member of the Tenth Circuit Court of Appeals; he was joined by two district judges, Arthur Mellott and Delmas Carl Hill; all three had grown up in parts of Kansas where few Blacks lived. Representing the school board was Lester Goodell, a former county prosecutor who constantly interjected sarcastic remarks when Carter answered questions from the judges, who let Goodell sneer at Carter without comment. Carter had just asked his first witness, a former school board member, why the board had not used its power to end segregation in Topeka when Goodell jumped up and—as Perry Mason always did—objected to the "incompetent, irrelevant, and immaterial" question. It was none of these things—in fact, it was the central issue in the case—but Judge Huxman sustained Goodell's meritless objection, firmly admonishing Carter that the only issue was whether the board was "furnishing adequate facilities" for Black children in separate schools. "If they are doing that, then what they are thinking about is immaterial," Huxman added.

After several witnesses testified about the conditions in Topeka's White and Black grade schools, listing the facilities each school had and the level of their teachers' training and experience, Oliver Brown took the stand as the named plaintiff. His nervousness showed in his speaking so quietly that Judge Huxman asked him to raise his voice, and he stumbled over how many blocks his home was from the all-Black Monroe school. But he described how Linda had to walk through the railroad switching yards to the school bus stop, telling the judges the bus was often late, and that "many times she had to wait through the cold, the rain, and the snow until the bus got there." And then Linda had to wait thirty minutes until the school gate was unlocked. She later recalled the bitter winter cold: "I remember walking, tears freezing up on my face because I began to cry because it was so cold, and many times I had to turn around and run back home."

Carter's prize witness was Louisa Holt, an assistant professor of sociology at the University of Kansas in Lawrence, who also worked with children at the prestigious Menninger Clinic in Topeka; in addition, she had two children in its public schools. Carter's first question went directly to the main issue in the case: "Does enforced legal separation have any adverse effect upon the personality development of the Negro child?" Her answer was equally direct:

> The fact that it is enforced, that it is legal, has more importance than the mere fact of segregation by itself does because this gives legal and official sanction to a policy which is inevitably interpreted both by white people and by Negroes as denoting the inferiority of the Negro group. Were it not for the sense that one group is inferior to the other, there would be no basis—and I am not granting that this is a rational basis—for such segregation.

Carter next asked how segregation affected the "learning process" of Black children. "A sense of inferiority must always affect one's motivation for learning since it affects the feelings one has of one's self as a person," she replied.

It was not a surprise to Carter or his fellow lawyers that the panel's decision, handed down on August 3, 1951, upheld Topeka's policy of grade-school segregation. Writing for the panel, Judge Huxman cited *Plessy v. Ferguson* as binding precedent for the "separate but equal" doctrine. He also reviewed the trial testimony, finding that "the physical facilities, the curricula, courses of study, qualification of and quality of teachers, as well as other educational facilities in the two sets of schools are comparable." In other words, if the schools are roughly equal, they can remain separate. However, and surprisingly to Carter, Huxman looked beyond brick-and-mortar comparisons, quoting Louisa Holt's testimony almost verbatim:

> Segregation of white and colored children in public schools has a detrimental effect upon the colored children. The impact is greater when it has the sanction of the law, for the policy of separating the races is usually interpreted as denoting the inferiority of the Negro group. A sense of inferiority affects the motivation of a child to learn. Segregation with the sanction of law, therefore, has a tendency to retard the educational and mental development of Negro children and to deprive them of some of the benefits they would receive in a racially integrated school system.

One might conclude, reading Judge Huxman's opinion, that it was internally inconsistent. If segregation made Black children feel inferior, and therefore not equal to White children, was that not a violation of the "separate but equal" doctrine of *Plessy*? Does that doctrine apply to other than material things like railway cars, such as the feelings of inferiority that segregated schools imposed on Black children? One might also ask of *Plessy*, equal in respect to what? Just the quality of buildings and teachers, or the fact of segregation itself, as a "badge of inferiority"? Two decades later, Judge Huxman reflected on this inconsistency. "We weren't in sympathy with the decision we rendered," he said of the panel he headed. "If it weren't for *Plessy v. Ferguson*, we surely would have found the law unconstitutional. But there was no way around it—the Supreme Court would have to overrule itself."

In the next chapter, we'll see how the Supreme Court justices—after some intense behind-closed-doors struggle—dealt with Judge Huxman's challenge, and the often violent aftermath of that historic decision. But I think it useful and enlightening to have first looked at the struggles within these five communities, very different in geography, racial composition, and ties to the Jim Crow system. And to introduce readers to the people involved in these cases: parents, children, school officials, lawyers, and judges. Each had a role to play—for good or ill—in the struggle for equality in a nation still tied to its past in ways that continue to divide its citizens.

9

"War against the Constitution"

DECEMBER 9, 1952, was a cool, rainy Tuesday in Washington, D.C. Promptly at 1:30 in the afternoon, Chief Justice Fred Vinson led his eight colleagues from behind a velvet curtain to their high-backed leather seats at the Supreme Court's bench. Every one of the three hundred seats in the Court's ornate chamber was filled, about half of them with Blacks who had begun lining up early that morning outside the Court's marble edifice, across from the Capitol building. Another four hundred people stood in a long line outside the courtroom and down the broad stairway on which reporters and photographers were clustered beneath umbrellas.

As we have seen, each of the five cases before the justices that afternoon reflected a different piece of the racial mosaic in midcentury America, across a wide arc of the country's geography: Clarendon County in South Carolina was part of the Deep South, more than 70 percent Black but governed entirely by Whites. Prince Edward County in Virginia was closely balanced in race, with a substantial number of Black farmers who owned their land. The District of Columbia was the nation's capital, whose Black residents were more educated and affluent than many southern Whites. New Castle County in Delaware sat just below the Mason-Dixon line, the most northerly of the seventeen states that imposed the Jim Crow system on its schools. Kansas, with some quarter-million students in public schools, segregated just a few hundred Black children in four elementary schools in Topeka, the state's capital.

But the question before the Supreme Court in these cases involved more than the students in five school districts. The real question was whether the country that held itself up to the world as the beacon of democracy, during a period of Cold War tensions and anticolonial ferment, could appeal to the "colored" peoples of Africa and Asia while more than a third of its states prevented Black and White children from attending school together. It was this question, and the issues of foreign policy it raised, that gave a special urgency and importance to the arguments in the school cases.

Sitting before the justices on their bench were stacks of legal briefs, submitted by the parties on both sides, reaching almost two feet in height. Since the basic issue in all the school cases was whether the Constitution's Due Process and Equal Protection clauses prohibited school segregation, the briefs dealt with that question with similar case citations and analysis; they differed primarily in the details of each case, especially the disparities of school funding and facilities between the White and Black schools. One brief, however, stood apart from the others and deserves mention here, since it raised an issue of global scale and significance. This was the brief of the U.S. government as an *amicus curiae*, or "friend of the court." The justices often invite the solicitor general (the Justice Department's top lawyer for federal agencies) to submit briefs, and sometimes to join the oral arguments, in cases in which the government is not a formal party but has an interest in a case's outcome. To prepare the brief, Acting Solicitor General Robert Stern chose Philip Elman, a career Justice Department lawyer who had served in the solicitor's office for seventeen years, from 1944 to 1961. A Harvard Law School graduate and former law clerk to Justice Felix Frankfurter (who would vote on the school cases), Elman had prepared the government's *amicus* briefs in the *McLaurin* and *Sweatt* cases on graduate and law school segregation.

For his new assignment, Elman looked to another department for assistance; the State Department, headed by Dean Acheson, had asked that its views be conveyed to the justices. Elman included in his brief a letter from Acheson to Attorney General James McGranery about the effect of racial discrimination on American foreign relations: "As might be expected, Soviet spokesmen regularly exploit this situation in propaganda against the United States, both within the United Nations and through radio broadcasts and the press, which reaches all corners of the world." Acheson pointed to Jim Crow schools:

> The segregation of schoolchildren on a racial basis is one of the practices in the United States that has been singled out for hostile foreign comment in the United Nations and elsewhere. Other peoples cannot understand how such a practice can exist in a country which professes to be a staunch supporter of freedom, justice, and democracy.

Secretary Acheson concluded that racial discrimination "remains a source of constant embarrassment to this government in the day-to-day conduct of its foreign relations; and it jeopardizes the effective maintenance of our moral leadership of the free and democratic nations of the world." The justices were certain to read the government's brief carefully, since the Court's decisions in the school cases would be read and scrutinized by America's friends and foes alike.

* * *

Many people assume that Thurgood Marshall argued the *Brown* case before the Supreme Court, since his name is always associated with it. Actually, his NAACP deputy, Robert Carter, spoke for Linda Brown and the other Black grade-school children in Topeka, as he had before the lower court panel in the case. Despite the panel's finding that the Black and White grade schools in Topeka were "substantially equal" in quality, Carter tried to point out the inequalities disclosed in the case record, but the justices wanted to hear instead about Carter's position on the *Plessy* case. After all, that was the central issue before the Court, not the number of blocks that Linda Brown traveled to the all-Black Monroe school. Carter danced around the question until Justice Frankfurter, who peppered him with questions, forced a direct answer. "I have no hesitancy in saying that the issue of 'separate but equal' should be faced," Carter said, "and should squarely be overruled."

In response, the young and inexperienced lawyer for the state of Kansas, Paul Wilson, doggedly clung to the *Plessy* case for precedent and dismissed the social science testimony that Judge Huxman had cited approvingly in his panel opinion. None of Topeka's Black children, Wilson claimed, had shown evidence of "some detriment that the rest of the population does not suffer" and thus had no basis for challenging their segregation. Wilson faced only a few questions and sat down well before his time expired.

After Carter and Wilson concluded their arguments in the *Brown* case, Marshall took the lawyers' lectern to argue for the Black children in Clarendon County in the *Briggs* case. Having already argued and won a half-dozen cases before the justices, Marshall "hovered imposingly over the lectern as he addressed the justices familiarly, but respectfully," recalled another of Marshall's deputies, Jack Greenberg. He took up where Carter had left off, with an attack on the constitutionality of racial classifications, reminding the justices of the Court's 1927 decision in *Nixon v. Herndon*, which struck down all-White primary elections in Texas. "States may do a good deal of classifying that is difficult to believe rational," Justice Oliver Wendell Holmes had written, "but there are limits, and it is too clear for extended argument that color cannot be made the basis of a statutory classification" that deprives Blacks of rights that Whites enjoy. Marshall followed Carter in directing his argument to Justice Frankfurter, who asked more than fifty questions during Marshall's hour at the lectern. His response to Frankfurter's most important question, about the general power of states to make legislative classifications, impressed the professorial justice. "I think that when an attack is made on a statute on the ground that it is an unreasonable classification, and competent, recognized testimony is produced," Marshall replied, "I think that the least that the state has to do is produce something to defend their statutes." Frankfurter beamed. "I follow you when you talk that way," he told the NAACP's lead counsel.

If the Jim Crow system had any chance of survival, it needed a lawyer who would defend segregation with more fire and conviction than Wilson had shown. South Carolina had such a lawyer in John W. Davis, a legendary advocate who had argued more cases before the Supreme Court than any lawyer since Daniel Webster; Davis had also served as solicitor general and was the (losing) Democratic presidential candidate in 1924. Now seventy-nine and a senior partner in a powerful Wall Street law firm, he remained fiercely loyal to the "southern way of life" and the Jim Crow system he had grown up with and still found more comfortable than the racial and ethnic melting pot of New York City. Marshall had challenged Davis to "produce something" to defend the Jim Crow schools in Clarendon County and the rest of South Carolina. Davis shouldered his load without bending an inch. The lawmakers who adopted the Fourteenth Amendment, Davis argued, had not intended to prevent the states from separating Black and White students. Before he left the lectern, Davis posed his own question for the justices, asking them to consider whether "the wishes of the parents, both white and colored, should be ascertained before their children are forced into what may be an unwelcome contact." The Black parents of Clarendon County, he failed to note, had clearly expressed their wishes by joining and supporting the first lawsuit against Jim Crow schools in the Deep South.

None of the lawyers who followed Marshall and Davis to the lectern, in arguments that spanned three days, matched their oratorical skills or provided the justices with different reasons to strike down or uphold school segregation. The arguments concluded at 3:50 p.m. on December 11, 1952, and Chief Justice Vinson thanked all the lawyers who had spoken during twelve hours of oratory. "Any description of the oral arguments must make clear how dull they were," Jack Greenberg later wrote. More than a dozen lawyers, on both sides, had stood up and sat down without making a single memorable statement or reaching an emotional climax. One of the most divisive issues in American politics, which moved many people to passionate defense or outraged opposition, had been argued in words that were mostly soft and flat. After the Court adjourned, none of the lawyers who spoke with reporters outside was willing to predict the outcome of the cases, although Davis was overheard saying "I think we've got it won, five-to-four, or maybe six-to-three."

Counting Supreme Court votes before the justices announce their decisions is a favorite parlor game of lawyers, although Davis did not list those he counted on either side. The outcome of the school cases depended on the tally of votes at the closed-door meetings of justices in their ornate conference room, at which no official records are kept, mostly because all votes at conference are tentative and subject to change until the decision is officially released to the press and public. But justices are allowed to take notes, and some are released after a justice dies or retires.

The justices met for the first time to discuss the school cases on December 13, 1952, two days after the arguments ended; the sketchy notes of Justices Harold Burton and Robert Jackson are the only records that survive, but they paint a picture of deep divisions at this first conference. Chief Justice Vinson, a native Kentuckian, led off the discussion and made clear his reluctance to end the Jim Crow system. Jackson noted Vinson's fear that striking down school segregation would mean "complete abolition of public school system in South—serious." Burton indicated Vinson's probable vote on *Brown* as "*Aff?*" The question mark suggested that the chief justice had not expressed a firm position on the issue but was leaning toward affirming the lower court decision that upheld public school segregation in that case. The next justice to speak, Stanley Reed, was another Kentuckian who had served the New Deal administration of Franklin Roosevelt in several posts, including a stint as solicitor general. His support for segregation was evident in a comment to one of his law clerks after the Court ruled that restaurants in Washington could not refuse service to Blacks. Reed, who lived with his wife in the ritzy Mayflower Hotel near the White House, exclaimed, "Why, this means that a nigra can walk into the restaurant at the Mayflower and sit down to eat at the table right next to Mrs. Reed!" He obviously did not relish such an event. It was thus no surprise that Reed expressed his intention to "uphold segregation as constitutional" in the school cases, according to Jackson's notes.

As the discussion continued around the conference table, it became clear that at least one justice, Reed, would vote to uphold Jim Crow schooling, while another three—Chief Justice Vinson and Justices Jackson and Tom Clark, the latter a native Texan—indicated they were still undecided in the cases. This prospect of a split Court, even with a majority to strike down school segregation, upset Frankfurter, a liberal in politics but cautious in deploying the Court's power to effect social change. Frankfurter was a compulsive note scribbler and reminded himself in one he wrote while the cases were before the Court of "the psychological truth that change, especially drastic change, takes time" and that changes in "deeply rooted social habits" were "best promoted when firmly designed but not precipitously expressed." To avoid a fractured vote that would fail to satisfy either side in this debate, Frankfurter urged his colleagues at their first conference on the cases to order the lawyers on both sides to return to the Court for another round of argument. He clearly hoped that deferring a decision for another year would encourage southern officials to begin planning for a gradual change to integrated schools. To keep the lawyers busy, Frankfurter proposed that they brief and argue questions about the intentions of the Fourteenth Amendment's framers in regard to school segregation and the Court's power to hold it unconstitutional, if the framers had not intended to ban the practice. The justices, perhaps relieved, accepted Frankfurter's proposal, and dozens of lawyers began digging through musty records of the congressional and state debates over adoption of the Fourteenth Amendment.

The preparations on both sides were abruptly interrupted on September 8 with the shocking news that Chief Justice Vinson had died in his sleep of a heart attack. Vinson was sixty-one, paunchy, and got his exercise shuffling cards at President Truman's poker table, but there had been no forewarning of his death. Justice Frankfurter's reaction to Vinson's death was characteristically acerbic: "This is the first indication I have ever had that there is a God." His prayers for judicial leadership were quickly answered by President Dwight Eisenhower, who had swept into office in 1952 with the greatest margin in history over his Democratic opponent, Adlai Stevenson. During his election campaign and eight months in office, the new president had avoided taking sides on school segregation or the Supreme Court cases. Privately, however, Eisenhower had confessed to friends that he could see why White parents objected to having a "big black buck" sit next to their daughter in school. To replace Vinson as chief justice, Eisenhower paid off a political debt by naming California governor Earl Warren to his seat; Warren had swung the California delegation to Eisenhower at the Republican convention, heading off a serious challenge by Ohio senator Robert Taft. In return, Eisenhower promised Warren that he would have the next open seat on the Court. (Eisenhower later said he hadn't meant the chief's seat, but Warren insisted he fulfill his bargain.)

Whether the Court would have voted unanimously to strike down school segregation if Vinson had lived is another "what if" question, but it was quickly answered by Warren. Within a few weeks of taking his seat, the hearty and solicitous Warren won over the justices: he sought Frankfurter's counsel, soothed Jackson's hurt feelings at having been passed over for the post, and asked Hugo Black to preside at his first conference, which pleased the longest-serving justice. And he brightened the Court's dimmer lights— Harold Burton, Tom Clark, and Sherman Minton—with his glow.

* * *

The second round of arguments in the school cases had been rescheduled after Vinson's death and began on December 7, 1953. Stacked before each justice were briefs that reflected six months of hard labor by lawyers and historians who had struggled to answer the two basic questions Justice Frankfurter had posed: Did the Fourteenth Amendment's framers intend to outlaw school segregation? If not, did the Court have the power to perform that task itself? Each side put its best gloss on the reports of debates in Congress and the state legislatures, but in the end they reached similar conclusions: the evidence was equivocal on both issues. How the justices should decide the cases was still an open question.

The oral arguments on these questions spanned three days and were, by all accounts, boring and unproductive. Jack Greenberg, who sat with Marshall at the counsel table, labeled his argument "uninspiring." Richard Kluger wrote in his masterful chronicle of the school cases, *Simple Justice*, that Marshall gave "one of his least creditable performances before the Court." The only lawyer who displayed any emotion at the lectern was John W. Davis, now eighty and making his last Supreme Court argument. Proclaiming South Carolina's "good faith and intention to produce equality for all of its children of whatever race or color," he choked up as he concluded, "Here is equal education, not promised, not prophesied, but present. Shall it be thrown away on some fancied question of racial prestige?" Tears flowed down his cheeks as Davis returned to his seat. Even Marshall was moved by his opponent's emotion. But one lawyer in the courtroom whispered to another, "[T]hat sonofabitch cries in every case he argues."

Marshall had reserved some time to answer Davis, and he spoke the next morning. Greenberg recalled that "Thurgood's rebuttal was his best argument ever." Marshall opened with a bow to his aged adversary. "As Mr. Davis said yesterday, the only thing the Negroes are trying to get is prestige," he began. "Exactly correct. Ever since the Emancipation Proclamation, the Negro has been trying to get . . . the same status as anybody else regardless of race." Marshall took the justices on a verbal tour of Clarendon County and its Black and White children: "They play in the streets together, they play on their farms together, they go down the road together, they separate to go to school, they come out of school and play ball together. They have to be separated in school." Marshall ended by deploring South Carolina's "determination that the people who were formerly in slavery, regardless of anything else, shall be kept as near that state as possible, and now it is the time, we submit, that this Court should make clear that is not what our Constitution stands for."

The second round of arguments concluded on December 10, but five months passed before the public learned of the Court's decisions in the five school cases. Even more than Frankfurter, the new chief justice was determined to forge a unanimous Court around a brief and forceful opinion. Only if the justices spoke with one voice, in words the American people could understand, would the Court be able to help the nation heal its racial wounds.

Earl Warren set himself an ambitious task and spent months cajoling his colleagues. Three justices required the full Warren treatment. Felix Frankfurter wanted an unequivocal ruling that school segregation violated the Fourteenth Amendment, but he also wanted to give southern districts time to comply with the Court's mandate; he proposed to Warren a judicial decree allowing school officials to proceed with "all deliberate speed" in moving toward integration. Robert Jackson wanted the Court to admit frankly that ending segregation had no explicit constitutional warrant; he drafted a concurring opinion that read like the fable about the emperor with no clothes. Warren agreed to Frankfurter's proposal of a third round of arguments on the issue of implementation of a decree to end school segregation and convinced Jackson to drop his concurring opinion. Stanley Reed posed the greatest challenge to Warren's unrelenting charms; the courtly Kentuckian had drafted a dissent arguing that the Fourteenth Amendment provided Blacks only "an opportunity to obtain facilities substantially equal to his neighbors for himself." But Reed finally succumbed to Warren after more than twenty lunchtime discussions. After Frankfurter and Jackson climbed aboard his bandwagon, Warren offered Reed the last seat: "Stan, you're all by yourself in this now. You've got to decide whether it's the best thing for the country." Reed decided that holding out for segregation was not the best thing for the country, or for the Court.

* * *

The Supreme Court's chamber was not crowded on May 17, 1954. Thurgood Marshall had gotten a tip from a friend and took a train to Washington that Monday morning. He entered the chamber as Chief Justice Warren presided over admission of lawyers to the Court's bar. Justice Clark then read an opinion in an antitrust case, followed by Justice William Douglas, who read two opinions in cases dealing with corporate negligence and labor picketing. Most of the news reporters present that day were lounging in their basement quarters when the Court's press officer stuck his head in the door. "Reading of the segregation decisions is about to begin in the courtroom," he informed them. The reporters dashed up the stairs to witness the historic moment. "I have for announcement," Warren began, "the judgment and opinion of the court in No. 1—*Oliver Brown et al. v. Board of Education of Topeka*." Reading in a "firm, clear, unemotional voice," Warren left reporters initially unsure who had won. "The Court's ruling could not be determined immediately," the Associated Press flashed in its first bulletin. By the time Warren made clear who had won, reporters began dashing out of the chamber to file their stories, all headlined with the historic and momentous news.

At this point, as with the *Dred Scott* opinion of Chief Justice Taney, we can better understand what Warren was reading from the bench by reading his opinion, with only minor editing.

Brown v. Board of Education of Topeka, Kansas

Appeal from the United States District Court for the District of Kansas
MR. CHIEF JUSTICE WARREN delivered the opinion of the court.

These cases come to us from the states of Kansas, South Carolina, Virginia, and Delaware. They are premised on different facts and different local conditions, but a common legal question justifies their consideration together in this consolidated opinion. In each of the cases, minors of the Negro race, through their legal representatives, seek the aid of the courts in obtaining admission to the public schools of their community on a nonsegregated basis. In each instance, they had been denied admission to schools attended by white children under laws requiring or permitting segregation according to race. This segregation was alleged to deprive the plaintiffs of the equal protection of the laws under the Fourteenth Amendment....

The plaintiffs contend that segregated public schools are not "equal" and cannot be made "equal," and that hence they are deprived of the equal protection of the laws. Because of the obvious importance of the question presented, the Court took jurisdiction. Argument was heard in the 1952 Term, and reargument was heard this Term on certain questions propounded by the Court. Reargument was largely devoted to the circumstances surrounding the adoption of the Fourteenth Amendment in 1868. It covered exhaustively consideration of the amendment in Congress, ratification by the states, then-existing practices in racial segregation, and the views of proponents and opponents of the amendment. This discussion and our own investigation convinced us that, although these sources cast some light, it is not enough to resolve the problem with which we are faced. At best, they are inconclusive. . . .

An additional reason for the inconclusive nature of the amendment's history with respect to segregated schools is the status of public education at that time. In the South the movement toward free common schools, supported by general taxation, had not yet taken hold. Education of white children was largely in the hands of private groups. Education of Negroes was almost nonexistent, and practically all of the race were illiterate. In fact, any education of Negroes was forbidden by law in some states. Today, in contrast, many Negroes have achieved outstanding success in the arts and sciences, as well as in the business and professional world. It is true that public school education at the time of the amendment had advanced further in the North, but the effect of the amendment on northern states was generally ignored in the congressional debates. Even in the North, the conditions of public education did not approximate those existing today. The curriculum was usually rudimentary; ungraded schools were common in rural areas; the school term was but three months a year in many states, and compulsory school attendance was virtually unknown. As a consequence, it is not surprising that there should be so little in the history of the Fourteenth Amendment relating to its intended effect on public education.

In the first cases in this Court construing the Fourteenth Amendment, decided shortly after its adoption, the Court interpreted it as proscribing all state-imposed discriminations against the Negro race. The doctrine of "separate but equal" did not make its appearance in this Court until 1896 in the case of *Plessy v. Ferguson*, involving not education but transportation.... And in *Sweatt v. Painter*, the Court expressly reserved decision on the question whether *Plessy v. Ferguson* should be held inapplicable to public education.

In the instant cases, that question is directly presented. Here, unlike *Sweatt v. Painter*, there are findings below that the Negro and white schools involved have been equalized, or are being equalized, with respect to buildings, curricula, qualifications and salaries of teachers, and other "tangible" factors. Our decision, therefore, cannot turn on merely a comparison of these tangible factors in the Negro and white schools involved in each of the cases. We must look instead to the effect of segregation itself on public education....

Today, education is perhaps the most important function of state and local governments. Compulsory school attendance laws and the great expenditures for education both demonstrate our recognition of the importance of education to our democratic society. It is required in the performance of our most basic public responsibilities, even service in the armed forces. It is the very foundation of good citizenship. Today it is a principal instrument in awakening the child to cultural values, and preparing him for later professional training, and in helping him to adjust normally to his environment. In these days, it is doubtful that any child may reasonably be expected to succeed in life if he is denied the opportunity of an education. Such an opportunity, where the state has undertaken to provide it, is a right which must be made available to all on equal terms.

We come then to the question presented: Does segregation of children in public schools solely on the basis of race, even though the physical facilities and other "tangible" factors may be equal, deprive the children of the minority group of equal educational opportunities? We believe that it does.... Such considerations apply with added force to children in grade and high schools. To separate them from others of similar age and qualifications solely because of their race generates a feeling of inferiority as to their status in the community that may affect their hearts and minds in a way unlikely ever to be undone. The effect of this separation on their educational opportunities was well stated by a finding in the Kansas case by a court which nevertheless felt compelled to rule against the plaintiffs: "Segregation of white and colored children in public schools has a detrimental effect upon the colored children. The impact is greater when it has the sanction of the law, for the policy of separating the races is usually interpreted as denoting

the inferiority of the group. A sense of inferiority affects the motivation of a child to learn. Segregation with the sanction of law, therefore,
has a tendency to retard the educational and mental development of
Negro children and to deprive them of some of the benefits they would
receive in a racially integrated school system."

Whatever may have been the extent of psychological knowledge
at the time of *Plessy v. Ferguson*, this finding is amply supported by
modern authority. Any language in *Plessy v. Ferguson* contrary to this
finding is rejected.

We conclude that, in the field of public education, the doctrine of
"separate but equal" has no place. Separate educational facilities are inherently unequal. Therefore, we hold that the plaintiffs and others similarly situated for whom the actions have been brought are, by reason
of the segregation complained of, deprived of the equal protection of
the laws guaranteed by the Fourteenth Amendment.

It is so ordered.

Before the Court adjourned that historic morning, Chief Justice Warren
took care of the one remaining school case on the docket, *Bolling v. Sharpe*.
Because the Fourteenth Amendment's equal protection clause applies only to
state laws and policies, Warren looked to the Due Process clause in the Fifth
Amendment for a peg on which to hang the decision striking down school
segregation in the District of Columbia; his brief—and again unanimous—
opinion noted that "the concepts of equal protection and due process, both
stemming from our American ideal of fairness, are not mutually exclusive. . . .
But, as this Court has recognized, discrimination may be so unjustifiable as
to be violative of due process." He found the necessary constitutional peg in
the "liberty" interest protected against governmental deprivation by the Fifth
Amendment. "Liberty under law extends to the full range of conduct which
the individual is free to pursue, and it cannot be restricted except for a proper
governmental objective," Warren wrote.

Segregation in public education is not reasonably related to any proper
governmental objective, and thus it imposes on children of the District
of Columbia a burden that constitutes an arbitrary deprivation of their
liberty in violation of the due process clause. In view of our decision
that the Constitution prohibits the states from maintaining racially
segregated public schools, it would be unthinkable that the same
Constitution would impose a lesser duty on the federal government.

The *Bolling* decision became the first in which the Court "incorporated" the Fourteenth Amendment's equal protection guarantee into the liberty interest of the Fifth, a step that made *Bolling* a precedent in many later cases involving federal laws that discriminated against racial, religious, and ethnic minorities.

In both its brevity and its phrasing in words almost anyone could understand, Warren's unanimous *Brown* opinion was intended to educate the American people about the education of their children, both White and Black, and to explain why the Constitution required that classrooms in every state be integrated. Let me point out four significant facts about the opinion that may have escaped newspaper readers at the time, who looked mostly at headlines and bottom lines. First, Warren made clear that the Court's decision did not turn on whether the separate schools in each case were equal or unequal in quality; in fact, he stressed, the Court would have made the same decision even if the schools were "substantially equal." Second, Warren and his colleagues viewed the institution of public schooling as the primary source of learning to be good citizens and to take part in civic affairs. Segregated education, Warren explained, could not produce good citizens if one group of students are considered inferior by another group, solely on the basis of race; segregated education runs counter to the American ideal of equality for all citizens. Third, Warren's opinion found the evil of segregation in its damaging psychological toll on Black children, who all understood that White people in their communities considered them inferior and didn't want a "big black buck" sitting next to their little White girls (a fear that prompted hundreds of lynchings of Black men who even "scared" White girls). It's worth noting that Warren's opinion borrowed liberally, even verbatim, from Louisa Holt's testimony at the initial *Brown* hearing in Topeka, and that was included almost verbatim in Judge Huxman's opinion in that case. It's fair to say, I think, that Holt—an unassuming sociologist and mother of children in the Topeka schools—played as significant a role in ending school segregation as more famous people like Marshall and Warren.

Fourth, and most important, the Court's opinion did not order the admission of any Black children to White schools (or vice versa). Adopting the go-slow approach that Frankfurter had urged, the Court scheduled another round of briefs and arguments for April 1955 on the issue of implementation of desegregation plans, inviting the solicitor general and the attorneys general of all states that required or allowed school segregation to express their views and submit any desegregation plans they had adopted. This move put any actual integration off for at least another year, during which—the justices hoped—White and Black school officials and parents would be working together to ensure that integration would begin peacefully. It turned out to be a vain hope, a testament to the ignorance of well-meaning White men about the depth of the racism that still infected most southern Whites and many in the North as well.

Chief Justice Warren again presided over the three days of "implementation" arguments that began on April 11, 1955. It quickly became clear to the justices that integration would not soon happen in communities in which the Jim Crow system was firmly entrenched. Speaking for the school board in Clarendon County, S. Emory Rogers tried Warren's patience. Rogers requested the Court to issue an "open order" that would impose no time limits or conditions on the county. Warren asked if school officials would "immediately undertake to conform" to the Court's decree.

"I am frank to tell you," Rogers answered, that he doubted whether "the white people of the district will send their children to Negro schools."

Warren pressed him: "You are not willing to say here that there would be an honest attempt to conform to this decree, if we did leave it to the District Court?"

"No, I am not. Let us get the word 'honest' out of there," Rogers replied.

"No, leave it in," Warren shot back.

Rogers remained defiant: "No, because I would have to tell you that right now we would not conform—we would not send our white children to the Negro schools."

Lawyers saw Warren flush with anger. "We thought he might charge Rogers with contempt" one recalled.

Rogers was telling the truth. The White parents in Clarendon County resisted integration for years, until forced to "conform" to a federal court order. Despite this clear warning of impending trouble, Warren spoke again for a unanimous Court in the "implementation" opinion, issued on May 31, 1955. Unlike his opinion in the first *Brown* case, what became known as *Brown II* merits quotation of the only four words most people ever learned from it: integration must proceed "with all deliberate speed." That's the only guidance the Court gave to school officials about planning for and implementing actual integration. And if "deliberate speed" sounds a bit like an oxymoron, it was clearly understood in the Jim Crow states as "much deliberation and very little speed."

Asked by a friend what he thought of the Court's decision, Marshall differed from those who criticized its lack of deadlines and guidelines. Some people, he said, "insist on having the whole hog," but "I think it's a damn good decision!" He outlined a plan for the NAACP to file suits against every school board that refused to abandon school segregation and march through the courts from Maryland through Texas, just as Sherman's army had marched through the Confederacy a century before. "You can say all you want," Marshall assured a friend, "but those white crackers are going to get tired of having Negro lawyers beating 'em every day in court. They're going to get tired of it."

* * *

Marshall completely misread the fierce determination of "white crackers" in the Deep South to maintain the Jim Crow system of segregated schools. One southern politician after another denounced the Court's decision. It was "the most serious blow that has yet been struck against the rights of the states in a manner vitally affecting their authority and welfare," Virginia's powerful senator Harry Byrd complained. "I shall use every legal means at my command to continue segregated schools in Virginia," echoed Governor Thomas Stanley, a cog in the Byrd machine. "No matter how much the Supreme Court seeks to sugarcoat its bitter pill of tyranny," Governor Marvin Griffin of Georgia railed, "the people of Georgia and the South will not allow it." In South Carolina, where the first lawsuit against school segregation had been filed in Clarendon County, Governor James Byrnes said that his state "will not now nor for some years to come mix white and colored children in our schools." Governor Fielding Wright of Mississippi, the most intransigent of the Deep South states, proclaimed, "[W]e shall insist upon segregation regardless of consequences."

Facing what became a policy of "massive resistance" to integration, the term adopted by Virginia politicians, NAACP lawyers filed dozens of suits in southern federal courts—between 1955 and 1960, federal judges held more than two hundred school hearings—and won at least partial victories in most. But lawyers in almost every southern state, beholden to racist politicians, did not "get tired of it," as Marshall had predicted. And those politicians were reflecting the views of their White constituents. According to Gallup polling, in 1940 only 2 percent of southerners (and 40 percent of northerners) supported school integration, not a surprising finding at that time. By 1956, two years after the *Brown* decision, those numbers had risen somewhat, to 15 percent among southerners and 61 percent in the North; even by 1963, a year of civil rights activism across the South, only 31 percent in that region supported school integration, while 73 percent did in the North. Put another way, even by 1963 almost 70 percent of southerners opposed integration. And of those 70 percent, a substantial number were prepared to battle integration in the streets, with raucous and sometimes violent resistance.

It would be impossible to list, let alone discuss, the hundreds of integration cases that followed the two *Brown* decisions and the scores of protests— many vocal but peaceful, others disruptive or violent—that were sparked by lower court desegregation orders. One such case, however, merits recounting here, not only because the violent resistance to judicial orders was encouraged by a state governor but also because, for the first time, scenes of clashes between screaming protesters and uniformed army troops appeared on millions of television screens in homes across the country, a medium that would soon eclipse newspapers and magazines as most people's primary source of news. A video of mob violence is worth a thousand news articles, to adapt a common phrase. And it was the defiance by Arkansas governor Orval Faubus of court orders in 1957 that nine Black students be admitted to Central High School in the state's capital of Little Rock that caused the Supreme Court to, in effect, lose its collective temper.

The case of *Cooper v. Aaron* began in 1955 with the Little Rock School District's approval of a plan for "phased" integration of the city's schools over a ten-year period, beginning in September 1957 with Central High, then the district's other high schools and junior highs, and finally its grade schools, first with the upper grades and concluding in 1967 with first graders in integrated classrooms. The Little Rock board made no bones that its plan was designed to produce "the least amount of integration spread over the longest period of time." The glacial pace of the plan failed to satisfy the Arkansas NAACP, however, and its lawyers filed suit against the board in February 1956. Six months later, federal judge John E. Miller endorsed the ten-year plan as a "good faith" effort to "ultimately bring about a school system not based on color distinctions." The Eighth Circuit federal appellate court in St. Louis upheld Miller's decision and cleared the path for nine Black students to enter Central High on September 3, 1957.

Although most Whites in Little Rock supported the school board's "phased integration" plan, news reports of the judicial order inflamed the city's racial bigots, who began waving Confederate battle flags and vowing to block the school's doors to Black students. The night before the "Little Rock Nine" were expected at Central High, Governor Faubus spoke to the state on television. Warning that "blood will run in the streets" if the nine Black students entered the school, Faubus announced that he had ordered National Guard troops to surround Central High and keep them out. The next morning, eight of the nine gathered at the home of Daisy Bates, the young president of the state's NAACP chapters, and left in station wagons for the short drive to their new school. Fifteen-year-old Elizabeth Eckford did not ride to school with the others. Walking alone, holding her head high, she tried to enter Central High and was turned away by soldiers with bayonets. A menacing crowd surrounded Elizabeth and began yelling, "Get her! Lynch her." Someone hollered, "Get a rope and drag her over to this tree!" Protected by a White NAACP member, Elizabeth finally escaped the mob by getting on a city bus.

Americans across the country witnessed Elizabeth Eckford's dignity in the face of lynch-mob hysteria on their television screens. Many people had never seen the face of racism so clearly, and calls began for federal intervention to end the Arkansas insurrection led by a governor who had sworn to uphold the Constitution. Pressure mounted on President Eisenhower to intervene, but he took no action. National Guard troops blocked Central High's doors to the Little Rock Nine until September 20, when a federal judge ordered Faubus to remove the troops. Little Rock police then escorted the Black students into the school, but an unruly mob stormed the building and the nine youngsters barely escaped with their lives through a side door.

Faced with the prospect of televised lynchings, Eisenhower interrupted his golfing vacation in Newport, Rhode Island, and summoned Faubus to meet with him and Attorney General Herbert Brownell. After receiving a stern lecture behind closed doors, Faubus emerged, sounding coopera-tive: "The people of Little Rock are law abiding, and I know that they expect to obey valid court orders. In this they shall have my support." By inserting the qualifying term "valid" in his statement, Faubus had given himself a loophole through which he crawled as soon as he returned to Little Rock. The cocky governor did not consider the Constitution a "valid" document in Arkansas, and he refused to provide the Little Rock Nine with state protection after the local police withdrew in the face of menacing mobs. This outright defiance finally spurred Eisenhower to act. On September 23, he issued a proclamation entitled "Obstruction of Justice in the State of Arkansas" that commanded "all persons engaged in such obstruction to cease and desist therefrom, and to disperse forthwith." The president also directed the secretary of defense to "use such of the armed forces of the United States as he may deem neces-sary." The next day, one thousand paratroopers of the 101st Airborne Division arrived in Little Rock from Fort Campbell, Kentucky, and quickly ringed Central High. The city's racists lacked the guts to battle paratroopers, and the Little Rock Nine finally began their classes. During the remainder of the school year, a band of White students harassed them unmercifully while school officials turned their heads. It was a hard year for the Black students, but on May 27, 1958, the first Blacks graduated from Central High.

Shortly before the graduation ceremony, the Little Rock school board asked federal judge Harry Lemley to delay any further integration until January 1961. The board's lawyers argued that school integration "runs counter to the ingrained attitudes" of many Little Rock Whites. They also pointed to Governor Faubus, who had persuaded the Arkansas legislature to pass laws authorizing him to take over local school boards that admitted any Black students to White schools. Judge Lemley held a three-day hearing at which school officials—all of them White—testified about the "chaos, bedlam, and turmoil" at Central High. The judge did not ask who had caused the chaos but granted the school board's petition on June 20 1958, resegregating all Little Rock schools for more than two years.

Judge Lemley's move precipitated a legal storm, as NAACP lawyers sought and obtained a stay of the judge's order from the Eighth Circuit appellate court in St. Louis, which reversed his ruling on August 18 after a hearing before all seven of the circuit judges. All but one signed an order that rebuked both Judge Lemley and the Arkansas officials who refused to obey judicial orders, putting into italics their admonition that "*the time has not yet come in these United States when an order of a federal court may be whittled away, watered down, or shamefully withdrawn in the face of violent and unlawful acts of individual citizens in opposition thereto.*" Despite this stern language, NAACP lawyers were stunned when the Eighth Circuit judges, abruptly and without explanation, reversed themselves on August 21 and stayed their own order until the Little Rock school board could file an appeal with the Supreme Court, which would have consumed months of delay. The NAACP then asked the Supreme Court to step in and end the legal chaos.

Although the justices had scattered around the country during their summer recess, Chief Justice Warren summoned them back to Washington for a "special term" on August 28, more than a month before the Court's traditional opening session on the first Monday in October. Little Rock schools were scheduled to open on September 15, and Warren wanted to decide this momentous case before the class bells rang.

Despite the short notice for this early session, the courtroom was packed with spectators, lawyers, and reporters. Richard Butler, the school board's lawyer, began his argument with an appeal for delay. "All we're asking," he said, "is for time to work this thing out in a climate of calm rather than a climate of hysteria." Warren listened politely to Butler's assurance that he was not speaking for the "law defiers" in Little Rock. "I know you're not," Warren soothingly replied. But the chief's smile quickly faded when Butler spoke for the chief law defier in Arkansas. "The point I'm making is this," Butler said, "that if the governor of any state says that a United States Supreme Court decision is not the law of the land, the people of that state, until it is really resolved, have a doubt in their mind and a right to have a doubt." Warren was astounded. "I have never heard such an argument made in a court of justice before," he shot back, "and I've tried many a case, over many a year. I never heard a lawyer say that the statement of a governor, as to what was legal or illegal, should control the action of any court." Warren would not tolerate this challenge to judicial authority, especially from a governor who thumbed his nose at the Supreme Court.

After Butler endured this rebuke, Thurgood Marshall took the lectern for the Black plaintiffs. He was just as angry as the chief justice, and his voice rose as he spoke for Little Rock's Black children. "I think we need to think about these children and their parents," he said, "these Negro children that went through this every day, and their parents that stayed at home wondering what was happening to their children, listening to the radio about the bomb threats and all that business." Marshall's voice filled the chamber with outrage. "I don't know how anybody under the sun could say, that after all these children and those families went through for a year, to tell them: All you have done is gone. You fought for what you considered to be democracy and you lost. And you go back to the segregated school from which you came. I just don't believe it."

The justices did not believe it either and scolded Governor Faubus with a single voice. On September 29, the Court handed down its written opinion in *Cooper v. Aaron*. Never before—or since—has every justice personally signed an opinion. The justices professed astonishment that Faubus and Arkansas lawmakers would claim "that they are not bound by our holding in the *Brown* case." The Court's opinion treated the defiant officials like schoolroom dunces. It was their "determination to resist this court's decision in the *Brown* case" which had "brought about violent resistance to that decision in Arkansas." Had the Arkansas officials not read the Constitution? Article 6 makes the Constitution "the supreme law of the land." Had the officials not all taken oaths "to support this Constitution?" The justices took out their paddles: "No state legislator or executive or judicial officer can wage war against the Constitution without violating his undertaking to support it." And who had the power to interpret and enforce the Constitution? "It follows that the interpretation of the Fourteenth Amendment enunciated in the *Brown* case is the supreme law of the land," the justices told the Arkansas officials. Looking beyond Little Rock to politicians in other states who might be tempted to emulate Governor Faubus, the Court demanded "the obedience of the states" to "the command of the Constitution" that federal court orders must be obeyed.

But the Arkansas officials did not learn their lesson, despite this stern judicial lecture. Defying the Court once again, Faubus and the state legislature closed down Little Rock's schools for an entire year. Going back to federal court, NAACP lawyers won a ruling in 1959 that reopened the schools. By spring 1960, Central High had 1,500 White students and just 5 Blacks. Litigation over the Little Rock schools dragged on for years, raising the question once again: What good is the Constitution if government officials refuse to obey its commands? What the Arkansas politicians finally obeyed was not the Supreme Court, but the commands of public opinion. In 1960 Little Rock's voters finally tired of chaos and turmoil in their schools and elected a new school board that moved toward compliance with court orders. But the images of the violent mobs in the streets around Central High and of the army troops who pushed back rioters at bayonet point lingered in the minds of millions of White Americans and convinced many that school integration might expose their children to danger. In that respect, the Supreme Court's invitation to proceed with "all deliberate speed" in dismantling Jim Crow schools had produced the deliberate obstruction and delay that blocked any effort to bring about the meaningful integration of America's schools.

(As a footnote, the federal government's *amicus* brief in the *Brown* cases had warned that Soviet propagandists would trumpet America's "chaos and turmoil" to Third World audiences around the globe, many struggling to shake off the yoke of White colonial domination. Sure enough, Soviet news outlets made hay of the Little Rock violence: the organ of the communist youth movement ran a sensational story about the conflict, complete with photographs of National Guard troops with bayonets, under the headline "Troops Advance against Children!" *Izvestia*, a major Soviet newspaper, told its readers, "[R]ight now, behind the facade of the so-called 'American democracy,' a tragedy is unfolding which cannot but arouse the ire and indignation in the heart of every honest man." In the ongoing battle for the hearts and minds of "colored" people in Africa and Asia, the United States was in danger of losing its claims to moral superiority and the virtues of democracy.)

What we have seen in these school cases, from Clarendon County in South Carolina to Little Rock in Arkansas, raises the question at the heart of our inquiry into the causes and effects of systemic racism and the resulting inequality in American society. If court orders can be enforced only at bayonet point, the racism of substantial numbers of White citizens has infected the crucial institution of public school education to an extent that leaves millions of Black and Brown children in schools, particularly in majority–Black and Brown cities, that are clearly inferior to majority-White schools in big-city suburbs, small towns, and many rural areas, both North and South. The impact of this resegregation of American schools, as we will see, extends well past the graduation ceremonies of those Black and Brown students who manage to obtain their high school diplomas.

* * *

Readers may be interested in an update on the current racial composition of the schools involved in the *Brown* cases. The following numbers are for high schools in the 2019–20 school year, from the National Center for Educational Statistics.

In Summerton, South Carolina, Scott's Branch High had 209 Black, 6 White, and 3 Hispanic students. Clarendon Hall, the former private "seg school," had 184 White and 3 Black students. Seventy years after the *Briggs* case began, Summerton's high schools remain almost completely segregated. Things clearly haven't changed much during those decades.

Prince Edward County, Virginia, defied an integration order and closed all its public schools from 1954 until 1959, when finally forced to reopen them by the Supreme Court. During these years, White students went to "seg schools" and Black children attended "Freedom Schools" in churches and homes, but these schools had no necessary facilities. Prince Edward High School in Farmville in 2019–20 had 332 Black, 241 White, 25 Hispanic, and 8 Asian students. From outright defiance to complete integration is quite a change.

Public schools in Washington, D.C., in 2019–20 were 68 percent Black, 18 percent Hispanic, and 10 percent White, but schools and housing were disproportionately Black in northeast and southeast D.C. and largely White in the high-income northwest. John Philip Sousa Middle School in southeast D.C. was 100 percent White in 1950. In 2019–20 it had 235 Black students and no White. The District's private and religious schools remained mostly White; the prestigious Sidwell Friends (high school of Malia and Sasha Obama) had 163 Black and 565 White students; Gonzaga College High (all male) had 100 Black and 744 White students. In sum, Washington's public schools were heavily Black and Hispanic in 2019–20, its private and religious schools more than three-fourths White.

In Wilmington, Delaware, in 2019–20 the formerly all-Black Howard High School (now Howard Technical High) had 564 Black, 69 White, and 188 Hispanic students. Brandywine High, which includes Claymont students, had 344 Black, 311 White, and 75 Hispanic students. When I lived in New Castle from 1950 to 1954, William Penn High School was all White by law. Sixty-five years later it had 1,004 Black, 525 White, and 550 Hispanic students. New Castle County also has several private and religious high schools that were predominantly White.

In 2019–20 Topeka, Kansas, had three high schools: Topeka High had 249 Black, 618 White, and 554 Hispanic students; Highland Park High had 208 Black, 175 White, and 370 Hispanic students; Topeka West High had 154 Black, 543 White, and 232 Hispanic students. The Advanced Placement classes in these schools, however, remained predominantly White.

"Two Cities—One White, the Other Black"

WE CAN LOOK back at the 1960s—and the extension of that decade into the mid-1970s—through several different lenses, depending on where we stand on the divisive issues of those years. One view, perpetuated through the pervasive media of television and movies, is of an endless Summer of Love with tie-dyed hippies flocking to San Francisco to enjoy "sex, drugs, and rock-and-roll." There certainly were hippies, many of them flamboyant in dress and libidinous in behavior. They had a lasting influence on mass culture, as sexual puritanism gave way to the slogan "If it feels good, do it" and as drug paranoia and legal prohibition proved incapable of stemming the ingestion of mind-altering vapors, pills, and powders, and "Question Authority" be-came a mantra. One measure of these changes comes from the Beatles: their 1964 hit "I Want to Hold Your Hand" was high-school-cute; by 1968 (with very disruptive years in between) they were asking, "Why Don't We Do It in the Road?"

Sixty years later, nostalgia has replaced the reality that hippies were a col-orful sideshow to the greater erosion of respect for unquestioned authority, whether from parents, pastors, or politicians. That erosion grew into outright rebellion as young people (advised not to trust anyone over thirty) realized that the older White men who controlled social and political institutions, particularly at the top in Washington, D.C., had lied about "winning" an un-winnable war in Vietnam, at the cost of more than fifty thousand American lives (and the deaths of more than 2 million Vietnamese on both sides of their civil war). These same men, in both political parties, profited from what President Dwight Eisenhower, in his farewell address in 1961, labeled and deplored as the "military-industrial complex," while at the same time these men were starving the programs that allowed many Americans of all races—from the Mississippi Delta to Appalachian "hollers" and decaying urban ghettos—to feed, clothe, and house their families. And many of these White men, backslapping and deal-making politicians in state legislatures and both houses of Congress, were kept in safe seats by White constituents who shared their racism, considered Black people inferior, and were determined to resist programs like affirmative action in education and employment as "stealing" benefits from more qualified Whites.

It was the confluence of these two factors—entrenched racist politicians and their racist constituents, and the human and financial cost of the Vietnam War—that turned the 1960s and 1970s into decades of protest and suffering for many Blacks in both the South and the North. Protests against Jim Crow segregation and voting discrimination won pathbreaking victories in congressional passage of the Civil Rights Act in 1964 and the Voting Rights Act of 1965, over fierce opposition from Dixiecrats in Congress. But these victories came at the cost of dozens of lives lost to racist killers, hundreds injured by police dogs and clubs, and thousands arrested, including children who insisted on marching for their rights. During these same decades, racial tension in many northern and western cities, sparked by constant police harassment and brutality, flared into riots that took dozens of lives, mostly Black, and saw thousands of homes and businesses go up in flames.

At the same time, between 1964 and 1975, the Vietnam War took an extra toll on Black Americans, not only the 7,243 Black troops who died in the war but also in robbing needed safety-net programs on which many Black families depended, in order to pay for the munitions, ships, planes, and all the other costs of a foreign war. Government officials have calculated that the war cost $168 billion (roughly $1 trillion in today's dollars), with a final cost, mostly in veterans benefits and interest, of more than $350 billion ($2 trillion now). These sums may not shock those of us who have experienced a global pandemic whose financial toll at this writing is well over $5 trillion. But during the 1960s and 1970s, government spending on the war cut into social program budgets, many of them (Head Start, food stamps, housing subsidies, and many others) helping Black families avoid poverty.

* * *

In my view, the most perceptive comments about the link between the Vietnam War and Black America came from a brash young Black man who grew up in Louisville, Kentucky, one of six children of a railway laborer. We now know Cassius Marcellus Clay as Muhammad Ali, the world heavyweight champion who relinquished his title after refusing military induction in 1966, based on his Muslim faith and opposition to the Vietnam War; his draft conviction was overturned by the Supreme Court in 1971, and he became an international sports icon before his death in 2016. Asked why he opposed the war, Ali responded in characteristic form: "Man, I ain't got no quarrel with them Viet Cong," later adding, "No Viet Cong ever called me nigger." He elaborated: "Why should they ask me to put on a uniform and go ten thousand miles from home and drop bombs and bullets on brown people in Vietnam while so-called Negro people in Louisville are treated like dogs and denied simple human rights?" We can appreciate Ali as perhaps the greatest boxer ever and as a consummate showman, but he also had a deep faith and understanding of how the war was harming both the "brown" Vietnamese and Black Americans alike. In this respect, Ali was more perceptive than many Whites who believed their leaders long after the war turned into an unwinnable "quagmire" that exposed the "best and brightest" government officials and think-tank "experts" as naïve and callous, for whom phony "body counts" were the only metric in their bloodless calculations. No one who looks back on the 1960s and 1970s should ignore the lessons that later architects of war failed to heed. That a boxer from the Black streets and gyms in Louisville understood the linkage between the Vietnam War and American racism is a tribute to him (and many other Blacks) and a lasting scar on the White American "elite" whose hubris blinded them to on-the-ground reality, both abroad and at home.

* * *

Many people assume that protests against Jim Crow segregation began on December 1, 1955, when Rosa Parks, a Black seamstress and secretary of the NAACP chapter in Montgomery, Alabama, was arrested for refusing to relinquish her seat on a city bus to a White man, under rules that gave Whites priority in seating. Her arrest sparked the Montgomery Bus Boycott, as Blacks stayed off the buses for an entire year, finally winning a Supreme Court decision in November 1956, holding bus segregation unlawful.

Rosa Parks became a civil rights icon during her long life; she died in 2005 at ninety-two in Detroit, where she lived for decades after leaving Montgomery. A recipient of the Presidential Medal of Freedom in 1996, she became the first woman whose body lay in state in the Capitol rotunda after her death. Parks has been justly praised for her courage in breaking an unjust and unconstitutional law, but she was not the first to challenge Jim Crow laws. Back in 1942, during a war against Nazi racism and genocide, a group of Black and White activists in Chicago formed the Congress of Racial Equality, adopting the nonviolent approach of Mohandas Gandhi to fighting British imperial rule in India. CORE members picketed Chicago businesses that wouldn't hire Blacks and conducted sit-ins at segregated lunch counters. In 1947, a group of eight White and eight Black men began the first "Freedom Rides," testing segregation on buses traveling between states in the Upper South (Virginia, North Carolina, Kentucky, and Tennessee). These early Freedom Riders were arrested and jailed several times, despite a 1946 Supreme Court ruling that struck down interstate bus and railroad segregation (although the "separate but equal" doctrine of *Plessy v. Ferguson* still allowed intrastate segregation).

CORE became an influential civil rights group, especially in training protesters in nonviolent tactics and helping to found the Student Non-violent Coordinating Committee (SNCC or, colloquially, "Snick") after lunch counter sit-ins resumed (after CORE's Chicago sit-ins during the 1940s) at a segregated Woolworth lunch counter in Greensboro, North Carolina, on February 1, 1960. The four Black male students—David Richmond, Franklin McCain, Ezell Blair Jr., and Joseph McNeil—from all-Black North Carolina Agricultural and Technical State University wore jackets, white shirts, and ties while they waited for service at Woolworth, having each ordered a never-served cup of coffee, and they remained in their seats until the store closed. They came back the next day with twenty more students and were harassed by Whites but not arrested. Their ranks swelled to more than three hundred that first week; the Black students were joined by three White female students—Eugenia "Genie" Seaman, Marilyn Lott, and Ann Dearsley—from the all-female University of North Carolina campus in Greensboro, who drew taunts of "nigger lover" for their courage. By this time, lunch counter sit-ins and picketing were spreading across the South, with sympathy picketing of Woolworth and other chain stores in northern cities to pressure their managers to end segregation in their southern stores. Ironically, Clarence Harris, the White Woolworth store manager in Greensboro, ended lunch counter segregation on July 25, 1960, by serving four of his own Black employees.

The sit-ins provoked several incidents of harassment and violence, as Black and White students endured having coffee, ketchup, and sugar dumped on their heads by jeering Whites, many of them high school students, while others were dragged from their seats and arrested by White police. They responded with a campaign they called "Jail, Not Bail," as hundreds of students were crammed into overflowing cells in Nashville and other cities, including Jackson, Mississippi, which sent protesters to the notorious Parchman Prison Farm, where Black inmates toiled on a huge cotton plantation, providing revenue for the racist state government. During its ultimately successful campaign against lunch counter segregation, SNCC enlisted more than seventy thousand Black and White students into its "Freedom Army," many of whom later became prominent in civil rights activism and as elected officials, from city councils to Congress.

Two other campaigns by SNCC and CORE members, however, provoked violent resistance and the murders (actually, modern-day lynchings) of several dozen civil rights workers. On May 4, 1961, thirteen Black and White students, led by CORE director James Farmer, climbed aboard Greyhound and Trailways buses in Washington, D.C., headed through Virginia, the Carolinas, Georgia, Alabama, and Mississippi to their final destination in New Orleans. Violence broke out in Rock Hill, South Carolina, where SNCC leader John Lewis was beaten. (Lewis was later anointed the "Conscience of Congress" for his integrity as a long-serving House member from Georgia, honored in 2011 with the Presidential Medal of Freedom from Barack Obama, and after his death in July 2020 lay in state in the Capitol rotunda.) When one of the Greyhound buses reached Anniston, Alabama, on May 14, a mob of two hundred Whites prompted the driver to keep going, but it was pursued by Whites in cars; when the bus blew a tire a few miles out of town, a mob member threw a flaming rag into it. While the bus burst into flames, the Freedom Riders were brutally beaten as they crawled through doors and broken windows. Photos of the burning bus ran on the front pages of almost every U.S. newspaper and in the pages of *Life*, *Time*, and other magazines, horrifying Blacks and White sympathizers across the country. And when the Riders reached Birmingham on another bus, they were again attacked at the terminal by a mob armed with baseball bats, tire irons, and bicycle chains. It later emerged that Birmingham's racist police commissioner, Eugene "Bull" Connor, had sent word through a deputy to local Ku Klux Klan leaders, promising them fifteen minutes to beat the Riders with no police interference. (Connor also, in May 1963, unleashed police dogs and trained fire hoses on hundreds of Black children, some as young as five, who marched through Birmingham to protest Jim Crow laws, again horrifying those who witnessed the police brutality on television.) The initial Freedom Riders never made it to New Orleans after more bus station violence and arrests in Jackson, Mississippi. Not until Rev. Martin Luther King Jr. called Attorney General Robert Kennedy did the federal government dispatch federal marshals to

Alabama on May 29, 1961, to protect the Riders. Attacks continued, however, as successive Freedom Rides (with more than seven hundred Riders)
pressured the slow-acting Kennedy administration into demanding that
Greyhound, Trailways, and other bus companies stop complying with local
and state Jim Crow laws on their buses and take down "Whites Only" signs in
their terminals, lunch counters, water fountains, and restrooms.

* * *

Maintaining and enforcing segregation on buses and in terminals provoked
Whites, many of them Klan members, to beat and bomb the Freedom Riders.
But White racists were even more determined to keep Blacks from voting,
especially in towns and counties across the Deep South with Black majorities;
the prospect of Black sheriffs threatened White rule by intimidation and violence, including murder. After the Freedom Rides ended bus segregation,
activists in the SNCC, led from 1963 to 1966 by John Lewis, began planning a
"Freedom Summer" in 1964 and enlisted hundreds of high school and college
students to live in small towns and rural counties, along with local residents
who risked White retaliation, for voter registration drives. These activists also
set up "Freedom Schools" to educate Blacks—many of them barely or not
at all literate—in how to pass the tests that White registrars manipulated to
keep even well-educated Blacks from voting. The volunteers also kept records
of who applied to vote and the phony reasons for "failing" the tests, records
they planned to submit to the Justice Department as evidence of massive racial discrimination, and to make the case for federal action and laws to dis-
mantle the Jim Crow voting system.

The Freedom Summer succeeded in some counties in registering large
numbers of Blacks, mainly counties with solid White majorities and thus less
concerned with losing offices, especially sheriffs, the most powerful officials
in most counties. However, voting rights activists—including White students
from northern colleges—in majority-Black counties, especially in Mississippi
and Alabama, risked their lives in driving down back dirt roads to visit a Black
sharecropper or going out at night from the houses they shared with Black
families. More than two dozen lost their lives in the voting rights campaign,
even years before the 1964 Freedom Summer. Each deserves a story, even a
book, but I will tell brief stories of seven people, Black and White, men and
women, who paid with their lives for challenging the murderous White men
who refused to obey laws that protected Black citizens in their right to vote.
And I'll just list here the names of other civil rights martyrs and the places

they died: **Louis Allen**, Liberty, Mississippi; **Henry Hezekiah Dee** and **Charles Eddie Moore**, Meadville, Mississippi; **Jimmie Lee Jackson**, Marion, Alabama; **Johnathan Daniels**, Hayneville, Alabama; **Vernon Dahmer**, Hattiesburg, Mississippi; **Clarence Triggs**, Bogalusa, Louisiana; **Wharlest Jackson**, Natchez, Mississippi. There were more murders, and the bodies of some victims were never found, but these martyrs to the cause of freedom deserve mention.

May 7, 1955 * Belzoni, Mississippi

Rev. George Lee, a minister and businessman, was the first Black person registered to vote in Humphreys County, Mississippi, and used his pulpit and his printing press to urge others to vote. White officials offered Lee protection from harassment on the condition he end his voter registration efforts, but he refused and was murdered by shotgun blasts into his car from a passing vehicle. Later investigation turned up several White suspects, but intimidation of potential witnesses prevented any prosecutions.

June 12, 1963 * Jackson, Mississippi

Medgar Evers, who directed NAACP operations in Mississippi, was leading a campaign for integration in Jackson when he was shot and killed by a sniper at his home. His death stunned civil rights workers, who feared more killings. Police arrested a known racist, Byron De La Beckwith, for the murder; his fingerprints were on the murder rifle. At his first trial, Mississippi's racist governor, Ross Barnett, came into the courtroom to shake Beckwith's hand in full view of the jury. After two all-White juries deadlocked on a verdict, Beckwith was released in 1964.

June 21, 1964 * Philadelphia, Mississippi

James Earl Chaney, Andrew Goodman, and **Michael Henry Schwerner,** young civil rights workers on a CORE voting drive, were arrested by a deputy sheriff and then released into the hands of Klansmen who had plotted their murders. They were shot, and their bodies were buried in an earthen dam, discovered two months later, after an intensive FBI search and tips from an informant. These were the highest-profile murders during the voting drives. The FBI identified a dozen Klansmen and sheriff's deputies as participants in the executions; state officials refused to prosecute anyone, but seven were convicted in federal court of depriving their victims of civil rights; they received light sentences and returned to their county as heroes to Whites, causing more fear among Blacks.

March 11, 1965 * Selma, Alabama

Rev. James Reeb, a Unitarian minister from Boston, was among many White clergymen who joined the Selma marchers after the attack by state troopers at the Edmund Pettus Bridge. Reeb was beaten to death by White men while he walked down a Selma street, eating an ice cream cone. Three White men, all known racists, were indicted for the murder but acquitted by an all-White jury. Outrage at Reeb's murder spread across the country, and President Lyndon Johnson invoked his name in sending the Voting Rights Act to Congress, which enacted it in August 1965.

March 25, 1965, Selma highway, Alabama

Viola Gregg Liuzzo, a housewife and mother from Detroit, drove alone to Alabama to help with the Selma March after seeing televised reports of the attack at the Edmund Pettus Bridge. She was ferrying marchers between Selma and Montgomery when she was shot and killed by a Klansman in a passing car. Her death prompted President Johnson to appear on television to announce that her killers—four Klansmen, one an FBI informant—had been arrested. They were later acquitted of murder in state court by all-White juries, but were later convicted in federal court of violating Liuzzo's civil rights. Two were sentenced to ten years in federal prison, one died before sentencing, and the FBI informant's case was dismissed.

The murders of Black activists (their lynchings, in truth) were not the only deaths of Black people by southern White racists during these turbulent years. The American public was shocked by the brutal murder in August 1955 of Emmett Till, a fourteen-year-old Black boy from Chicago, killed while he was visiting relatives in the small town of Money, Mississippi. Emmett had supposedly committed one of Jim Crow's gravest offenses by flirting and making suggestive comments to twenty-one-year-old Carolyn Bryant, a White woman who operated a small grocery store. Her husband, Roy, and his half-brother, J. W. Milam, seized Till from his great-uncle's house and beat and mutilated him before shooting him and dumping his body into the Tallahatchie River, where it was found three days later. An all-White jury acquitted Bryant and Milam of Till's kidnapping and murder in September 1965. The next year, Carolyn Bryant admitted to *Look* magazine that Till had not propositioned her, and both Roy Bryant and Milam confessed to his murder, now protected by the Constitution's Double-Jeopardy clause from further prosecution. Photos of Emmett's bloated and mutilated body in the open-casket funeral in Chicago that his mother insisted on, as thousands filed by the casket and attended the funeral, exposed millions of White Americans to the murderous racism that still gripped the Deep South.

Eight years later, in September 1963, millions more Americans, White and Black, were appalled by the murders of four young Black girls—Addie Mae Collins, Denise McNair, Carole Robertson, and Cynthia Wesley—as they prepared for Sunday services at the Sixteenth Street Baptist Church in Birmingham, Alabama. They died from the blast of a dynamite bomb placed under the church steps; the FBI identified four Klan members—one known as "Dynamite Bob" for his favored explosive—but none was charged. President John F. Kennedy deplored the murders, urging that they "awaken the entire nation to a realization of the folly of racial injustice and hatred and violence," and called on all Americans "to unite in steps toward peaceful progress before more lives are lost."

Unfortunately, as we've seen, racist hatred, violence, and murder has continued from those blood-stained days into the present, as the killings of unarmed Black men and women by White police and vigilantes have spurred millions of Americans of all races to awaken and unite to combat endemic and systemic racism, from which no city or town has been spared. The 1960s and 1970s, in a very real sense, are still with us. We can no longer ignore this violent reality.

* * *

We'll return now to Detroit, to look at the impact of racism on its residents—and those of surrounding counties—during the turmoil of these decades. In particular, we will closely examine, from its filing in August 1970 through the Supreme Court's decision in July 1974 in *Milliken v. Bradley*, a challenge to segregation in Detroit's almost-all-Black public schools and the almost-all-White schools in the city's suburbs.

The *Milliken* case was decided at the tail-end of a decade of urban revolts that swept across the country, from Newark to Los Angeles, leaving death and destruction in their wake. Angry and frustrated, inner-city Blacks lashed out at the White police who pushed them off their stoops and street corners and goaded them with racial epithets. Between 1964 and 1967, more than twenty urban ghettos blew up and burned. The Watts riots in Los Angeles, the most violent since World War II, began on a hot August night in 1965 with White cops dragging a young Black driver from his car and clubbing a young Black woman who objected. Within hours, hundreds of cops in riot gear confronted an unruly crowd that showered them with rocks and bottles. Over the following week, hundreds of stores were looted and firebombed, thirty-four people were killed, and hundreds were injured. The Watts riot shocked the American people, but it was not the most deadly of the urban insurrections of the 1960s. Detroit erupted in 1967 after the police raided an after-hours bar (known as a "blind pig") whose patrons were Black; the rioting that followed culminated in forty-three deaths, $50 million in property damage, and the occupation of the city by seventeen thousand U.S. Army and National Guard troops.

In the wake of the Detroit riot, White residents fled from the city in droves. By 1970, the city's Black population had grown to 660,000, some 44 percent of the total; during the preceding decade, the White population within the city limits had declined by 350,000, while the suburban White population swelled by just that number. The trend was clear; Detroit was becoming a Black city surrounded by a ring—or noose—of White suburbs in the three surrounding counties. Most of these suburbs, including two of the largest, Dearborn and Warren, had just a handful of Black residents in 1970. Just 13 of Dearborn's 104,000 residents were Black, as were only 132 of Warren's population of 179,000. Hardly any Blacks lived in such upper-income suburbs as Sterling Heights, Birmingham, and Madison Heights; just 71 of the 125,000 residents of these three cities were Black, some living with White families as housekeepers. Some 86 percent of all Blacks in the Detroit metropolitan area lived within the city in 1970, and most of the remainder lived in working-class suburbs like Inkster and Pontiac and labored in the auto plants in those towns.

The segregation of Detroit and its suburbs was even more pronounced in the area's public schools. Although Blacks and Whites lived within the city limits in roughly equal numbers in 1970, the city's neighborhoods were clearly separated by race. The vast majority of Detroit's census tracts were more than 90 percent White or Black, and the city's public schools mirrored this residential segregation. In 1970, more than 70 percent of the schools were virtually all White or all Black, with more than 90 percent of their students in the majority race. The phenomenon of White flight had already begun in Detroit, as White families with school-age children either moved to the suburbs or sent their children to private and parochial schools. The steady flow of Whites from the city to the suburbs became a virtual stampede after the 1967 riot.

Given the segregation in Detroit's schools, it is hardly surprising that NAACP lawyers filed a lawsuit in federal court in August 1970 on behalf of "all school children in the city of Detroit, Michigan, and all Detroit resident parents who have children of school age." Verda Bradley was the Black mother whose name appeared first on the caption, but some of the plaintiffs were sympathetic White parents who felt their children were being denied an integrated education. Michigan's Republican governor William Milliken headed the list of defendants, which included the Detroit and Michigan boards of education. The case of *Bradley v. Milliken* (the party names were reversed when the case reached the Supreme Court) landed on the docket of District Judge Stephen J. Roth, a former prosecuting attorney, state court judge, and attorney general of Michigan before his nomination to the federal bench in 1962 by President Kennedy. (Roth was an immigrant from Romania, brought to Detroit at the age of five by his parents to escape the anti-Semitism of that regime, and became active in Detroit's Jewish community.)

Judge Roth held several rounds of hearings in the *Milliken* case and considered desegregation plans from both sides before he ruled in June 1972 that Detroit officials had intentionally segregated the city schools by building new schools well inside neighborhood boundaries rather than placing new schools in areas that would draw students of both races. Roth also found that school officials had allowed transfers from schools in racially "transitional" areas, allowing White students to escape from largely Black schools. The judge's finding that Detroit had practiced de jure (established by law) segregation did not surprise anyone, given the clear evidence in the testimony and records at the hearing. But one aspect of Roth's decision shocked the residents of the White suburbs that ringed Detroit. He ordered a "multi-district" remedy that would include fifty-three suburban districts in a desegregation plan under which 310,000 students would be bused across district lines to new schools. White children would ride buses from their suburban homes into city schools, and Black children would sit in suburban classrooms that had never had Black students. Judge Roth made clear in his opinion that "no school, grade, or classroom" in the Detroit metropolitan area would have a racial balance "substantially disproportionate to the overall pupil racial composition" of the three-county area covered by his order.

Judge Roth noted in his opinion that school district boundaries in Michigan—like those in most states—were drawn by the state legislature. "School district lines," he wrote, "are simply matters of political convenience and may not be used to deny constitutional rights." Roth found nothing sacrosanct about school district boundaries, pointing out that state lawmakers had often redrawn district lines to consolidate rural schools, and that several districts covered by his order included two or three towns. He placed the blame on state officials for allowing the Detroit school board to build schools and draw attendance zones in ways that produced the segregation he found to be an "official" policy.

Outrage from Whites flooded the area's newspapers and radio shows. One parent objected to sending his children to school in "dirty, violent, undesirable Detroit." The fact that some 300,000 children in the three-county area were already bused to school did not change many minds. "No kid of mine is going to get on a bus," one White mother said. "I'd go to jail first." Some parents admitted that they had joined the White flight to the suburbs expressly to avoid the city schools. "[M]y kids weren't going to go to that school down there," as one put it.

School officials in forty-four of the fifty-three suburban districts that had been included in Judge Roth's busing order filed appeals with the Sixth Circuit Court of Appeals, claiming there was no evidence they had done anything to segregate any school in their districts and that they bore no responsibility for the segregation in Detroit's schools. Lawyers for the suburban districts complained that they had not even been parties to the NAACP lawsuit until Roth dragged them in by judicial order. The appellate judges upheld his order in 1973, however, finding that the Michigan Board of Education had adopted policies that "fostered segregation throughout the Detroit Metropolitan area."

When the appeal from the Sixth Circuit decision reached the Supreme Court in 1973, the stakes were high. Two years earlier, the Court had upheld a large-scale busing order in North Carolina's largest city, in *Swann v. Charlotte-Mecklenburg County Board of Education*. In that case, however, the schools in Charlotte and the county that encircled it were in one large school district. The Court's decision in *Swann* did not address the issue in *Milliken*, of an order that would bus White and Black students across dozens of school district lines. There were many northern cities whose school boards had juggled attendance zones to separate Black and White students, and NAACP lawyers would certainly follow up a victory in *Milliken* with similar cases in Kansas City, St. Louis, Chicago, Cleveland, Philadelphia, Boston, and other cities with largely Black schools and White suburbs. If the Supreme Court upheld Judge Roth's order, suburbs would no longer be "safe havens" for Whites.

Oral argument in *Milliken* began on February 27, 1974. Frank Kelly, Michigan's attorney general, went first in defending the state. He quoted Judge Roth's comment at the initial hearings: "This lawsuit is limited to the city of Detroit and the school system; so that we are only concerned with the city itself, and we're not talking about the metropolitan area." Kelly asserted that Roth had a hidden agenda, quoting a later statement: "The task that we are called upon to perform is a social one—which the society has been unable to accomplish—to attain a social goal through the education system by using law as a lever." Kelly urged the justices not to hold Governor Milliken responsible for the long-ago acts of the Detroit school board.

William Saxton, a partner in one of Detroit's most prestigious law firms, argued for the forty-four suburban districts that had appealed Judge Roth's order. He did not contest his findings that Detroit officials had deliberately segregated their schools, "aided and abetted by acts of certain officials of the state government." But the suburbs had done nothing to deserve judicial finger-pointing. "You will search this record in vain to find one whit, one jot, of evidentiary material that any suburban school district committed any de jure act of segregation, either by itself, in complicity with the state, or complicity with anyone else," Saxton claimed.

J. Harold Flannery, a partner in another of Detroit's leading firms and himself a suburban resident, followed Saxton to the lectern to argue for the NAACP. He stressed Judge Roth's findings that acts of state and local officials had "caused housing segregation and school segregation to be mutually supportive, mutually interlocking devices, with the result that black families and black children were confined to a small portion of the tri-county area," unable to escape Detroit's Black ghetto. Flannery shared his time with Nathaniel Jones, the NAACP's general counsel and a future Sixth Circuit judge. Given the residential segregation in Detroit and its origins in official acts, Jones argued, any "Detroit-only" remedy for school segregation would result in "the perpetuation of a black school district surrounded by a ring of white schools." This was true, the justices certainly knew, not only of Detroit but of almost every large city as well.

After the oral arguments concluded, the justices met to discuss and vote on the *Milliken* case in their closed-door conference room. Discussion must have been heated, as the justices traded pointed barbs in their later opinions. Chief Justice Warren Burger was particularly upset that district judges like Stephen Roth had not heeded his warning in the *Swann* opinion that only proof of a "constitutional violation" could justify remedies such as busing, even within a single district. Burger exercised his prerogative as chief to assign the *Milliken* opinion to himself. But he did not write for a unanimous Court. For the first time since the *Brown* decision in 1954, the justices were split in a school case, voting by a 5–4 margin to reverse Judge Roth. Their single-vote division reflected the right-wing stamp that Richard Nixon placed on the Court during his first term as president. Nixon, who had denounced advocates of "instant integration" as "extremists" during his 1968 presidential campaign, followed his appointments of Warren Burger and Harry Blackmun to the Court with two justices to fill the seats of Hugo Black and John Harlan, who both resigned from the Court in September 1971 and died of cancer before the year ended. Their replacements, Lewis F. Powell Jr. and William H. Rehnquist, joined the Court in January 1972 and cast their first votes on school integration in the *Milliken* case.

Nixon could not have picked two justices more hostile to Judge Roth's order, and their clear opposition to judicial orders in school cases had been instrumental in Nixon's decision to add them to the Court. Powell, a prominent Richmond lawyer, had served as chairman of both the Richmond and Virginia school boards. Under his leadership the boards had done nothing to integrate Richmond's schools. When he stepped down as chairman in 1961, exactly two Black children attended classes with White students in Richmond. Rehnquist, a brash young lawyer from Phoenix, had served as law clerk to Justice Robert Jackson during the Supreme Court's deliberations on the *Brown* case. During his Senate confirmation hearings in 1971, a memo he wrote to Jackson in 1953 surfaced. "I think *Plessy v. Ferguson* was right and should be reaffirmed," Rehnquist had stated, arguing that states should be able to operate segregated public schools; he had opposed a Phoenix school integration plan, writing to a newspaper, "We are no more dedicated to an 'integrated' society than we are to a 'segregated' society." Only one senator voted against Powell's confirmation, but twenty-six opposed Rehnquist for his thinly veiled racism. The fifth and deciding vote in *Milliken* came from Justice Potter Stewart, a stalwart Republican from Cincinnati.

Chief Justice Burger's opinion for this narrow majority, handed down on July 25, 1974, stopped the school buses at the Detroit city limits. He conceded that school district boundaries "may be bridged where there has been a constitutional violation calling for inter-district relief," but he deplored "the notion that school district lines may be casually ignored or treated as a minor administrative convenience" by lower court judges. Burger dismissed the findings in Judge Roth's opinion. "The record before us," he wrote, "voluminous as it is, contains evidence of de jure segregated conditions only in the Detroit schools; indeed, that was the theory on which the litigation was initially based and on which the District Court took evidence." As Burger read the trial record, "disparate treatment of white and Negro students occurred within the Detroit school system, and not elsewhere, and on this record the remedy must be limited to that system." He professed dismay at the consequences of Roth's order: "The metropolitan remedy would require consolidation of fifty-four independent school districts historically administered as separate units into a vast new super school district" and would turn Roth into "the 'school super-intendent' for the entire area." Burger and his conservative colleagues sent the case back to Judge Roth for a desegregation order applied only to Detroit, al-though there were only a handful of White students to shift into "integrated" classrooms.

The four dissenters in *Milliken* had never been on the losing side of a school case. Thurgood Marshall, in particular, felt betrayed by the majority and answered Burger's thirty-page opinion with one that was longer and more detailed and that undertook to review Judge Roth's order "for what it is, rather than to criticize it for what it manifestly is not." Speaking for Justices William O. Douglas, William Brennan, and Byron White, Marshall took the unusual step of reading portions of his opinion from the bench, his tone both sad and scornful as he answered Burger point by point. He began with the *Brown* decision, two decades earlier. "This Court recognized then that remedying decades of segregation in public education would not be an easy task," Marshall said. "Subsequent events, unfortunately, have seen that predic-tion bear bitter fruit. But however embedded old ways, however ingrained old prejudices, this Court has not been diverted from its task of making a 'living truth' of our constitutional ideal of equal justice under law." "After 20 years of small, often difficult steps toward that great end, the Court today takes a giant step backwards," wrote the Court's first Black justice.

After this pointed rebuke, Marshall began his dissection of Burger's ma-jority opinion. He first noted that in Michigan, school district lines were set by the state and did not follow the boundaries of cities and towns; of the eighty-five districts in the Detroit metropolitan area, "seventeen districts lie in two counties, two in three counties. One district serves five municipalities; other suburban municipalities are fragmented into as many as six school districts." Not only had the state taken actions that created and maintained segregated schools in Detroit, a point Burger had conceded, but "it was well within the state's powers to require those districts surrounding the Detroit school district to participate in a metropolitan remedy," Marshall wrote. The Court's ruling, he predicted, would increase segregation in Detroit as "white parents withdraw their children from the Detroit city schools and move to the suburbs in order to continue them in all-white schools." The reversal of Judge Roth's order would guarantee "that children in Detroit will receive the same separate and inherently unequal education in the future as they have been unconstitutionally afforded in the past." He was right about the future, as we'll see.

Marshall ended his dissent with a paragraph that expressed his dismay at the Court's capitulation to the growing White backlash to school integration: "Desegregation is not and was never expected to be an easy task," he reminded the majority.

> Racial attitudes ingrained in our Nation's childhood and adolescence are not quickly thrown aside in its middle years. But just as the inconvenience of some cannot be allowed to stand in the way of the rights of others, so public opposition, no matter how strident, cannot be permitted to divert this Court from the enforcement of the constitutional principles at issue in this case. Today's holding, I fear, is more a reflection of a perceived public mood that we have gone far enough in enforcing the Constitution's guarantee of equal justice than it is the product of neutral principles of law. In the short run, it may seem to be the easier course to allow our great metropolitan areas to be divided up each into two cities—one white, the other black—but it is a course, I predict, our people will ultimately regret. I dissent.

* * *

Thurgood Marshall's prophecy of continued turmoil over busing was almost immediately confirmed. The most vociferous and violent reaction to a judicial busing order came in Boston, the state capital and center of the nineteenth-century abolitionist movement. Three months after the *Milliken* ruling, in September 1974, classes were set to begin in Boston schools under a desegregation order by federal judge W. Arthur Garrity; his plan would bus high school students from the heavily Black neighborhood of Roxbury to all-White South Boston High, and students from "Southie" (as residents called their mostly Irish enclave) would be bused to Roxbury High. Urged to resist busing by the Boston school board's racist chair, Louise Day Hicks, crowds in Southie pelted the buses carrying Black students with rocks and racial slurs; Boston's mostly Irish cops intervened only after protesters tried to tip over a bus. Gloria Joyner, a Black mother of two high school students, rode the bus from Roxbury to South Boston; she described the escort required to keep the buses and children safe from White mobs: "Our four buses were escorted by three police cruisers, 10 motorcycles, and a state helicopter overhead looking for rooftop snipers." Jean McGuire, a bus safety monitor, recalled the scene when the bus with Black kids pulled up at Southie High: "Bricks coming through the windows. Signs hanging on buildings, 'Nigger Go Home.' Pictures of monkeys. The words. The spit. People just felt it was all right to attack children." Meanwhile, White students refused to board buses for Roxbury, launching a year of turmoil throughout the city, during which some twenty thousand White students fled to private and parochial schools; moving to Boston's wealthy suburbs was too costly for most working-class Whites. "Stop Forced Busing" became a rallying cry in cities across the country, as school boards and judges watered down or abandoned busing plans, fearful of becoming another Boston.

During the two decades from 1960 to 1980, largely as a result of White flight from cities to suburbs, the social and economic status of Blacks continued to lag far behind those of Whites. Some dry statistics will reveal the barriers they faced. In 1960, only 20.1 percent of Black adults had finished high school, less than half the White rate of 43.2; the gap narrowed somewhat by 1980, with 51.2 percent of Blacks with high school diplomas, compared to 68.8 percent of Whites. The gap in family income hardly budged during those years: Black income was 55 percent of the White level in 1960; it went up a bit, to 61 percent, in 1970, but then fell back down to 58 percent in 1980, and stayed at that not quite three-fifths level through 2018, at 59 percent of White income (a figure reminiscent of the infamous "three-fifths clause" in the Constitution, a not-coincidental fact, in my opinion). In 1960, 55 percent of Blacks lived in poverty; the numbers dropped to 33.5 percent in 1970 and 32.5 percent in 1980. (The poverty rate for Blacks stayed above 30 percent until 1994.) Many of those above the official poverty level were still just scraping by, especially single mothers who juggled work and child care on minimum-wage budgets or were forced to rely on welfare programs with onerous and demeaning conditions, including unannounced visits to "catch" men living with welfare recipients. The current effect of these Scrooge-like cuts on Blacks is severe: although the poverty rate for all Blacks had decreased to 23 percent in 2018, 39 percent of single Black women with children lived in poverty, and 55 percent of Black families with children are currently headed by unmarried women. The long-term effect of these numbers on the life chances of today's Black children—10 million under eighteen in 2020—is certain to keep many in the poverty their families have endured for generations.

A few other measures of Black-White disparities should not be surprising: in 1980, the presidents of all eight Ivy League universities were White men; not a single CEO of a Fortune 500 company was Black (in 2020 there were three, down from an all-time high of six); only 17 Blacks were among the 435 members of the House of Representatives (4 percent) and none in the

Senate; and only 43 Blacks served among 825 federal judges (5 percent, about one-third of proportionate parity), with one (Thurgood Marshall) on the Supreme Court. These institutions, of course, are the backbone of a society created and governed by privileged White men. Dislodging them to a position of parity with Blacks (and with Hispanics, Asians, Native Americans, and women as well) is a long-term project, having had considerable (but not yet adequate) success in the past few years. But as recently as 1980, the Black-White disparity in these institutions was appalling.

In my opinion, as we look back, the legal system and the mostly White judges who issue rulings from its courts have twice failed America's Black children, first in the "all deliberate speed" concession in 1955 to southern racists in *Brown II* and second in the "buses stop at city limits" ruling in the *Milliken* case. The result of these decisions, returning many American schools to the Jim Crow segregation the Supreme Court supposedly ended with the first *Brown* ruling, is a sad commentary on the deep-rooted racism the courts proved powerless to eradicate.

"All Blacks Are Angry"

THURGOOD MARSHALL WAS right.

Close to a half-century after his prediction—and his lament—that America faced a future in which our major metropolitan areas will "be divided up into two cities—one white, the other black," that forecast is more true now than it was in 1974. Even earlier, in response to the Detroit riot in 1967, President Lyndon Johnson appointed a National Advisory Commission on Civil Disorders, headed by Governor Otto Kerner of Illinois, to examine the causes of urban outbursts and to recommend programs to prevent further disorder. Issued in 1968, the 426-page Kerner Commission report (which became a bestseller, as concerned Americans bought 2 million copies) warned, "Our nation is moving toward two societies, one black, one white—separate and unequal." The report was a lacerating indictment of White complacency and disregard for the plight of poverty-stricken Blacks: "What white Americans have never fully understood—but what the Negro can never forget—is that white society is deeply implicated in the ghetto. White institutions created it, white institutions maintain it, and white society condones it." Half a century later, the Commission's recommendations, almost identical to the demands of today's Black Lives Matter and other civil rights movements, remain un-fulfilled: government programs to expand the safety net that protects many Blacks from falling into deeper poverty; support to fund and train more di-verse and community-sensitive police forces; and the investment of billions—now perhaps trillions—to provide decent and dispersed low-income housing to break up residential segregation in cities with substantial Black populations. It was in these increasingly Black cities that racial inequality created and fu-eled the no-longer-suppressed anger that spawned deadly violence in Detroit and other cities from Newark to Los Angeles, most often in response to police brutality against Blacks.

This chapter, building on the historical record of White racism we have examined, will attempt to explain how systemic racism has created the "two societies" in which most Black and White Americans live in fragile coexistence, much like the Cold War hostility between the United States and the Soviet Union. During the turbulent decades since the Kerner Commission and Thurgood Marshall sounded the tocsin, the relative status of Black Americans has lagged far behind that of Whites, notwithstanding the emergence and growth of a substantial Black middle class; in 2018, 31 percent of Black households earned $50,000 or more, compared to 44 percent of Whites. However, middle-class Blacks are still at a disadvantage compared to Whites with equivalent levels of education and employment. To cite one indicator, the average household income of Black couples with college degrees is roughly 80 percent of that for comparable White couples, an income gap of about $16,000 per year. It's also true that many middle-class Blacks have moved into formerly nearly-all-White suburbs, although a second wave of White flight has turned some former "safe havens" for Whites into majority-Black suburbs; for example, Prince George's County in Maryland, bordering Washington, D.C., as of 2019 was 65 percent Black, 19 percent White, and 15 percent Hispanic, with a median family income of $82,580, making it the wealthiest majority-Black county in the nation. Other large metropolitan areas, in all regions of the country, have seen an influx of Blacks (and Hispanics) into suburban communities.

Not surprisingly, the Black middle class is increasingly portrayed as the norm in the media, especially films and television. It's almost a rule today that TV commercials include token Blacks (preferably with cute children) mingling with middle-class White families. What we don't see portrayed in the media, except as violent criminals, are poor and inner-city Blacks, not a prime demographic group for selling up-scale products. But it's the two-thirds of Blacks in the working class and below it who bear the brunt of systemic racism, as measured by lower rates of education, employment, and income, and higher rates of poor health, "excess deaths," and criminal victimization. It is this group, roughly 25 million of the country's 42 million Blacks, that is largely confined to "hyper-segregated" inner-city neighborhoods whose residents lack many basic public services—especially quality schools and healthcare—and that places them in environments in which they are more likely than Whites to die early, go to prison, become victims of domestic violence, and subsist on low-paid jobs or public welfare, often both. Not surprisingly, residential hyper-segregation is closely linked to poverty and its disabilities; one-half of Blacks have lived in the lowest income quartile of urban neighborhoods for at least two generations, as poverty is passed on from parents to children in these blighted areas, making it virtually impossible for these Black children to move up the income ladder. In contrast, only 7 percent of White families have lived in similar low-income neighborhoods for two generations or more.

* * *

Over the past five decades, social scientists have produced hundreds of studies and data that point to systemic racism as the root cause of White-Black disparities on a wide range of social indicators. To measure its devastating impact on Blacks, we start with the "two cities" and "two societies" view of America's metropolitan areas, in which about 80 percent of Blacks now live. Residential segregation is best measured by what demographers call the dissimilarity index (DI) on a scale from 0 to 100: an index score of 0 means the metro area is completely integrated, with Whites and Blacks in equally proportionate numbers in each neighborhood (with figures based on census tracts of roughly five thousand residents, which generally track neighborhoods). A DI of 100 means that Blacks and Whites are completely separate in their respective neighborhoods. (These extremes don't exist in any metro area.) The DI also indicates the percentage of residents of the smaller racial group (Black or White) who would have to move to another neighborhood in order to achieve complete integration. For example, a DI of 70 means that 70 percent of metro residents (White or Black) would have to move. Demographers generally consider any DI of 70 and above to indicate hyper-segregation, a situation in which Whites and Blacks rarely interact with each other outside of workplaces, creating social isolation, which in turn leads to a lack of personal interaction (the kind we have with our neighbors, for example) that fosters racial stereotypes and attitudes among both racial groups: the White belief that Blacks are violent and that it's best to stay out of their turf, and the Black belief that Whites don't think Black lives matter. Not everyone in either group holds these beliefs, of course, but enough do to create tension between them and the potential for violence.

It's notable that every one of the twenty-four metropolitan areas (MAs) with more than a million residents has a DI above 70, an indication of racial hyper-segregation. They range from the Los Angeles–Long Beach MA at 70.5, up to Detroit at 86.7 in 2018. Fourteen of these MAs have a DI above 75, largely because of the concentration of Blacks in center cities and of Whites in surrounding cities and counties. In addition to Los Angeles and Detroit, these hyper-segregated MAs include New York, Chicago, Cleveland, Philadelphia, St. Louis, Baltimore, and Kansas City, all of them end-points for southern Blacks who joined the First Great Migration to the North between 1900 and 1930. Even as the Black middle class grew in subsequent decades, those who moved into largely White neighborhoods and suburbs left behind the "truly disadvantaged" Blacks in decaying neighborhoods as breeding grounds for crime and family disruption. It's true that DI scores have trended downward since the 1980s, but hyper-segregation remains high in most major MAs, largely a result of White racial bias. Few White suburbanites would now mind a Polish or Greek or even Japanese neighbor, but many still feel less than welcoming to even middle-class Blacks moving in next door. The story of Ossian Sweet in Detroit in 1925, told in chapter 6, is still relevant in White neighborhoods whose residents use tools such as restrictive zoning laws and even fencing to keep Blacks out.

* * *

Given the continuing national debate about the causes of and potential cures for centuries of racial discrimination and inequality, it's instructive to go back several decades and look closely at works that explored and tried to account for the persistence of these racial disparities. There is a large and expanding number of books that address this issue, but two stand out as significant in reaching a wide audience beyond the ivy-covered walls of academia. The first, a book-length government report (widely reviewed, both favorably and neg-atively), was the product of a young, politically ambitious scholar, Daniel Patrick "Pat" Moynihan, with a doctorate in sociology and postgraduate work at the London School of Economics. After a brief stint as a policy advisor to New York's Democratic governor W. Averell Harriman and volunteer work on John Kennedy's presidential campaign, Moynihan landed a low-level job in the Labor Department in 1961, rising by 1965 to assistant secretary in Lyndon Johnson's administration. That year, he completed a report entitled *The Negro Family: The Case for National Action*. Moynihan, from a tight-knit Irish Catholic family, was sensitive to family issues; his father had deserted his wife and children when Moynihan was ten, which may well have prompted his study of Black families.

Delving into census data and other measures of racial inequality, Moynihan was struck by one statistic: in 1950, the rate of "out-of-wedlock" births among White women was about 2 percent, and that of Blacks was slightly higher, at 5 percent. By 1965, however, although the rate for White women had crept up to 3 percent, that for Black women, many still in their teens, had mushroomed to 25 percent. (As of 2015, the unmarried-mother rate for White women had reached 36 percent, just half the Black rate of 72 percent.) Even in 1965, this disparity shocked Moynihan. Although he acknowledged the impact of slavery and Jim Crow laws on Black families as a factor in creating and perpetuating the poverty in which more than half lived at that time, he placed more emphasis on the "matriarchal structure" of Black culture and the consequent inability—as he saw it—of Black men to embrace fatherhood and function as authority figures, especially for their male children. In a semantic blunder he most likely later regretted, and which fueled his academic critics, Moynihan titled—in capital letters—the longest chapter of his report, "A TANGLE OF PATHOLOGY." In that chapter, he wrote that "at the heart of the deterioration of the fabric of Negro society is the deterioration of the Negro family. It is the fundamental source of the weakness of the Negro community at the present time." Most people, of course, associate the term "pathology" with its medical use to describe serious illness and disease. Many of Moynihan's critics faulted him for—in their minds—casting blame for this Black "pathology" on its victims and giving credence to stereotypes of Black men as "shiftless" and uncaring of their paternal responsibilities. Moynihan dismissed welfare programs as essentially paying Black women—even though far more poor White women relied on government aid to support their families—for having too many children; this later gave rise to Ronald Reagan's false and racist denunciations of "welfare queens" who supposedly preferred welfare to working. Moynihan, in fact, wrote, "The steady expansion of welfare programs can be taken as a measure of the steady disintegration of the Negro family structure over the past generation in the United States." He advocated, instead, as linchpins of LBJ's War on Poverty, job-training programs that would provide young Black men with marketable skills that would, presumably, give them incomes sufficient to support a couple and their children. Whatever modest benefits these programs achieved for their participants, they did little or nothing to stem the rising tide of single-parent, unmarried-mother families, in which more than half of all Black children now live.

Moynihan attributed the "pathology" of Black family structure to a culture based upon matriarchy, which presumably sent a message to Black men that they were not needed, or even welcome, in raising families and caring for children. But if the roots of this pathological matriarchal culture were planted during slavery—when marriage between Blacks was often prevented and during which slave families were literally torn apart, with slave owners selling children and their parents to different owners—Moynihan did not explain why, as recently as 1950, only 5 percent of Black families were headed by single, unmarried women. He was distressed that this rate had grown fivefold by 1965. But something must have happened during this fifteen-year span to cause that growth. Moynihan attributed this to two factors: one was "welfare dependency," which gave Black women the bare necessities to support themselves and their children without having to work at low-skill, low-paying jobs. Most studies of poverty, in fact, showed that Black women would prefer working to welfare, despite White stereotypes of "welfare queens."

A second factor cited by Moynihan was the high level of unemployment among Black men, especially young men with poor education and few skills. However, although the rate of Black male unemployment was, in 1965, twice that of Whites (8.1 versus 4.1 percent), the vast majority of Black men in the labor market (that is, working or seeking work) were employed. True, their wages lagged well behind those of White men, but to say they could not support families was untrue. And in 1965, three-quarters of Black families lived in households with two parents. That figure was lower than for White families, but hardly the kind of national crisis that Moynihan painted. As a well-meaning White liberal, Moynihan did not welcome the embrace of his report by conservatives who employed it as a political weapon against welfare programs and as evidence that such programs encouraged Black women to have illegitimate children (read "bastards") who would drain the public coffers and create further generational cycles of poverty and welfare dependency. By focusing on the "pathology" of Black family structure, Moynihan unwittingly provided ammunition to conservatives (most of them Republicans) who pointed to his report as proof that Blacks themselves, both men and women, were to blame for their poverty and for the social ills (drug use, violence, and other forms of crime among them) that festered in Black ghettos and threatened to spill into White neighborhoods.

Moynihan and his report had many critics, on both the right and the left. But none answered the report with greater detail and vehemence than William Ryan, a psychology professor at Boston College. He started writing a rebuttal in 1966, shortly after the Moynihan Report was issued, which was published in 1971 as *Blaming the Victim*. Although Ryan's book was not as widely reviewed as its target, its title became a watchword for those—mostly academics—who expanded on Ryan's argument that systemic (or institutional) racism was at the core of racial inequality rather than a symptom in the "pathology" of Black family structure. Ryan defined "blaming the victim" as a "process of identification . . . whereby the victim of social problems is identified as strange, different—in other words, as a barbarian, a savage." These are harsh words, but Ryan was harsh in his criticism of academics whose work became fodder for right-wing politicians and propagandists who claimed that Blacks were inherently less intelligent than Whites, a view held by at least a quarter of the American public (and, in my opinion, a greater percentage who conceal their belief in Black inferiority in responding to pollsters' questions on this charged topic).

Among the academics Ryan excoriated in the revised edition of his book were Arthur Jensen and Edward Banfield. Jensen, a psychology professor at the University of California, Berkeley, wrote an article for the *Harvard Educational Review* in 1969 titled "How Much Can We Boost IQ and Scholastic Achievement?" Jensen's answer to his rhetorical question was "not much," since, he claimed, 80 percent of the IQ variance in populations was the result of genetic factors (over which we have no control), the remainder due mostly to environmental factors, such as poverty, poor nutrition, and other social ills. Jensen pointed to IQ studies that supposedly showed Blacks lagging roughly 10 IQ points behind Whites. The "science" of IQ testing has been widely criticized as culturally biased in favor of Whites and is rejected by most geneticists, but Jensen gave "scholarly" cover to believers in Black inferiority.

Edward Banfield, a Harvard political scientist whose book, *The Unheavenly City: The Nature and the Future of Our Urban Crisis*, was published in 1970, argued that Black "culture" was expressed by Black males in risk-taking and fighting. Most controversial, and most offensive to Ryan and other adherents of the systemic racism explanation of urban poverty, was Banfield's claim that residents of Black ghettos actually *liked* their neighborhoods of deteriorating housing, poor schools, and crime. Banfield also argued that what he called "conceptual intelligence" was lacking in poor Blacks, making them so "present-oriented" that they cannot look ahead and plan ways to escape their poverty. Instead, they pursue only instant gratification in using alcohol, drugs, and indiscriminate sex to block out the grimness of their present (and future) life. It seems bizarre to claim that poor Blacks actually prefer ghetto life to that of stable, two-parent, middle-class life, especially when that claim is made by a White Harvard professor. Even more damaging is Banfield's related claim that this preference is rooted in the "lower intelligence" of Blacks, consigning them to successive generations of poverty, with no tools to escape its grip.

In the 1976 revision of his book, Ryan looked back to the previous decade of the 1960s as a time of optimism—which he shared—for Black progress, with the passage in 1964 of the Civil Rights Act, the Voting Rights Act of

1965, and the presidential declaration of a War on Poverty. Ten years later, Ryan confessed to pessimism: Martin Luther King was dead, along with his "dream" of eventual racial equality; the civil rights movement "seemed to be withering and splintering"; and the War on Poverty was "doing all the wrong things—following all the formulas for blaming the victim so precisely that it was downright eerie." By 1976, alarmed by the seemingly "scientific" works of Jensen, Banfield, and others who turned Moynihan's "pathology" of Black family structure into political weapons, Ryan lamented that he had "underestimated the scope and severity of the counterattack mounted in the past few years against the Equality Revolution of the 1960s." He wrote that the "generic formula of *Blaming the Victim*—justifying inequality by finding defects in the victims of inequality—has been retained, but in a much wider, more malevolent and dangerous form, particularly in the resurgence of ideas about hereditary defects in Blacks, the poor, and working people in general."

And by 1976 Ryan had broadened the scope of his analysis in terms that have found echoes in recent years—especially by socialist and progressive politicians like Bernie Sanders and Elizabeth Warren—in denunciations of "the 1 percent" whose ostentatious wealth rests on exploitation of the bottom half of American workers. We are now all victims, Ryan wrote about the White middle class:

> Others own America, we're just workers, whether we realize it or not. Some of us may think we're flying high and are much better off than those below us, but, in the end, we're just "house niggers," allowed better food than the "field niggers" and wearing fancier clothes. But none of us owns even a corner of the cotton field. Massa owns it all, and Massa—the two or three percent who essentially own America— is the real problem.

Ryan's pessimistic words, more than four decades ago, remind us that inequality, both of race and class, is rooted so deeply in the social, political, and economic institutions of American society that its "owners" have little to fear from "socialist" and "progressive" movements that rail against them, especially because these owners also own the two major political parties that depend on corporate support and spending, regardless of "populist" rhetoric aimed at the White working class by politicians in both parties. In this sense, the racism that underlies the "grievance politics" of these White voters shows that Moynihan—who went on to serve four six-year terms in the Senate as a New York Democrat from 1977 to 2001—bested Ryan in the battle over which kinds of programs and policies would best tackle urban poverty and assist its victims, largely Black and Hispanic, in moving out of the economic basement. A prototypical "New Deal liberal," Moynihan later expressed regret that his report was widely cited by right-wing politicians and "neoconservative" think-tank writers—many of them former liberals—as proof that redistributionist New Deal programs and their War on Poverty successors had failed, attributing that failure to defects that were inherent in the violence-prone "gangstas" who populated America's Black urban ghettos and committed heinous crimes against Whites. Blaming the victims of systemic racism for their acts of rebellion against its perpetrators is still a staple of right-wing rhetoric.

One use of the "Black savage" stereotype, going back to the slavery and Jim Crow eras, illustrates its continuing political appeal to White voters. During the 1988 presidential campaign between Michael Dukakis and George H. W. Bush, a Black inmate in Massachusetts, where Dukakis was the Democratic governor, was given a weekend pass from the prison where he was serving a life-without-parole sentence for murder. This inmate, Willie Horton, did not return to the prison but instead went to Maryland, where he was arrested for robbing, assaulting, and raping a young White woman. Bush's campaign strategists convinced him to make Horton—whose mug shot, looking savage, was featured in Bush's television ads—the face of Dukakis's alleged "soft on crime" position, although he had no role in Horton's weekend release and opposed that program for murderers. Bush repeatedly referred to Horton in speeches and debates; his bare-knuckle campaign manager, Lee Atwater, said of White voters, "[B]y the time we're finished, they're going to wonder whether Willie Horton is Dukakis' running mate." Playing the "savage" card proved a winning hand for later politicians; Donald Trump used it in calling Mexicans "rapists" and "animals," even bringing the parents of young women who had been murdered by "illegals" to his side at raucous campaign rallies. This naked appeal to racism and nativism draws upon stereotypes of Black and Brown men as inherently lacking the intelligence to become "civilized," no matter what remedial programs try to accomplish. Just as painting one's political adversaries as "soft on crime" proved a winning strategy for Nixon and later right-wing politicians, so charging them with being soft on Black "thugs" and Brown "invaders," as Trump labeled them, proved the appeal of racism and xenophobia to a significant segment of White voters in the 2016 presidential election, enough to propel Trump to the White House (with thanks to the archaic Electoral College, that group of unknown people who actually cast the deciding votes).

* * *

To better understand this book's major thesis of systemic racism and inequality, based in large part on White fear of Black violence—from slave revolts and thousands of lynchings to police and White vigilante killings of supposedly threatening Blacks—we will look at the treatment of people the eminent Black Harvard sociologist William Julius Wilson called "the truly disadvantaged" in his 1987 book with that title, updated and expanded in 2012. Wilson and his Harvard colleague Robert J. Sampson have offered in their work and more recent studies a compelling theory—buttressed by empirical data—that locates the source of racial disparities, particularly in crime rates, in the structure of communities and neighborhoods that inflict what I call systemic violence on their Black residents. Most significant, Wilson and Sampson present the concept of "racial invariance" to show that such disadvantaged environments operate almost equally on the Blacks and Whites who live in them. In other words, crime rates for Blacks and Whites vary only slightly among those of both races—especially young men—from equivalent disadvantaged environments. However, far more Blacks than Whites, in percentage terms, live in such environments, providing a persuasive explanation for the higher crime rates among Blacks, most evident in violent crimes such as homicide, rape, and assault. Turning the tables, let's assume that far more Whites than Blacks, proportional to their racial groups, live in such disadvantaged environments (which they don't, of course). Under Wilson and Sampson's "racial invariance" thesis, violent crime rates among Whites would be at least double the Black rates. In other words, environment and not race is the most significant factor in explaining differing crime rates (and rates of other social ills as well).

Wilson and Sampson outlined their theory in a 2018 article that looked back at their earlier 1995 article, "Toward a Theory of Race, Crime, and Urban Inequality." They wrote:

> [W]e advanced a theoretical strategy that was primarily structural but that also incorporated cultural arguments regarding race, crime, and inequality in American cities. In contrast to psychologically based relative deprivation theories and the subculture of violence thesis, we viewed the race and crime linkage from a contextual framework that highlighted the very different community contexts of Blacks and Whites. Our basic thesis was that macrosocial patterns of residential inequality by race gave rise to the social isolation and ecological concentration of the truly disadvantaged, which in turn led to structural

barriers and behavioral adaptations that undermined social organization and hence the control of crime and violence.

Among the evidence they cite for these propositions is a longitudinal study of over 20 million children and their parents, whose authors—headed by Harvard economist Raj Chetty—found that "very few black children grow up in environments that foster upward economic mobility across generations" and that "fewer than 5 percent of black children currently grow up in areas with the poverty rate below 10 percent and more than half of black fathers present. In contrast, 63 percent of white children grow up in areas with analogous conditions." Consequently, vastly more Black than White children grow up in environments that produce higher rates of crime and social deprivation.

The focus in Wilson and Sampson's work on "macrosocial patterns of residential inequality" looks at population aggregates and not the individuals who make up this aggregation. But in acknowledging the "behavioral adaptations" of individuals to their impoverished neighborhoods and their low status in the wider society, Wilson and Sampson raised—but did not answer—the question of the role of these individual adaptations in varying rates of crime and violence; some of those adaptations are, in fact, the commission of crimes and violence.

* * *

It is at the intersection of aggregate neighborhood characteristics and individual behavior that the racial invariance thesis finds substantial corroboration. We know that hyper-segregated, dilapidated, low-income, and low-education neighborhoods have significantly higher rates of crime and violence than more affluent areas. We also know that far more Blacks and Hispanics than Whites live in such run-down neighborhoods. If these neighborhoods "produce" crime, almost as a commodity, they inevitably produce criminals, whose "adaptations" to their environment can be understood in the context of limited means to make a decent living through steady employment.

But why this persistent racial disparity in violent crime, which remains fairly consistent regardless of crime rates going up or down? Here, it's instructive to employ a theory that's been around, with modifications, for more than eighty years. Back in 1937, a Yale social psychologist, John Dollard, along with several colleagues, published *Caste and Class in a Southern Town*. Dollard spent several months in the mid-1930s, during the Great Depression, doing fieldwork in the town of Indianola, Mississippi (he changed its name in his book). The Delta town, with a population then of about 3,500, was the seat of Sunflower County, the site of Mississippi's notorious Parchman Prison Farm, whose mostly Black inmates toiled on an eighteen-thousand-acre cotton plantation owned by the state. Indianola was then, and still is, about three-quarters Black and one-quarter White; during Dollard's fieldwork, no Blacks were registered to vote, and Whites held all the county posts and power.

Dollard's goal was to examine, through interviews and observation, relations between the two races and to understand how Indianola's Blacks dealt with their hugely inferior positions. What he discovered, not surprisingly, was that in Jim Crow Mississippi, almost all Blacks adopted a "front" of servility and deference in dealing with Whites. He also found that this "front" concealed a simmering anger and resentment against Whites, again not surprising. What Dollard did find surprising was the very high incidence of violence in the Black community against other Blacks. Often fueled by liquor and disputes over women, Blacks were prone to fights in which injuries were mostly inflicted by knives, clubs, feet, and hands; only rarely were guns involved, and few fights ended with someone's death. But it could have deadly consequences if a Black person—even accidentally—threatened or injured a White person of whatever social rank, and all Blacks knew and most heeded that rule.

Out of these observations, Dollard outlined a psychological theory to explain the prevalence of Black-on-Black violence in this small town, the site of several gruesome lynchings some thirty years earlier. In a 1939 book, *Frustration and Aggression,* he labeled it the "frustration-aggression-displacement" (F-A-D) theory. In basic form, it posits that high levels of Black frustration about being treated badly by Whites—both individually and as a group—is expressed in anger and aggression, which in turn is displaced onto other Blacks to avoid potential punishment (lynching or imprisonment) for assaulting a White person. The theory itself is not complicated; many studies with laboratory animals and of animals observed in the wild show a strong link between frustration and aggression, most often over food and sex, at much higher levels in confined and crowded environments and frequently displaced onto others who didn't create the initial frustration. For humans, that aggression is most often targeted against persons in their immediate environment, even—and especially—family members. It's important to note that the F-A-D theory applies equally to Whites and Blacks, although for Whites—often the kind denigrated by other Whites as "trailer trash"—the source of frustration is more likely their own low status in society compared to that of more affluent and higher-status Whites. The victims of violent crimes by Whites are overwhelmingly, as with Blacks, people in their immediate environment, especially family members. Applying the F-A-D theory to 2018 violent crime statistics, 84 percent of those murdered by Blacks were other Blacks (2,600 of 3,114 cases where the race of victim and offender is known), while 91 percent (2,667 of 2,991) of White victims were murdered by other Whites. One finding in my research surprised me, and I expect will surprise most readers. Using 2018 statistics, I calculated that, on a per capita basis, twice as many Blacks were murdered by Whites (0.56 per 100,000) than Whites by Blacks (0.26 per 100,000). The raw numbers are small, to be sure: 234 Blacks out of the total U.S. Black population of 42 million were murdered by Whites, and 514 Whites out of the total U.S. White population of 197 million were murdered by Blacks. But that two-to-one disparity is exactly opposite what most people, White and Black alike, would likely say if asked which race is more likely to murder those of the other race. The myth of Black predators lusting to kill Whites is simply untrue, despite the claims of race-baiting politicians hoping to frighten White voters.

It's less surprising that (although not broken down by race) 81 percent of murder victims in 2018 were known to the perpetrators, and more than 50 percent were in the same extended family: spouses, children, in-laws, grandparents. Some portion of these murders—we don't know how many—are likely the result of displacing frustration onto nearby targets. Much of domestic violence against spouses, partners, and children falls into this "displacement" category. And, as many studies have shown, children who witness or experience violence—inside or outside the home—are more likely to commit violent crimes themselves. Since two to three times as many Black children as White are exposed to violence, higher rates of violence among Blacks as adults is predictable. Again, as Wilson and Sampson argue, environment and not race is the determining factor in the etiology of violent crime. But the link between social frustration and violent aggression is perfectly complementary with the racial invariance concept. One is macro in approach, the other micro; taken together, they help us to better understand the complex of factors that result in violent crime.

In 1968, two Black psychiatrists, William H. Grier and Charles M. Cobbs, published a book titled *Black Rage*, which was widely and favorably reviewed, with a revised and updated edition in 2000, from which the following excerpts come. Drawing upon their sessions with Black clients and close knowledge of the urban Black environment, Drs. Grier and Cobbs spoke to Americans of both races in words many might not have wanted to hear. Here's the part that will help put this chapter in better context:

> The American black man is unique, but he has no special psychology or exceptional genetic determinants. His mental mechanisms are the same as other men. If he undergoes emotional conflict, he will respond as neurotically as his white brother. In understanding him we return to the same reference point. Since all other explanations failed, we must conclude that much of the pathology we see in black people had its genesis in slavery. The culture that was born in that experience of bondage has been passed from generation to generation. Constricting adaptations developed during some long-ago time continue as contemporary character traits. That they are so little altered attests to the fixity of the black-white relationship, which has seen little change since the birth of this country. . . .
>
> Persisting to this day is an attitude, shared by black and white alike, that blacks are inferior. This belief permeates every facet of this country and it is the etiological agent from which has developed the national sickness. . . . The nation became involved in a bizarre system of reasoning about slaves. No longer were they simply unfortunate beings caught up in an economic system which exploited their labor. Now they were to be sub-human—quasi-humans who not only preferred slavery but felt it best for them. The American had to hide from himself and others his oppression of blacks. To be safe, the entire country had to share in the denial. . . .
>
> In the second half of the twentieth century the posture of the nation generally is only slightly changed. Long after slavery, many whites are haunted by a vision of being oppressed, exposed to the whims of a powerful cruel *black* man. To dissipate the fantasy, increasing barriers have had to be erected. In reality it seems a remote possibility that blacks might overthrow their oppressors and enslave them. But all men have the capacity to deceive themselves, and the entire country has participated in devising humiliating laws and customs. Pseudo-scientific theories of racial superiority have been elaborated and unreasoning fears of blacks have become a part of the national character. How else to explain such massive preparations for such an unlikely attack? . . .
>
> Because there has been so little change in attitudes, the children of bondage continue to suffer the effects of slavery. There is a timeless

quality to the unconscious which transforms yesterday into today. The obsessions of slave and master continue. Both continue a deadly struggle of which neither is fully aware. It would seem that for most black people emancipation has yet to come. . . .

And of the things that need knowing, none is more important than that all blacks are angry. White Americans seem not to recognize it. They seem to think that all the trouble is caused by only a few "extremists." They ought to know better. . . . Aggression leaps from wounds inflicted and ambitions spiked. It grows out of oppression and capricious cruelty. It is logical and predictable if we know the soil from which it comes. People bear all they can and, if required, bear even more. But if they are black in present-day America they have been asked to shoulder too much. They have had all they can stand. They will be harried no more. Turning from their tormentors, they are filled with rage. . . . The growing anger of Negroes is frightening to white America. There is a feeling of betrayal and undeserved attack. White people have responded with a rage of their own.

With both sides driven by rage, or at least by simmering anger, even if sublimated, and with fewer Whites than Blacks, I think, willing to admit theirs, and most eager to deny it, it's understandable that explosions of rage will be blamed on Black and White "extremists" whose crimes are solely their fault, as expiation for our national complicity in creating the conditions that produce these crimes.

* * *

Most people, especially those for whom violent crime is a salient political issue (in August 2020, shortly before the elections, 74 percent of Republicans said it was "very important" in their candidate choice, as opposed to 46 percent of Democrats) would likely think crime rates are increasing, and consequently that prison populations are also growing. In fact, the opposite is true. Between 2006 and 2018, the Black imprisonment rate dropped by 34 percent, along with a 26 percent decline for Hispanics and 17 percent for Whites. This is a consequence, of course, of the long-term declining violent crime rate, in which fewer convicted offenders are being sent to prison, and more are released after doing their time. But it's still true, as the Pew Research Center reported in 2018, that the Black imprisonment rate was nearly twice that of Hispanics and more than five times that of Whites. What Michelle Alexander, in her influential and widely read 2010 book, *The New Jim Crow: Mass Incarceration in the Age of Colorblindness*, portrayed as a consequence of White fears of Black men is still a serious problem, notwithstanding the declining rate of Black imprisonment.

All of this, I'm sure, will be hard for many Whites to believe, since evidence shows the widespread prevalence of the belief that Blacks are predisposed by inherent and heritable characteristics to commit violent crimes, what might be called the "bad genes make bad dudes" explanation. This opinion, of course, is rooted in racial stereotypes: that Blacks as a group are less intelligent, more prone to violence, less attached to family, and less willing to work hard and obey laws than Whites. These beliefs, expressed in numerous polls over decades of research, mark those Whites who hold them as what I call "active racists" and includes about a third of the White population. Admitting to these beliefs, by definition, makes one a racist, despite offended denials. In my estimate, roughly another third or more of Whites are "passive racists," those who admit that Blacks have been and still are victims of discrimination but make no effort—in their schools, workplaces, and communities—to press for social changes that would reduce this discrimination and its effects on Blacks. Such "passive racists" actually impede such efforts, as the widespread NIMBY (Not in my back yard) campaigns against low-income housing in White neighborhoods, halfway houses for released inmates, and school integration plans have demonstrated. Fear of lowered property values becomes a cover for "I don't want them in my neighborhood, although I'm not a racist" excuses for such exclusion. It may seem unduly harsh to label as racist people who would never use the N-word or believe Blacks are inferior to Whites, but those in this group give tacit support to racism by their unwillingness to support or join in efforts to combat systemic racism. My estimate of their numbers is admittedly just that, but numerous polls and studies buttress my estimate. On the hopeful side, the number of White "antiracists" has grown in recent years, including those who march with Blacks for racial justice and against systemic police harassment and brutality—including murder—of Blacks. This "antiracist" group also includes Whites who advocate for low-income housing, criminal justice reform, workplace diversity, and greater school integration. Of course, it's that first one-third of "active racists" whose hostility to Blacks (and Hispanics and Asian Americans, even legal immigrants) has fueled very recent outbursts of racial violence: the Charleston church murders in 2015; the Charlottesville neo-Nazi violence (including the murder of Heather Heyer) in 2017; the assault-rifle massacre of twenty-two people, mostly Hispanic, at the El Paso Walmart in 2019; and the murder of six Asian women in Atlanta in March 2021 are only the most notorious among scores of violent attacks on Blacks and other non-White groups.

* * *

Putting together the differing perspectives of the root causes of crime by Blacks—from sociology, social psychology, psychology, and psychiatry—it seems clear that violent behavior is primarily affected by residential segregation, especially in densely populated, hyper-segregated neighborhoods, with almost all violence inflicted on other, nearby Blacks. Here, some recent statistics will flesh out this argument, the opposing side of which argues that Black crime rates exceed those of Whites because Blacks are inherently more "violent" and "criminal" than Whites—that is, *because* they are black. In a 2016 Reuters/Ipsos poll of Trump supporters, almost half (48 and 46 percent, respectively) agreed with these negative attributes. A bit more than half, of course, did not agree. But the first group had roughly 30 million members among Trump's 2016 supporters, enough to elect him president along with hard-right members of Congress in heavily White districts with below-average education levels, a significant minority bloc in Congress. Those politicians are more likely to push for longer sentences, more prisons, and ending or restricting parole, despite pretending to support systemic criminal justice reform. Swirling below opposition to real reform such as sharply cutting sentences, decriminalizing drug use, and community-based correctional facilities are racist currents.

It was the crack cocaine epidemic in the 1980s and 1990s that sent thousands of Blacks to prison for mandatory five-year sentences for possessing 5 grams of crack, while it took 500 grams of powder cocaine—both made from the same plant—to merit five years. Even though crack is more powerful than powder in its effect, this 100-to-1 disparity reflected fears of Blacks high on crack robbing or assaulting Whites, although most Black crime stemming from drugs was against other Blacks, most often during "turf wars" between rival gangs. Most Whites—many of them affluent professionals—could afford their cocaine habit and didn't need to rob anyone. The racism behind these disparate punishments was so clear (and embarrassing) that Congress, in the Fair Sentencing Act in 2010, finally increased the trigger for five-year sentences from 5 grams of crack to 28, reasoning that 5 grams was intended for personal use but 28 grams or more presumed trafficking it. The law also eliminated mandatory five-year minimum sentences, giving judges more discretion in sentencing. But it did little to reduce the skyrocketing violence of the "crack wars" in the 1980s and 1990s, during which cities with large Black populations saw their murder rates shoot up. Detroit's rate, at one point the nation's highest, was 58.2 per 100,000 in 1985, and the police chief estimated that 65 to 70 percent of the city's murders were drug related. By 2018, the murder rate had dropped to 38 per 100,00, a one-third decline, although still more than seven times the national rate.

Many people, alarmed by news reports of spikes in murders in cities like Chicago (although murders declined there by 35 percent from 2016 to 2019) don't know that rates for almost all criminal offenses have dropped by half since the late 1990s. This is most clearly seen in the national murder rate. Calculated as the number of murders for every 100,000 residents (with separate figures for national, state, and local rates), the national rate has fallen from a high of 10.2 in 1980 to 4.96 in 2019. In other words, an "average" city with a million residents would see 102 murders in 1980 but only 50 in 2019, a drop of more than half. In fact, the national murder rate did not fall below 8.0 per 100,000 residents between 1971 and 1993, except for two years at 7.9; in contrast, the rate has been at 5.0 or below in every year since 2009. Tally them up, and close to 150,000 people, about half of them Black, did not get murdered because of that drop. Some drops have been dramatic: in New York City, for example, the 1990 murder rate was 30.9 per 100,000 residents; by 2019 that figure had dropped 88 percent to 3.83, a truly astounding development.

*　*　*

The debate between Moynihan and Ryan back in the 1960s and 1970s foreshadowed the two opposing sides in today's debate over the root causes of racial and ethnic inequality. The first, generally espoused by self-identified "conservatives," places most of the blame for inequality on Blacks themselves. Those who point to the "individual responsibility" (or the lack thereof) of Blacks, and to a lesser extent Hispanics, for their inequality are significantly more likely than self-identified "liberals" to consider Blacks to be basically inferior to Whites. Not surprisingly, in the current era of extreme partisan divides on social issues, White Republicans hold more disparaging views of Blacks than do White Democrats. Over the past two decades, polling by the National Opinion Research Center at the University of Chicago has measured racial attitudes by party affiliation. Three questions illustrate this partisan divide. One asked respondents whether they believe that Blacks "lack the motivation and willpower to lift themselves out of poverty." In 1996, 55 percent of White Republicans (WRs) and 47 percent of White Democrats (WDs) agreed. By 2016, the same percentage of WRs (55) agreed, but only 26 percent of WDs.

A related question, far more explosive in political terms, asked whether Blacks were "less intelligent" than Whites as a group. In 1996, 38 percent of both WRs and WDs agreed; by 2016, both groups had rejected this foundational belief of White supremacy, but by less (26 percent) among WRs than WDs, although one out of six WDs (18 percent) agreed that Blacks were less intelligent than Whites. A third question tested the centuries-old stereotype that Blacks are "inherently lazier" than Whites. In 1996, 53 percent of WRs agreed, as did 46 percent of WDs, another shocking result. But again, by 2016 there were fewer in both groups who agreed with the stereotype; however, 42 percent of WRs agreed, but only 24 percent of WDs, a significant partisan difference.

The NORC study reveals that roughly a third of all Whites (Republicans more than Democrats) view Blacks as unmotivated, less intelligent, and inherently lazier than Whites. This is hard-core racism, held by a hard-core group of Americans who believe themselves superior to Blacks (and other races and ethnic groups as well). Predominantly older, more rural, and less educated, their numbers and political influence will shrink as they succumb to the actuarial tables, assuming that "millennials" and younger people maintain their current, more liberal racial views. This assumption, of course, is just that; past generations have experienced shifts of varying degrees toward more conservative views as they age.

Another survey, by the Pew Research Center in 2020, revealed the unwillingness of Whites to acknowledge the historic roots of racial inequality. Respondents were given two choices to identify the causes of discrimination: that it is "built into the laws and institutions" of American society, or that discrimination is "based on the prejudice of individuals"—in other words, the prejudices of individual employers, landlords and realtors, government officials, police officers, school teachers and administrators, and other functionaries of private and public institutions with whom Americans of all races must deal in their daily lives. Only 19 percent of Whites chose the "built into the laws and institutions" answer, a shorthand definition of systemic racism; 70 percent of Whites lay the blame for discrimination on prejudiced individuals, presumably acting outside and in violation of the laws and norms that govern their institutions.

Of course, systemic and individual racism are not mutually exclusive categories. Every social institution employs individuals who feel empowered to treat Blacks and other minorities as "less deserving" than Whites of the benefits of that institution. But in no institution has there been a greater and more debilitating impact on Blacks—especially today's Black children—than in education, as we'll see in our concluding chapter.

12

"The Basic Minimal Skills"

RESIDENTIAL SEGREGATION IS rooted in historical White racism; there's no denying that fact. And it's also an undeniable fact that public school segregation is a direct consequence of residential segregation. As we saw in chapter 10, the Supreme Court's *Milliken* decision in 1974 effectively cemented the "neighborhood school" system in which schools—going back at least seven decades—were purposely placed well inside racial and ethnic neighborhoods, and school attendance boundaries were often gerrymandered to reduce the number of Black and Brown students in largely White schools. Those efforts to keep minority and White students in separate schools as much as possible have largely survived campaigns, both legal and political, to foster real integration, thanks to *Milliken* and later judicial decisions that cited it as precedent.

One result of what might be called educational hyper-segregation is that majority-White school districts receive significantly more funding per student than majority-Black (and -Hispanic) districts. In 2019, low-income districts with 75 percent or more of minority students received 19 percent less funding, about $2,600 per student, than affluent districts with more than 75 percent Whites. In several states, including Oklahoma and Arizona, the per-pupil disparities exceed 30 percent. More disturbing, low-income minority districts received 11 percent less (about $1,500 per student) even than districts with a majority of poor Whites, although both groups get shafted by receiving lower funding than affluent White districts. Several states have even greater disparities between poor-minority and poor-White districts: Washington state gives poor-minority districts 59 percent less, a shortfall of about $11,000 per student; in New Jersey, the disparity is 32 percent, or $7,300 less per student. These disparities obviously affect the quality of the education of Black kids in poor districts; their schools also have fewer credentialed teachers and fewer facilities—science labs, music programs, and more—than White kids get.

These statistics, and the funding disparities they reveal, are the direct result of a 1973 Supreme Court decision that rivals *Milliken* in its damaging impact on Black and Brown students in cities across the country. The story of this case, *San Antonio Independent School District v. Rodriguez*, is worth telling as an example of judicial disregard of children who have the disadvantage of living in school districts with high numbers of minority students and high levels of poverty, two closely related barriers to quality education.

The name of Demetrio Rodriguez appeared first among those on the complaint filed in the federal court of San Antonio, Texas, on July 10, 1968. Six other parents of children in the Edgewood Independent School District, located in the sprawling Hispanic barrio on the West Side of San Antonio, added their names to the suit against a long list of school and state officials. The suit charged that Edgewood children, and those of all other poor families in Texas, suffered from inferior education because of the inequitable property tax basis of the state's school financing system. The Edgewood parents asked the federal court to find the system in violation of the U.S. Constitution and to order the state to equalize the funding of all one thousand school districts in Texas.

Demetrio Rodriguez was the logical choice to head the list of plaintiffs in the complaint. The forty-two-year-old U.S. Navy and Air Force veteran had worked for more than fifteen years at Kelly Air Force Base, just south of his Edgewood home. The Rodriguez family lived in a neat white house on Sylvia Avenue, a street with no sidewalks or storm sewers. Roosters crowed in the neighbors' yards. Three of Rodriguez's four sons attended Edgewood Elementary School, just a block away across a dusty playing field. The school building was crumbling, classrooms lacked basic supplies, and almost half the teachers were not certified and worked on emergency permits. Rodriguez feared the Edgewood schools would not prepare his sons to compete for the good jobs that "Anglos" controlled in San Antonio. He became a grassroots community activist and helped to organize the Edgewood District Concerned Parents Association.

The parents group met with frustration in asking Edgewood school officials to improve the district's twenty-five schools, which enrolled twenty-two thousand students. Dr. Jose Cardenas, the district superintendent, explained sadly that he had no money to rebuild crumbling schools and hire more qualified teachers. Behind the gloomy financial figures lay ethnic statistics. More than 90 percent of Edgewood students were Hispanic, 6 percent were Black, and fewer than 5 percent came from the Anglo community that dominated San Antonio's business and political leadership. Faced with insurmountable financial barriers, the parents group turned for help to Arthur Gochman, a San Antonio native and the city's best-known civil rights lawyer, who was also well-connected to its business and political elite. At a meeting arranged by Demetrio Rodriguez, Gochman listened patiently to the parents, and then explained that the real source of poor schools for poor families was unfair funding between affluent, mostly White, school districts and those with poor families, mostly Hispanic and Black. He had recently read a federal court decision which struck down funding disparities between schools in Washington, D.C. Although this decision was limited to schools within one district, Gochman felt that its holding could be expanded on a statewide basis.

Gochman prepared the complaint with great care. The case rested upon two major claims, neither of which had been accepted by any federal court. One was that the Fourteenth Amendment to the U.S. Constitution included education as a "fundamental right" which states must provide on an equal basis to all students. The other was that poor families constituted a "suspect class," meaning they deserve special judicial protection against discrimination by state officials. Gochman added a third claim: Mexican Americans were a distinct racial and ethnic group and were included, like Blacks, in the "suspect class" category. If the federal court accepted any of these claims, judicial precedent required that Texas officials present a "compelling" reason to justify the property-tax basis of school funding. Gochman knew these claims rested on shaky legal foundations, but he supported each with a rock-solid factual argument.

Because the *Rodriguez* case challenged a state law on federal grounds, it came before a three-judge panel that would rule without a jury. There would be no courtroom dramatics in this case, which began slowly and wound through the court like a dry creek bed. Lawyers for the state asked the judges to dismiss the complaint, arguing that there was no legal basis for relief to the Edgewood parents. More than a year passed before the judges denied the motion in October 1969. The state then argued that the Texas legislature, which would not convene until January 1971, had authorized a committee study of school financing and should be allowed to act on the study. The state's lawyers predicted that legislative reform would equalize funding among districts and provide relief to the parents. Aware that the legislature had convened in January 1969 and had adjourned in May without acting on similar reform proposals, the judges reluctantly granted the state's go-slow motion, directing the defendants to advise the court every ninety days of progress by the committee. Despite these assurances, the Texas legislators came to Austin in 1971 and left without acting on school finance reform. Judge Adrian Spears of the federal panel lectured the state's lawyers at a hearing in December 1971:

> I think it is a little disconcerting to a court, when it abstains and does it on specific grounds that it wishes for the legislature to do something about it, and with education as important as it is to the citizenry of our state and our nation, for the legislature to completely ignore it. It makes you feel that it just does no good for a court to do anything other than, if it feels these laws are suspect, declare them unconstitutional.

Cheered by this expression of judicial sympathy, Gochman decided to dramatize the issues by contrasting Edgewood, the poorest of Bexar County's seven districts, with Alamo Heights, its most wealthy. The names alone illustrate the division—the Hispanic district at the city's edge, and the Anglo district on its heights. Wealth looks down on poverty in most cities, and despite its modest hills, San Antonio is no exception to this rule. Lawyers, doctors, and bankers lived in Alamo Heights; 54 percent of its male workers held executive or professional positions in 1970, against just 4 percent in Edgewood. Gochman drove home the disparities with simple charts, extracted from more than 100,000 pages of documents. School funding began with local property values: the 1970 figure for Edgewood was only $5,429 per student, while the Alamo Heights figure was $45,095. Even though Edgewood parents taxed themselves at the highest rate in the county, property taxes provided only $26 for each pupil. State funding added $222 and federal programs contributed $108, for a total of $356 for each Edgewood student. Parents in Alamo Heights, eight times wealthier in property, taxed themselves at the city's lowest rate and still raised $333 for each student. The state program added even more for Alamo Heights than for Edgewood, $225 per student, and federal funding of $26 gave a total of $594. With almost twice as much to spend on each student, Alamo Heights could afford better teachers; 40 percent had a master's degree, as opposed to just 15 percent in Edgewood. Gochman put his case into a nutshell with this figure: Edgewood parents would have to tax themselves at twenty times the rate of those in Alamo Heights to match their revenues from property taxes. This would require a tax of almost $13 for each $100 of property value. But the state imposed a property tax ceiling of $1.50. "The Texas system makes it impossible for poor districts to provide quality education," Gochman concluded.

Two days before Christmas in 1971, more than three years after the Edgewood parents filed their suit, the three-judge panel, like the Wise Men of old, brightened their holiday by ruling that the Texas school finance program violated the Equal Protection guarantee of the Fourteenth Amendment. The judges held that "wealth" discrimination was "suspect" under the Constitution and that education was a "fundamental" right, as Gochman had argued. The panel also ruled that not only had Texas been "unable to demonstrate compelling state interests" in basing school funding on property values, but it had failed "even to establish a reasonable basis" for the existing system. This latter holding meant the state had flunked even the most simple test for judging laws: whether the state presented the bare minimum of a "rational basis" for the challenged law. But the brightly wrapped Christmas package was empty: the judges granted the state two more years to reform the unlawful system.

Between the suit's filing and the court's grace period, Texas had been given six years to put its schools in order. But state officials had not expected the federal court ruling. "The initial reaction in Texas was one of surprise, bordering on shock," wrote Mark Yudof, a University of Texas law professor who had helped Gochman in the case. With the state's pocketbook at risk, the Texas attorney general hired a prominent lawyer to argue an appeal before the U.S. Supreme Court. Charles Alan Wright had become, at the age of forty-three, an acknowledged expert on federal litigation. He also had close ties with the Republican establishment and belonged to exclusive social and country clubs in Austin and New York. (He later served as Richard Nixon's lawyer during the Watergate scandal.) Wright was the ideal choice to defend the state's enormous financial stake in the status quo.

Other states and their nervous bondholders had stakes in the case as well. The attorneys general of twenty-five states filed friend-of-the-court briefs on the side of Texas. Supporting the Edgewood parents were the American Civil Liberties Union, the NAACP, and the National Education Association. Most unusual and ironic was the brief submitted by the San Antonio Independent School District, urging the justices to uphold the lower court ruling: the district was in fact the nominal defendant and was represented by Wright, whose argument the brief asked the justices to reject.

Wright began his Supreme Court argument on the morning of October 12, 1972, with a strategic concession: that the Texas school finance system was "imperfect" and produced substantial disparities between districts. But he then claimed that the lower court ruling to eliminate these disparities "would impose a constitutional straight jacket on the public schools of fifty states."

Wright urged that "the rational basis test is the appropriate test" of the Texas system, although the lower court had flunked the state on that easy test. He also argued that "very little is to be left of local government if the decision below is affirmed," although the local government he supposedly represented now asked for affirmance. Wright faced a final question from Justice William O. Douglas, who noted that the case record "pretty clearly demonstrated" that Mexican Americans suffered from unequal school funding. "The racial issue is in this litigation," Wright admitted. Although the case was brought by "particular plaintiffs who are Mexican American and who live in a district with low taxable resources," he argued that racial and ethnic factors were simply "a happenstance" in the case.

Arthur Gochman then replaced Wright at the lectern and quickly pointed out that "the poorest people live in the poorest districts and the richest people live in the richest districts." The heart of the case, he argued, was that district wealth "perfectly correlates" with district school funding. Gochman was questioned about his claim, adopted by the lower court, that education was a "fundamental right" under the Constitution. What about police and fire protection, or health facilities, one justice asked. "Where would you grade them, with respect to public education? Higher? Lower?" Gochman responded that "education affects matters guaranteed by the Bill of Rights." Unlike protection against crime, fire, and disease, education "is related to every important right we have as citizens."

Gochman gave a heated rebuttal to Wright's cold statement that Texas was required to give Edgewood students only a "minimum" level of education. "What kind of morass is Mr. Wright asking you to get into? What is a minimum? Are we going to have two classes of citizens—minimum opportunity students, and first class citizens?" Gochman ended his argument by noting that Wright's ostensible client, the San Antonio School District, "after seeing the decision of the trial court and the equity involved and the vast discrimination, filed a brief in support of the decision of the trial court."

The legal and financial stakes in the *Rodriguez* case were reflected in the length of the Court's opinions, which covered 137 closely printed pages. Ruling by a one-vote margin, the Supreme Court reversed the lower court and upheld the property-tax basis of America's public schools. The ruling was issued on March 21, 1973, two months after Nixon's second inauguration. Nixon had appointed four justices during his first term, and all four voted for Texas and its bondholders. The Warren Court had given way to the Burger Court, which almost invariably upheld the powers of state and local officials.

Justice Potter Stewart, who joined the Nixon appointees in this case, was a fellow Republican and predictable supporter of fiscal stability.

Chief Justice Warren Burger asked Justice Lewis Powell to write the Court's majority opinion. Powell was a perfect choice for the task, a former corporate lawyer from Richmond, Virginia, whose firm represented many owners of school bonds. He had also chaired both the Virginia and Richmond school boards, dragging his feet in responding to court-ordered integration plans. Powell's opinion dutifully and diligently canvassed the factual record of the *Rodriguez* case, finding "substantial disparities" in the funding of Texas school districts. But he considered the proper judicial test more important than facts. "Texas virtually concedes," he wrote, that its school finance system "could not withstand the strict judicial scrutiny" that the lower court had employed. Powell's approach, however, found "neither the suspect classification nor the fundamental interest analysis persuasive."

Powell first addressed the issue of wealth as a suspect classification ("suspect" in the sense of requiring closer judicial scrutiny to pass constitutional muster). The Court's previous opinions striking down laws discriminating against poor persons, he noted, affected only individuals. The problem with poor people in Texas was that they belonged to "a large, diverse, and amorphous class, unified only by the common factor of residence in districts that happen to have less taxable wealth than other districts."

Powell continued with a denial that education constituted a "fundamental right" that was essential to effective citizenship. He noted that education "is not among the rights afforded explicit protection under our federal Constitution." Two months earlier, he had joined an opinion holding that the Constitution protected a "fundamental right" to abortion, a term also not mentioned in the Constitution. Powell agreed that education was central to citizenship, but the Constitution did not "guarantee to the citizenry the most *effective* speech or the most *informed* electoral choice," using italics for an unstated implication that effective speech and informed voting were reserved for the more affluent (and Whiter) students in districts like Alamo Heights.

Powell's opinion reeked of privileged disdain for people like Demetrio Rodriguez and the Hispanic kids whose schools were literally falling apart: "Though education is one of the most important services performed by the State, it is not within the limited category of rights recognized by this Court as guaranteed by the Constitution. Even if some identifiable quantum of education is arguably entitled to constitutional protection to make meaningful the exercise of other constitutional rights, here there is no showing that the Texas system fails to provide the basic minimal skills necessary for that purpose." Powell's use of a word defined as "barely sufficient" and "negligible" to set a standard for educating Hispanic (and Black) kids speaks volumes about privileged racism. He also took an unnoticed slap in *Rodriguez* at Chief Justice Warren's *Brown* opinion, which singled out education as the most important state function and the foundation of good citizenship.

Justice Thurgood Marshall lamented the *Rodriguez* decision in his dissent, as he did the next year in *Milliken*: "The majority's holding can only be seen as a retreat from our historic commitment to equality of educational opportunity. . . . In my judgment, the right of every American to an equal start in life, so far as the provision of a state service as important as education is concerned, is far too vital to permit state discrimination." The Court's only Black member ended his dissent with disparaging remarks about Justice Powell's faith in Texas legislators. He wrote with obvious sarcasm that Powell's remarks "will doubtless be of great comfort to the schoolchildren of Texas' disadvantaged districts, but considering the vested interests of the wealthy school districts in the preservation of the status quo, they are worth little more." Marshall's dissent raised a basic question about American society: If education is not considered a "fundamental right" under the Constitution, what is? The Supreme Court has designated the Free Speech and Free Press clauses as protecting fundamental rights of free expression, but how effective can they be for those with only "the basic minimal skills" of reading and writing? In a real sense, Edgewood and Alamo Heights in San Antonio are separate and unequal parts of the "two societies" the Kerner Commission warned that America was becoming.

Demetrio Rodriguez spoke for the Edgewood parents in responding to the Court's decision: "The poor people have lost again." But their struggle for equal school funding was not lost. Twelve years later, in 1985, Rodriguez joined another suit, this one filed by the Mexican American Legal Defense and Education Fund, challenging the school finance system under the Texas state constitution. During those twelve years, the courts of six states had ruled that property-tax school funding violated state constitutions. Supreme Court Justice William J. Brennan, whose home state of New Jersey joined this parade, had urged lawyers for years to use state constitutions in seeking wider rights for their clients. It's little known that the Supreme Court does not review the rulings of state court judges that are based on their state's constitutional provisions, which judges can interpret more broadly—but not more narrowly—than Supreme Court precedent would allow; for example, the Court did not review an Oregon Supreme Court decision upholding a state referendum allowing physician-assisted suicide, even though the Court had upheld such a ban from the neighboring state of Washington against a federal constitutional challenge under the Due Process clause of the Fourteenth Amendment.

Ruling on April 30, 1987, Judge Harley Clark of the Texas State Court in Austin followed Brennan's lead. "If one district has more access to funds than another district," Clark wrote, "the wealthier one will have the best ability to fulfill the needs of its students." After decades of foot-dragging—one judge threatened to have the Texas legislators arrested and jailed if they failed to act on school financing reform—the tide began to turn: in 2017, the Edgewood district spent $10,412 for each student; the figure in Alamo Heights was just $8,622. Dollars do not measure the quality of an education, but they make it more likely students will get better teachers and facilities. And Edgewood finally had the funds to replace its crumbling schools. But the Supreme Court had turned a deaf ear to Black and Brown kids across the country: all the Constitution guaranteed them, five White justices ruled, were "the basic minimal skills" that kept good jobs out of reach. Combined with the *Brown II* and *Milliken* decisions, *Rodriguez* completed a triumvirate of cases that essentially reinstated Jim Crow segregation in the nation's largest cities. It is not coincidental that the Supreme Court majorities in each of these cases were composed of privileged White men. As a foundational institution in American society, the legal system has a failing grade in protecting another foundational institution, public education, from the damage inflicted on millions of Black and Brown children by inferior, segregated schools. Systemic racism is a reality for these kids, even without knowing its name.

* * *

At this point, we'll make a final visit to Detroit. I should point out again that my choice of Detroit, among the nation's twenty-five largest cities, to illustrate the impact of systemic racism and inequality on the nation's major cities was not to disparage the "worst" city and its residents in terms of poverty, residential segregation, and student achievement, but to explain those social ills as predictable consequences of Detroit's also being the "Blackest" major city. Rather than blaming the victims for their plight, as right-wing politicians and pundits routinely do, we need to look at the sources of inequality in American society.

In Detroit, a major source of its intractable racial disparities—compared to its suburban neighbors—is the appalling state of its public education system. This can best be illustrated with statistics about the performance of students in the city's public schools, as measured by scores on the National Assessment of Educational Progress (NAEP), known as the "Nation's Report Card." Beginning in 2009 and every two years since then, schools in twenty-seven of the largest school districts in a dozen states have administered identical tests in math and reading to students in fourth and eighth grades. Scores on the NAEP tests are separated into four categories: Below Basic, Basic, Proficient, and Advanced.

On each of the six administrations between 2009 and 2019, students in Detroit's public schools were dead last among the participating districts. Here are the results from the 2019 tests. Only 5 percent of Detroit fourth-graders scored Proficient in math, as compared to 40 percent of students in the combined districts; just 6 percent of Detroit fourth-graders were Proficient in reading, compared to 35 percent of the national total. Not even 1 percent in Detroit were rated as Advanced in either math or reading. Scores for the city's eighth-graders were only slightly better: 5 percent Proficient in math and 7 percent in reading; again, fewer than 1 percent scored at the Advanced level.

Even more disturbing are the percentages of Detroit students in the Below Basic category: 62 percent of fourth-graders in math and 77 percent in reading; 61 percent of eighth-graders in math and 59 percent in reading. Put another way, roughly nineteen of every twenty students in Detroit's elementary and middle schools lack proficiency in both math and reading, and almost two of every three cannot grasp even the most rudimentary skills in these subjects. It's also disturbing that, even in the top-ranked Charlotte-Mecklenburg district in North Carolina, 40 percent of Black students scored in the Below Basic category on the combined math and reading tests, although 24 percent were Proficient and 4 percent Advanced; in contrast, only 10 percent of White kids were Below Basic, with 41 percent Proficient and 27 percent Advanced. These racial disparities, in varying degrees, are found in all twenty-seven NAEP districts, a sobering indication of the daunting tasks ahead in reducing—and hopefully ending—them for coming generations of Black kids.

Table 12.1 shows the glaring disparities between Black and White students in twelve NAEP districts with substantial numbers of Blacks. The table lists the percentages of White and Black students who scored in the Below Basic (BB) category on the 2019 eighth-grade reading test, a critical skill for success in high school. It also includes the percentages of eighth-grade White and Black students scoring at the combined Proficient and Advanced (PA) levels on the 2019 reading test. TF indicates too few White students to compute.

Table 12.1

District	White BB	Black BB	White PA	Black PA
Detroit	TF	65	TF	5
Milwaukee	21	64	40	7
Baltimore	20	54	48	10
Philadelphia	31	53	27	13
Cleveland	37	52	23	10
Washington, D.C.	6	51	74	14
New York City	20	50	46	14
Houston	19	50	50	9
Atlanta	11	44	67	15
Miami-Dade	16	44	46	13
Chicago	12	42	55	16
Charlotte	12	41	54	18

As we can see, the gaps between White and Black students at both the bottom and top eighth-grade reading levels are large in each of these NAEP districts. In just two districts (Philadelphia and Cleveland) were more than 20 percent of White students in the Below Basic category; in every district, more than 40 percent of Black students scored in that bottom category. At the other end, again with the same two exceptions, in each district at least 40 percent of White students scored at the Proficient or Advanced levels, while no more than 18 percent of Black students scored at that level in any district. (Similar gaps are found in the fourth-grade math and reading tests and the eighth-grade math test.) Detroit's Black students may have scored at the bottom in these tests, but the Black-White gaps in every other district are wide and troubling for those hoping to close them.

* * *

Many of Detroit's current fourth- and eighth-grade students will be going into the city's high schools, which were 92 percent Black in the 2019–20 school year. It might be instructive to look at two of those high schools, Mumford and Martin Luther King Jr., and compare them with two high schools, Grosse Pointe North and Grosse Point South, just five miles away, in the upper-income suburb of Grosse Pointe (actually, five adjoining towns in one school district). We'll first compare the median household incomes of the two districts in 2018: Detroit's was $26,249, and Grosse Pointe's was $100,688, a fourfold disparity that will help in comparing their high schools. That same year, the average value of single-family homes in Detroit was $45,200, while homes in Grosse Pointe had an average value of $407,500, a ninefold disparity.

In the 2019–20 school year, Mumford High had 1,032 Black and 2 White students; King High had 1,062 Black and no White students. Grosse Pointe had a growing number of middle-class Black residents; Grosse Pointe North High had 822 White and 372 Black students; Grosse Pointe South High had 1,319 White and 104 Black students. In 2019, seniors in all four high schools took the Scholastic Assessment Test (SAT, or College Boards), which is graded on a scale of 200 to 800, with exams in both math and language skills (called the English test); the median score on each would be 500. The math and English scores are combined for a total score between 400 and 1600, with 1000 as the median. At Mumford High, the average math score was 383 and English was 393, for a total SAT score of 776 (a score in the bottom 7 percent of all students tested). At King High, math was 396 and English was 420, for a total score of 816 (the bottom 13 percent). At Grosse Pointe South High, the average math score was 592 and English was 578, for a total of 1170 (the top 30 percent). At Grosse Pointe North, math was 521 and English was 536, a total of 1057 (the top 40 percent). Keep in mind that roughly half the students in each school had scores above the average and half below it, but within fairly narrow ranges. And let's look at three of Michigan's premier universities, since the SAT is designed to inform college admissions officers about their applicants. Entering freshmen at the flagship University of Michigan in 2019 had average SAT scores of 1435; those at Michigan State University had average scores of 1210, and those at Wayne State University in Detroit an average of 1109, all averages also within a fairly narrow range. Now calculate the odds that a graduate of Mumford High or King High would have of enrolling at one of these universities, and the odds for graduates of the Grosse Pointe high schools. The answers are obvious.

Another quiz: using a 2019 Bureau of Labor Statistics report, Table 12.2 lists occupations in which Blacks (who comprised 12.3 percent of the labor force) are underrepresented by at least 50 percent of their labor force share and those in which they are overrepresented by at least 50 percent. From these lists, select those in which graduates of Mumford and King high schools would most likely find employment, and those in which graduates of the Grosse Pointe schools would find jobs, in most cases after college and professional training.

Table 12.2

Blacks Underrepresented	Blacks Overrepresented
Chief executives	Social service providers
Architects	Health aides
Engineers	Jail and prison staff
Physical scientists	Security guards
Biological scientists	Janitors
Lawyers	Maids and housecleaners
College professors	Laundry workers
Physicians	Taxi drivers

Again, the answers are obvious. It's also worth noting that the median incomes for the professional occupations range between $75,000 and $120,000, while the jobs that don't require college degrees provide incomes below $40,000. In this sense, schools (like those in Detroit and other heavily Black cities) that turn out students with no more than "basic minimal skills" in literacy and math are filling a need for low-skill workers upon which the economic system relies for its functioning. That's not what educators would like to admit, but it's an unfortunate fact, a legacy from the Jim Crow school and housing systems into which most Blacks were forced by law and White racism.

Going back to Detroit's grade schools, it's totally unrealistic to assume that any kids in the Below Basic category on the NAEP exams, even if they are granted a high school diploma, will be able to attend college, much less graduate with a degree in any field. These Below Basic students are, in cold, hard reality, consigned to lives of poverty, unemployment or minimum-wage jobs, single parentage for girls, lower life expectancy than middle-class adults (six years less in Detroit than in adjacent counties), and, for boys, a substantial likelihood of spending years behind bars; nationally, 37 percent of Black males between twenty and thirty-four years old and without a high school diploma are in prison. That's a pretty dire prospect for those Detroit kids.

For most Black kids in Detroit (and those in other highly segregated cities), starting far behind the kids who grow up in largely White city neighborhoods and suburbs begins literally at birth and is closely related to another factor that is more pronounced in Detroit but common to Black children across the country: the extremely high rate of single-parent families, almost all headed by women. Seventy-five percent of Black households with children under eighteen in Detroit are female-headed, the highest rate of the twenty-five largest cities. But even in other cities (including Philadelphia, St. Louis, Milwaukee, Memphis, and Baltimore) more than 60 percent of families are female-headed Black families.

There is no dispute about the huge disparity between Whites and Blacks in terms of female-headed households with children under eighteen. Census data from 2016 shows that 67 percent of Black children are raised in single-parent homes, compared to 25 percent of White children; Hispanics are in the middle at 42 percent. And 73 percent of Black children are born to unwed mothers, although roughly 10 percent of these households also have an adult male (often a brother or grandfather) living with them; just 29 percent of White mothers are unwed, as are 53 percent of Hispanic mothers.

The impact of these differences in family structure on urban Black children has significant life-chance consequences: single (and most often unmarried) Black mothers, not surprisingly, have much greater rates than White mothers of poverty, low education, unemployment or minimum-wage jobs, welfare dependence, and poor nutrition and health problems, including high rates of obesity, diabetes, and heart disease. And their children suffer from the consequences of these conditions, even before birth. The infant mortality rate in Detroit in 2016, at 15 deaths per 1,000 births, is almost three times higher than the national rate of 6 per 1,000 births. In Michigan as a whole, White babies average 7.3 pounds at birth; Black babies, 6.7 pounds. Studies show that this birth-weight disparity, even at half a pound, is connected to both mental and physical developmental problems in early childhood, including language facility and physical mobility.

These consequences of single Black motherhood illustrate the difficulties these young women—many of them teenagers themselves—face in raising their children. By the time Black kids in Detroit begin school, they are already well behind White kids, both in the city and the suburbs, in vocabulary and being read to by parents. A 2012 study by the Brookings Institution showed that fewer than half of children of low-income parents, of all races, are prepared for school with basic reading and number skills, putting them at an immediate disadvantage to their higher-income classmates. Another study measured the amount of time parents spent each day talking with their young children in mutual conversations. The higher-income parents spent almost a half-hour more than low-income parents in face-to-face conversation with their kids. Most likely because of work and family obligations, Black single mothers have even less time or inclination to converse with their young kids.

This "word gap" has significant impacts on both vocabulary and reading comprehension; the extra half-hour of child-parent talking exposed higher-income kids to an amazing 30 million more words by age five, and these kids had vocabularies almost twice as large as the low-income kids. As the Brookings study concluded, "children with higher levels of school readiness at age five are generally more successful in grade school, less likely to drop out of high school, and earn more as adults, even after adjusting for differences in family background." This "readiness gap" gives poor Black kids in Detroit little chance to catch up with White kids in school or later employment. It is the combination of all these disabilities—physical, social, and personal—that inflict what I call "systemic violence" on the Black residents of America's hyper-segregated cities.

As we all know, there are no easy solutions to the deep-rooted and complex problems this book has explored in their differing historical settings, short of a radical restructuring of the institutions that comprise the American social system. But that doesn't mean there aren't programs that will assist Detroit's Black residents—and those in every American city and town—to improve their lives and give their children an equal start in life. To skeptics, I reply that if we can't make this commitment to them, to whom do we owe our compassion and care? Every religion professes that concern for "the least of these" is a command that underlies and motivates every act we perform. Responsible citizenship requires that concern as well, since those in need—of all races—share our citizenship and deserve its protection and benefits.

* * *

This book has been framed by the lynching of Rubin Stacy in 1935 in Fort Lauderdale, Florida, and by the photograph of his bullet-riddled body hanging from a tree limb, with a little White girl—dressed in virginal white—standing just a few feet from his body, viewing it with an enigmatic smile, or perhaps a grimace. We don't know what her emotions really were, but it makes a difference. Whatever her reaction to Rubin's lynching, it was most likely passed on by her parents, and then to her children, and from them to succeeding generations, some probably still in Florida, others scattered around the country. We don't know the values and attitudes of this girl's parents or hers or those of her descendants, of course, but it might be fruitful to imagine ourselves in her place, and what we would have passed on to our children. And to imagine a society in which such atrocities no longer occur, especially the modern-day lynching of young men and women that is the tip of the iceberg of racism that lurks below the surface of the "two societies" into which all Americans have been divided, whether they realize that or not.

I've tried in this book to explore the historical record of American racism from the slavery of the colonial era to the present, in which modern-day lynchings of Black men and women, even children, at the hands of police and White vigilantes have provoked our national reckoning with the destructive consequences of systemic racism and inequality. The extent to which I have succeeded in this self-appointed task I leave to this book's readers. At the very least, I think you have—and hope you will take—an opportunity to think about this nation-defining issue, and hopefully join this debate as informed and concerned citizens. Our times demand no less of us.

Epilogue

I BEGAN WORKING on this book during the first year of Donald Trump's presidency, in 2017. I completed the manuscript shortly before the election on November 3, 2020, but decided to put off this epilogue until the presidential results were confirmed, assuming (rightly) that the outcome would have a significant effect on federal policies to deal with entrenched systemic racism. But like most political pundits on both the right and left, I assumed (wrongly) that a victory by Joe Biden would be followed by a peaceful transition of power, even with Trump's blustering that the election was somehow "rigged" and "stolen" from him by a nationwide conspiracy of "crooked" Democrats. Trump, after all, had fired up his "MAGA Nation" of devoted followers for months before voting began by claiming, dozens of times, "The only way we can lose is if the election is rigged."

The election was not rigged, as both Republican and Democratic local and state election officials agreed. But Trump refused to concede his loss to Biden, even after Christopher Krebs, the Homeland Security Department's top cybersecurity expert, assured a Senate panel that the election was "the most secure in American history." For this apostasy, Trump promptly fired Krebs. Even Trump's loyal attorney general, William Barr, enraged the lame-duck president by stating that the Justice Department "has not seen fraud of a scale that could have effected a different outcome in the election." Trump's anger at this perceived disloyalty prompted Barr to resign a post. He left with a tarnished reputation for doing Trump's bidding, until echoing his baseless "stolen election" claims became too much even for Barr to swallow.

Trump's last-ditch effort to nullify the electoral votes in several swing states Biden won, and to replace them with his loyalists, was planned for January

6, 2021, the day Vice President Mike Pence would open each state's certified tally of electoral votes in the Senate chamber and announce the total: 306 for Biden, 223 for Trump (ironically, the same margin by which Trump defeated Hillary Clinton in 2016). Pence, in effect, would be reading aloud the obituary of Trump's one-term presidency. Trump planned a rally on January 6 on the Ellipse behind the White House to exhort his most devoted fans to march to the Capitol to "Stop the Steal" and demand that the vice president disregard the certified tally sheets and announce Trump's victory. Trump believed (wrongly) that Pence had the power to reject the certified ballots of any state. The morning of the rally, he warned Pence of the retaliation that would follow disobedience: "You can either go down in history as a patriot, or you can go down in history as a pussy." That was Trump's ultimate insult to men who failed to obey his orders unquestioningly.

Pence refused to violate his oath to the Constitution, presiding over the Senate while, a mile away, some ten thousand flag-waving Trump loyalists heeded the president's call to march up Pennsylvania Avenue to surround the Capitol and shout "Stop the Steal" so loudly the senators could hear them. But even before Trump finished his harangue, groups of people, many in full military combat gear, were approaching the Capitol, which was protected only by movable metal barriers. Among the several hundred in the advance group were members of such violent, extremist elements of the broader and long-lasting White Christian Nationalist movement as the Proud Boys, Three Percenters, Boogaloo Bois, Oath Keepers, and several self-styled "militia" groups who trained for armed combat. Leaders and members of these groups heeded Trump's call to arms on January 6. "Be there," he urged. "Will be wild!"

What ensued was more than wild. With platoons of violent extremists at the fore, this quickly became an insurrection, defined in law as a violent effort to overthrow the government or disrupt any of Congress's essential business, which Pence was doing just as rioters breached the Capitol and headed for the Senate chamber, chanting "Hang Mike Pence" after Trump's "pussy" insult spread over Twitter. Secret Service agents hustled Pence and his family to a secure location, saved only by the quick thinking of a heroic Capitol Police officer, Eugene Goodman, who lured rioters up a staircase and away from the Senate chamber. The Capitol Police, overwhelmed and retreating, fought back against the rioters, and Officer Brian Sicknick, who was sprayed in the face with toxic bear spray, died the next day. A rioter who was crawling through a smashed window was shot and killed by an officer; another rioter was crushed to death as rioters fled from tear gas. The FBI, at this writing, has made some four hundred arrests of rioters on charges from trespassing to assault with intent to seriously injure a law enforcement officer.

Scenes of mayhem were broadcast live and endlessly rerun: invasions of both House and Senate chambers, parading a Confederate battle flag around the Rotunda, a rioter wearing a "Camp Auschwitz" sweatshirt, rioters crushing a police officer with a door while others yell, "Get his gun!" All of this happened among a sea of Trump flags, banners, and MAGA hats. Trump was reportedly "excited" to watch the rioting from the safety of the White House, but finally—and grudgingly—yielded to his horrified advisors with a short video urging rioters, some of them murderers, to "go home," assuring them, "We love you; you're very special."

A week after this riot, Trump was impeached by the House of Representatives for "incitement to insurrection." Although the vast majority of congressional Republicans rushed to Trump's defense against impeachment, perhaps the most honest and accurate statement came from Representative Liz Cheney of Wyoming, the third-ranking House Republican and a consistent conservative, who explained her vote—one of only ten Republicans—to impeach Trump:

> The President of the United States summoned this mob, assembled the mob, and lit the flame of this attack. Everything that followed was his doing. None of this would have happened without the President. The President could have immediately and forcefully intervened to stop the violence. He did not. There has never been a greater betrayal by a President of the United States of his office and his oath to the Constitution.

For this act of lèse-majesté, Cheney was formally censured by her state's pro-Trump Republican committee.

Nonetheless, as we know, after a chilling presentation of evidence of Trump's instigation of the riot by the House prosecutors, some in shockingly graphic video shot by rioters themselves, only seven of fifty Republican senators joined all fifty Democrats to convict Trump, ten short of the constitutional minimum of sixty-seven, or two-thirds of senators voting. Also needless to say, Trump, now in exile at his Mar-a-Lago resort in Florida, has vowed electoral revenge against Cheney and the sixteen other GOP apostates in the House and Senate. Time will tell whether these threats succeed or whether the Republican Party has been irrevocably splintered between Trump loyalists and those, like Cheney, who insist the party must disavow him and the violent

racist element that put her life and all those in the Capitol at risk that day—
one on which Trump told his followers, "Remember this day forever." For
most of us, January 6, 2021, will be remembered as we remember December
7, 1941, and September 11, 2001: dates that "will live in infamy," as President
Franklin Roosevelt said of the Pearl Harbor attack.

* * *

Some readers may question the relevance of this recounting to a study of systemic racism in American society. I do this for two interlocked reasons: first,
to note, as we've seen, that the majority of Trump's followers harbor racist
and nativist attitudes toward Blacks, Hispanics, and other ethnic minorities.
Although federal prosecutors and the FBI have thus far identified and charged
some four hundred rioters, thousands more—armed and angry—are spread
across the country. Calls for a "race war" against Blacks still spread through
the dark alleys of the internet. Every year of Trump's presidency was marked
by a dramatic rise in reported hate crimes against Blacks, Hispanics, Jews,
and Asians, all targets of Trump's hostility. What the FBI labels "domestic
violent extremism" is likely to find new targets among those who denounce
systemic racism and propose legislative measures to combat the historic inequality of Black Americans. Already, Black members of Congress who voted
to impeach Trump (and White members as well) have received death threats,
some directed against family members and children. To dismiss these dangers
as hyperbolic is to imitate the ostrich. The obstacles to significant and meaningful efforts to root out systemic racism include the potentially violent backlash from White racists, much like the violent and deadly resistance to school
integration after the *Brown* decision in 1954.

My second reason for looking back at the 2020 election and its violent
aftermath is that, for the first time in American history, the issue of systemic
racism was raised and discussed by a presidential candidate. During the campaign, Trump replied, "I don't believe that," when asked if systemic racism
existed in law enforcement, repeating his "few bad apples" refrain. Joe Biden,
for his part, promised that his administration would make a priority of
"rooting out systemic racism from our laws, our policies, our institutions, and
our hearts." Pressed by the Democratic Party's growing progressive wing and
his own commitment to racial justice (despite some earlier lapses, such as opposing busing as part of school integration plans, a stand he later recanted),
Biden released a lengthy and detailed policy and legislative agenda entitled
"Lift Every Voice: The Biden Plan for Black America" (borrowing the first

phrase from the song by the brother duo of James Weldon Johnson and John Rosamond Johnson, first performed in 1900 and now popularly called "The Black National Anthem"). The Biden Plan listed six goals:

- Advance the economic mobility of African Americans and close the racial wealth and income gaps.
- Expand access to high-quality education and tackle racial inequity in our education system.
- Make far-reaching investments in ending health disparities by race.
- Strengthen America's commitment to justice.
- Make the right to vote and the right to equal protection real for African Americans.
- Address environmental justice.

For each of these aspirational goals, the Biden Plan attached dozens of specific policies and programs, such as payments to Black farmers who had received far less in federal aid than more prosperous White farmers, a form of reparations that recalls Reconstruction-era promises of "forty acres and a mule" with few acres or mules actually granted to Black farmers. Political candidates routinely offer laundry-list "plans" to remedy real and perceived social ills, but Biden's was unique in squarely confronting systemic racism.

With the new administration just beginning at this writing, and with narrow majorities in both chambers of Congress (aided by Vice President Kamala Harris as the tie-breaking vote in an evenly divided Senate), the ultimate fate of Biden's plan and its components remains to be seen; as with the Supreme Court and the Roman Catholic papacy, one death or retirement can shift a body's ideological balance from right to left or vice versa. One thing is certain, however: the Republicans in Congress will do everything in their power (short of insurrection, we hope) to make Biden "a one-term president," as Senate minority leader Mitch McConnell had vowed (but failed) to deny Barack Obama a second term. The current rash of voter suppression laws proposed or enacted by poor-loser Republicans, more than 250 such laws in more than forty states, are clearly aimed at making it harder for Blacks and other minorities to cast their votes; this partisan assault on democracy was rightly denounced by President Biden as "Jim Crow in the 21st century."

* * *

There are many reasons Biden won the election and brought out a record number of voters. Two issues in particular were cited as "very important" in their presidential choice by a majority of voters in a preelection Gallup poll: the president's handling of the coronavirus pandemic by 62 percent, and race and ethnic inequality by 52 percent. Both of these issues also raise the deeper issue of systemic racism. Biden's relentless attacks on Trump for denying the dangers of Covid-19 and disparaging and even mocking proven mitigation behavior, such as mask wearing in public and maintaining social distancing at gatherings, proved effective, according to postelection polls. Trump's bungling of the pandemic response had a deadly effect on the public at large, but especially on Black Americans.

There's an old saying with more than a kernel of truth: "When White folks catch a cold, Black folks get pneumonia." The coronavirus story has lots of numbers: the daily and cumulative tally of infections, hospitalizations, and deaths. Many saw those numbers daily on their TV or computer screens and perhaps became numb as they went up or down. One number, however, reported on the WebMD site on February 18, 2021, literally jumped from my screen: "U.S. Life Expectancy Drops 1 Full Year Due to Covid-19." That's the biggest drop since World War II, and is certainly disturbing news. But the real news for me was this first statistic: "Black male life expectancy dropped by three years (71.3 to 68.3)." Black females had a 2.3-year drop, from 78.1 to 75.8. "By comparison," the report concluded, "white males had a decline in life expectancy of 0.8 years (76.3 to 75.5), while white women had a 0.7 decline (81.3 to 80.6)." There's no genetic or biological cause for these racial disparities. The causality, experts in the field agree, lies in the deprived social conditions that Blacks disproportionately endure, especially those in "the truly disadvantaged" group, who live below the poverty line: densely populated neighborhoods, overcrowded homes, multigenerational and extended families in one home, food insecurity and bad diets, jobs (such as restaurant and hotel workers, bus drivers, and grocery clerks) that require face-to-face contact, and higher levels than Whites of "comorbidities," or preexisting conditions, such as obesity, diabetes, hypertension, and circulatory problems, each of which carries a higher risk of severe Covid-19 and death. That helps explain why significantly more Blacks have been getting infected and dying of Covid-19 and its complications than Whites. As of February 2021, exactly one year after the first reported U.S. Covid-19 death, Blacks were 230 percent more likely to die than Whites. Put another way, 1 of every 645 Blacks died of Covid-19 that year, compared to 1 of every 825 whites. Or another: if Blacks died from Covid-19 at the same rate as Whites, roughly fifty thousand Blacks would still be alive at this writing, on the day the reported U.S. death toll reached 500,000. These figures are cause for mourning the victims, of course, but the racial disparity is deeply rooted in systemic racism that places Blacks at greater risk of early death and susceptibility to disease. Any other explanation would constitute a form of "blaming the victims" for exposing themselves to the virus, while holding their White suburban neighbors blameless for the conditions that more rapidly spread it.

A January 2021 report in the prestigious *Journal of the American Medical Association* summarized the relationship between Covid-19 and disparities in morbidity and mortality:

> Covid-19 is not simply a problem of people of certain races/ethnicities or socioeconomic position living in certain cities. Longstanding social inequities—and the living and working conditions they generate—are associated with many aspects of the pandemic, including its severity and timing.
>
> Furthermore, the profound economic impact of the pandemic, including the stay-at-home orders and other public health emergency policies necessary to contain [Covid-19], will likely only exacerbate inequities in the social determinants of health, including unemployment, poverty, food insecurity, poor quality education, lack of health insurance or paid sick leave, and lack of access to the Internet. These social conditions, driven by public policy choices, in turn may create a vicious cycle of increasing disease transmission and perpetuation of inequities in Covid-19 outcomes if underlying social factors are not considered and addressed. . . . The difficult but crucial task for local, regional, and national policy makers will be to address, in addition to downstream health care issues, the numerous upstream and midstream social factors associated with health and health care disparities.

Tackling these disparities, of course, will require both short-term and long-range programs to uproot systemic racism in the institutions on which all Americans depend: education, housing, employment, healthcare, and law enforcement. Not an easy task, but vitally necessary to bring together the "two societies, one black, one white—separate and unequal," of which the Kerner Commission warned in 1968.

* * *

Another date that should "live in infamy" as a stain on American society, along with the Capitol insurrection, is May 25, 2020. At about 8:00 p.m. that night, police in Minneapolis, Minnesota, arrested a forty-six-year-old Black man, George Floyd, for allegedly trying to pass a counterfeit $20 bill at a convenience store in the largely Black Longfellow neighborhood. Although witnesses agreed that Floyd had complied with orders (with a gun pointed at him) to get out of the car in which he was sitting, he resisted being shoved into the backseat of a squad car, telling the officers he was claustrophobic. He was handcuffed by Officer Derek Chauvin, who forced Floyd to lie prone on the pavement, next to a police car, with his cuffed hands behind his back. Chauvin then pressed a knee against Floyd's neck for nine minutes and twenty-nine seconds, the entire event captured on a passerby's phone camera. During his last minutes of life, Floyd repeatedly gasped "I can't breathe" and called for "Mama," who had died two years earlier. Floyd became still and un-responsive for two or three minutes before Chauvin, who had been chatting with three other officers at the scene during this time, finally lifted his knee from Floyd's neck. He was dead.

Before we look more closely at George Floyd's murder—Officer Chauvin, with a past record of complaints of excessive force against Blacks, was charged with several counts of homicide, including manslaughter and second-degree murder—one point needs to be set in boldface: **George Floyd would never have been arrested and killed by a police officer had he been a neatly dressed White person**. The store clerk would likely have accepted the sup-posedly phony bill without close scrutiny unless it was an obvious forgery, or would have returned it in exchange for a genuine bill; the White person would probably have said, "My goodness, I don't know where that came from," and leave, unmolested and still alive. But George Floyd was suffocated and died because, and only because, he was Black. Again, to dispute this fact is to imitate the ostrich.

George Floyd, of course, was hardly the first unarmed Black man or woman to be killed by police or self-appointed White vigilantes in recent years. One list in February 2021 included the names of 104 unarmed Black men, women, and children killed since George Zimmerman, a White armed "neighborhood watch" volunteer at a gated Florida apartment complex, shot and killed Trayvon Martin, a seventeen-year-old Black boy visiting relatives on the night of February 26, 2012. Trayvon was returning from a store with a bag of Skittles and a soft drink when Zimmerman accosted him and fatally shot him. After much public outcry and legal wrangling, Zimmerman was finally charged with second-degree murder; he pled not guilty, claiming he shot Trayvon in self-defense. A six-person jury acquitted him after a trial in July 2013.

I mention Trayvon's case and Zimmerman's acquittal because it sparked a movement with direct links to the eruption of massive, nationwide protests of George Floyd's murder, which spanned the country—from Boston to Los Angeles, Seattle to Miami—and spurred an estimated 15 to 20 million people of all races to march with banners and handmade signs saying "I Can't Breathe" and chanting "Say His Name—George Floyd." The most prominent banner at these marches read "Black Lives Matter." This was the name chosen for the movement founded in 2013 by three radical Black women and organizers: Alicia Garza, Patrisse Cullors, and Opal Tometi. The following year, in August 2014, the murder of eighteen-year-old Michael Brown by a White policeman in the majority-Black St. Louis suburb of Ferguson, Missouri, propelled Black Lives Matter (BLM) into national (and international) prominence through protest marches and organizing at the grassroots level. By the time of George Floyd's murder, BLM had become a symbol on both ends of the political spectrum, praised by progressives and attacked by President Trump (who called the BLM acronym a symbol of "hate") and his media megaphones as dangerous rioters and anarchists, although BLM leaders denounced the looting and arson at some protests by opportunists with no connection to the group. BLM activists helped organize and mobilize the massive turnout of Black voters and White sympathizers that propelled Biden to the White House, but most took a "wait and see" attitude toward Biden's promises of forceful action to combat systemic racism in law enforcement and other institutions.

There's no one person who can epitomize all the injuries inflicted on Black people by systemic racism, and few who successfully overcome the disability of a prison record. George Floyd was one of those few. Born in Fayetteville, North Carolina, in 1973, he moved with his single mother, Larcenia "Cissy" Floyd, to Houston, Texas, when he was two, living in a sprawling, red-brick public housing project known as "the Bricks" in the city's largely Black Third Ward, one of the poorest and most crime-ridden neighborhoods. Over six feet tall in middle school (he would grow to six-six) and known as "Big Floyd," he starred on his high school football and basketball teams, catching a touchdown pass in a state championship game. His athletic skill earned him a football scholarship to a Florida state college; he returned to Texas after two years for a year at Texas A&M University, Kingsville, where he played basketball but dropped out in 1995 to return to the Bricks in Houston and his family. Things went badly then: between 1997 and 2005, Floyd was jailed eight times for drug possession and other crimes, the first arrest for a $10 drug deal that cost him ten months in jail. In 2007, he was charged with armed robbery, pleaded guilty in 2009, and spent four years in prison, before his release on parole in 2013. By most (White) standards, Floyd was a dangerous ex-felon with few job prospects and most likely a chronic recidivist. But he turned his life around, becoming active in a Christian ministry that helped young Black men gain skills to keep them out of prison. The ministry also had a program in Minneapolis that included drug rehabilitation; Floyd had become addicted to prescription narcotics for old sports injuries and completed a ninety-day rehab program after moving from Houston, finding work as a security guard at a Salvation Army shelter for homeless men, and then as a nightclub bouncer. Known to patrons as "Friendly Floyd," he used his size (230 pounds) and quiet approach to defuse tense confrontations. Jovanni Thunstrom, the club's owner, found him a welcome employee, who came in early and stayed late. "Right away, I liked his attitude," he said of Floyd. "He would shake your hand with both hands. He would bend down to greet you." Floyd made a point of walking the club's female employees to their cars after dark as a protective measure.

We can look at George Floyd from radically different perspectives. Some would dismiss him as an ex-con who deserved what he got for trying to pass a phony bill. Others saw him as an example of redemption, helping young Black men and boys to avoid the violence and crime that prematurely ended too many lives and put others behind prison bars for years, some for life. Growing up in a neighborhood that showed all the effects of systemic racism—poor housing, poor schools, poor jobs, poor health—it's a sad commentary on American society that George Floyd is remembered more for his murder under the knee of a racist cop than for his efforts to overcome the disabilities and dangers that face every Black boy and girl in the Third Wards of every American city, all struggling to escape the systemic racism that rests solely on the skin color of their residents.

I'm writing these final words just hours after the jury in Derek Chauvin's trial returned guilty verdicts on all three homicide charges against him, on April 20, 2021. The case against Chauvin depended less on medical testimony and that of police officials who denounced him for egregiously violating on the proper use of force in making arrests than on the nine minutes and twenty-nine seconds of cellphone video of Chavin grinding his knee into George Floyd's neck, his hand in a pocket and his face glaring defiantly at horrified bystanders who pleaded with him to let his victim breathe. Hundreds of people outside the courthouse cheered and danced, some shedding tears, on hearing the guilty verdicts. In his comments shortly after the verdicts, President Joe Biden once again voiced his support for laws and policies to combat "systemic racism" in all American institutions, not only law enforcement.

With celebrations still going on across the country as I write, we need to soberly confront two realities: first, that these verdicts will not bring George Floyd back to life, or any of the thousands or Black men and women murdered in the name of lynch law before him; and second, that there will undoubtedly be more killings of unarmed Black and Brown people by police and self-appointed White vigilantes. Hopefully, fewer lives will be lost as police departments improve their recruitment and training programs and further break down the "blue wall of silence" that Minneapolis police officials renounced in testifying against one of their own. But this verdict may, again hopefully, stimulate efforts in both Congress and state legislatures to pass meaningful police reform.

Perhaps the best tribute to George Floyd came from his six-year-old daughter, Gianna. "Daddy changed the world," she said of the father she lost to White racism. It's too early to know if Gianna was right, but it's up to the rest of us to make that happen, with no guarantee of ultimate success in rooting out systemic racism. But, to quote again the challenge from Mother Jones of a century ago, "Pray for the dead, and fight like hell for the living." That's what we can—and must—do to honor the life and death of George Floyd, one of the thousands of Black men, women, and children—including Rubin Stacy in 1935—murdered only because their skin was dark. America must reckon with that bloody legacy or abandon the Constitution's promise of "equal protection of the law" to every person within the nation's borders. The reign of White Men's Law must end.

April 2021

Source Notes and Suggested Reading

Most historians these days, aside from those who toil in dusty, undigitized archives, rely heavily in their research on the internet. Vast amounts of information and data are posted daily, much of it previously available only in out-of-print books, obscure journals, and other hard-to-find sources. That's both a blessing and a curse for historians. Virtually all the material in this book, including much that I quote from books, is just a few clicks away from my screen. But there's also a lot more chaff to winnow through, much of it repetitive or off-topic. In searching for material, I use my judgment as to which sites are credible and reliable; much of what I use is from official sources: government reports, judicial opinions, census data, and social statistics. I also rely on the internet for biographical data, accounts of events, and links to original sources (what courts call "judicial notice" material, of verifiable accuracy). For my needs, I've found that Wikipedia entries are generally reliable, and most have citations to original and secondary sources.

I should also note that some of what I've written has been adapted (and most often substantially condensed and revised) from two of my earlier books: *A People's History of the Supreme Court* and *Jim Crow's Children: The Broken Promise of the* Brown *Decision*. In those books, I wrote about Supreme Court cases I also discuss in this book. Readers who wish to learn more about those cases can find fuller accounts in those two books, which I cite in the source notes; those books are copiously sourced for readers who might want to look more closely at particular cases. I also cite books by other writers on each chapter's topics and a separate listing of books on topics that recur in this one.

A final note about citations to Supreme Court opinions: the Court's official publication is *United States Reports*, with citation to case name, volume, first page, and year of decision, for example, *Plessy v. Ferguson*, 163 U.S. 537 (1895). The full text of opinions can be found on several legal websites by entering the case name.

PROLOGUE: "THEY'VE GOT HIM!"

Account of Rubin Stacy's lynching: Bryan Brooks, "The Day They Lynched Reuben Stacey" [*sic*], Fort Lauderdale *Sun-Sentinel*, July 17, 1988; Emma Sipperly, *The Rubin*

Stacy Lynching: Reconstructing Justice, Northeastern University School of Law, Civil Rights and Restorative Justice Clinic, Fall 2016.

Costigan-Wagner antilynching bill: "NAACP History: Costigan Wagner Bill," naacp. org; Robert L. Zangrando, "The NAACP and a Federal Antilynching Bill, 1934–1940," *Journal of Negro History* 50, no. 2 (April 1965): 106–17; see generally Philip Drey, *At the Hands of Persons Unknown: The Lynching of Black America*, 2005.

Genealogical data on Rubin Stacy and the Jones family: this material is taken from name searches on the Ancestry.com website (fee required) and U.S. and Florida census records.

CHAPTER 1: "THIRTY LASHES, WELL LAID ON"

Virginia settler cannibalism: Deborah Zabarenko, "Starving Virginia Settlers Turned to Cannibalism in 1609: Study," *Reuters News*, May 1, 2013; Dennis Montgomery, "Such a Dish as Powdered Wife I Never Heard Of," *Colonial Williamsburg Journal*, Winter 2007.

Case of Elizabeth Key: "Elizabeth Key Grinstead," Wikipedia entry; Taunya Lovell Banks, "Dangerous Woman: Elizabeth Key's Freedom Suit—Subjecthood and Racialized Identity in Seventeenth Century Colonial Virginia," *Akron Law Review* 41 (2008); "Elizabeth Key Grinstead, the Freedom Suit, and Colonial Virginia," americanhistoryusa.com.

Virginia slave code: "Slave Law in Virginia: A Timeline," shsu.edu.

Stono Rebellion: "Two Views of the Stono Slave Rebellion, South Carolina, 1739," nationalhumanitiescenter.org; Lisa Vox, "Impact of the Stono Rebellion on the Lives of Enslaved People," December 15, 2020, thoughtco.com; Mark M. Smith, *Stono: Documenting and Interpreting a Southern Slave Revolt* (Columbia: University of South Carolina Press, 2005).

New York arson plot: Douglas O. Linder, "The New York Conspiracy ('Negro Plot') Trials: An Account," famous-trials.com; "Trials Relating to the New York Slave Insurrection, 1741," Historical Society of the New York Courts, history.nycourts. gov.

Banning the teaching of slaves: Peter Irons, *Jim Crow's Children: The Broken Promise of the Brown Case*, 2002, 1–6 (hereafter Irons, *Jim Crow's Children*); see also Carter G. Woodson, *The Education of the Negro Prior to 1861* (1919); Henry Allen Bullock, *A History of Negro Education in the South* (1967).

Drafting of the Constitution: Peter Irons, *A People's History of the Supreme Court*, 1999, 17–82; James Madison, *Notes of Debates in the Federal Convention of 1787*, various editions (almost all quotes are from Madison's *Notes*).

General works: Lerone Bennett, *Before the Mayflower: A History of Black America*, 1962; Betty Wood, *Slavery in Colonial America, 1619–1776*, 2005; Edmund S. Morgan, *American Slavery—American Freedom: The Ordeal of Colonial Virginia*, 1975.

CHAPTER 2: "DEM WAS HARD TIMES, SHO' NUFF"

John Calhoun speech: Copies can be found on several websites; one is "Slavery a Positive Good—Teaching American History," teachingamericanhistory.org. See also Larry Edward Tice, *The "Positive Good" Thesis and Proslavery Arguments in Britain and America, 1701–1861* (Athens: University Press of Georgia, 1987). A recent biography is Robert Elder, *Calhoun: American Heretic*, 2021.

George Fitzhugh book excerpt: George Fitzhugh, *Cannibals All! Or, Slaves without Masters* (Richmond, VA: A. Morris, 1857). The only biography of Fitzhugh is Harvey Wish, *George Fitzhugh, Propagandist of the Old South*, 1943.

Jefferson Davis speech: for full text, see "Document: Farewell Speech, Jefferson Davis, January 21, 1861," teachingamericanhistory.org; for a biography, see William C. Davis (no relation), *Jefferson Davis: The Man and His Hour*, 1992.

Alexander Stephens speech: for full text, see "Alexander Stephens, Cornerstone Speech, Savannah, Georgia, March 21, 1861," American Battlefield Trust, battlefields. org; for a biography, see Thomas E. Schott, *Alexander H. Stephens of Georgia: A Biography*, 1996.

Excerpts of slave narratives: Ira Berlin, Marc Favreau, and Steven F. Miller, eds., *Remembering Slavery*, 1998; a complete collection of all 2,300 slave narratives can be found in the seventeen-volume *Slave Narratives: A Folk History of Slavery in the United States from Interviews with Former Slaves* (Washington, DC: Library of Congress, 1941). All narratives can be found online: "Born in Slavery: Slave Narratives from the Federal Writers' Project, 1936 to 1938," at loc.gov.

For general works on slavery and slaves, see Kenneth M. Stampp, *The Peculiar Institution: Slavery in the Antebellum South*, 1956; Federal Writers' Project, *These Are Our Lives* (slave narratives), 1939; Project Gutenberg, *Slave Narratives: An Online Anthology*, 2007; Paul Finkelman, *Defending Slavery: Proslavery Thought in the Old South*, 2003.

CHAPTER 3: "BEINGS OF AN INFERIOR ORDER"

Prigg case: *Prigg v. Pennsylvania*, 41 U.S. 539 (1842); Irons, *People's History*, 151–53; see also H. Robert Baker, *Prigg v. Pennsylvania: Slavery, the Supreme Court, and the Ambivalent Constitution*, 2012.

George Latimer rendition case: Irons, *People's History*, 152–53.

Anthony Burns rendition case: Irons, *People's History*, 153.

Dred Scott biography, Irons, *People's History*, 157–63.

Dred Scott case: The official citation is *Scott v. Sandford*, 60 U.S. 393 (1857). Discussion of Supreme Court decision, Irons, *People's History*, 163–78. See also Don E. Fehrenbacher, *The Dred Scott Case: Its Significance in American Law and Politics*, 1978; Amy Van Zee, *Dred Scott v. Sandford: Slavery and Freedom before the Civil War*, 2012.

Abraham Lincoln on "social equality" of races: *Collected Works of Abraham Lincoln*, vol. 3, quod.lib.umich.edu.

CHAPTER 4: "FIGHTING FOR WHITE SUPREMACY"

Freed slave reactions to emancipation: adapted from Lonnie G. Bunch, "Emancipation Evoked Mix of Emotions for Freed Slaves," *Washington Post*, September 7, 2012, washingtonpost.com.

Lincoln and Thirteenth Amendment: "I Am President of the United States, Clothed with Immense Power," *Atlantic*, October 29, 2012, wjml.blogspot.com.

Adoption of Fourteenth Amendment: Irons, *People's History*, 193–230.

Anna Baker and Klan night-riders: "Slave Narrative of Anna Baker," accessgenealogy. com.

Freedmen's Bureau and education of Black children: Irons, *Jim Crow's Children*, 7–11; also see Horace Mann Bond, *The Education of the Negro in the American Social Order*, 1934.

Colfax Massacre and *Cruikshank* case: Irons, *People's History*, 202–5; *United States v. Cruikshank*, 92 U.S. 452 (1875). Also see Charles Lane, *The Day Freedom Died: The Colfax Massacre, the Supreme Court, and the Betrayal of Reconstruction*, 2006; Leeanna Keith, *The Colfax Massacre: The Untold Story of Black Power, White Terror, and the Death of Reconstruction*, 2007.

On Reconstruction generally, see Eric Foner, *Reconstruction: America's Unfinished Revolution*, 1988; Eric Foner, *The Second Founding: How the Civil War and Reconstruction Remade the Constitution*, 2019; W. E. B. Du Bois, *Black Reconstruction in America: 1860–1880*, 1935; Harold Hyman, *A More Perfect Union: The Impact of the Civil War and Reconstruction on the Constitution*, 1973; Henry Louis Gates Jr., *Stony the Road: Reconstruction, White Supremacy, and the Rise of Jim Crow*, 2019.

CHAPTER 5: "THE FOUL ODORS OF BLACKS"

Supreme Court and Civil Rights cases: indictments in Philip B. Kurland and Gerhard Casper, eds., *Landmark Briefs and Arguments of the Supreme Court*, vol. 8, 307, 311–12, 355, 334–35 (hereafter *Landmark Briefs*).

Decision in *Civil Rights Cases*: *Civil Rights Cases*, 109 U.S. 3 (1883); Irons, *People's History*, 211–15.

Benjamin Tillman and Red Shirt massacres: "Benjamin Tillman," Wikipedia; "Ben Tillman Was a Racist, Terrorist, and Murderer," *Charleston City Paper*, February 5, 2014; "Tillman, Benjamin Ryan," *South Carolina Encyclopedia*, scencyclopedia. org; "South Carolina Red Shirts," Wikipedia; "Hamburg Massacre," Wikipedia; "Benjamin Tillman," Wikiquote.

Mississippi constitutional convention 1890: "Mississippi Constitution, 1890," Wikipedia.

Homer Plessy case: Irons, *People's History*, 221–32; Tourgée brief, *Landmark Briefs*, vol. 13, 62–63; Supreme Court opinions, *Plessy v. Ferguson*, 163 U.S. 537 (1895); also see Williamjames Hoffer, *Plessy v. Ferguson: Race and Inequality in Jim Crow America*, 2012; Steve Luxenberg, *Separate: The Story of Plessy v. Ferguson, and America's Journey from Slavery to Segregation*, 2019; C. Vann Woodward, *The Strange Career of Jim Crow*, 1955; Greg W. Gallagher and Alan T. Nolan, *The Myth of the Lost Cause and Civil War History*, 2000; Edward H. Bonekemper III, *The Myth of the Lost Cause: Why the South Fought the Civil War and Why the North Won*, 2015.

CHAPTER 6: "NEGROES PLAN TO KILL ALL WHITES"

W. E. B. Du Bois biography: "W. E. B. Du Bois," Wikipedia; for "Twentieth Century" quote, see W. E. B. Du Bois, *The Souls of Black Folk*, 1903 (several editions available); W. E. B. Du Bois, *The Philadelphia Negro*, 1899. An excellent biography is David Levering Lewis, *W. E. B. Du Bois: A Biography 1868–1963* (2009).

Sam Hose lynching: "At the Hands of Persons Unknown: The Lynching of Sam Hose," *Washington Post*, March 8, 2002.

The Great Migration: there are many books and articles on the Great Migration; see especially Nicholas Lehmann, *The Promised Land: The Great Black Migration and How It Changed America*, 1992; James N. Gregory, *The Southern Diaspora: How the Great Migrations of Black and White Southerners Transformed America*, 2007; Isabel Wilkerson, *The Warmth of Other Suns: The Epic Story of America's Great Migration*, 2013.

Woodrow Wilson and racism: Judson MacLaury, "The Federal Government and Negro Workers under President Woodrow Wilson," U.S. Department of Labor, March 16, 2000; "The Birth of a Nation," Wikipedia; "President Woodrow Wilson and His Racist Legacy," *Atlantic*, November 27, 2015.

Washington, D.C., race riot: "Washington Race Riot of 1919," Wikipedia; Abigail Higgins, "Red Summer of 1919: How Black WWI Vets Fought Back against Racist Mobs," July 26, 2019, history.com; Rawn James Jr., "The Forgotten Washington Race War of 1919," March 7, 2010, historynewsnetwork.org.

Chicago race riot: "Chicago Race Riot of 1919," Wikipedia; "The Chicago Race Riot of 1919," December 2, 2009, history.com; "The Red Summer of 1919," Chicago History Museum, chicagohistory.org; Cate Cauguiran, "Chicago Shootings: Family of Sincere Gaston, 1-Year-Old Killed in Chicago Shooting, Remember Toddler on 2nd Birthday," October 15, 2020, abc7chicago.com.

Elaine, Arkansas, massacre: "Elaine Massacre," Wikipedia; "What Was the Elaine Massacre?," *Smithsonian Magazine*, August 2, 2018, smithsonianmag.com; books include J. Chester Johnson, *Damaged Heritage: The Elaine Race Massacre and a*

Story of Reconciliation, 2020; Grif Stockley, Brian K. Mitchell, and Guy Lancaster, *Blood in Their Eyes: The Elaine Massacre of 1919*, 2001.

Elaine Massacre and *Moore v. Dempsey* case: *Moore v. Dempsey*, 261 U.S. 86 (1923); "Moore v. Dempsey," *Encyclopedia of Arkansas*, encyclopediaofarkansas.net.

Tulsa, Oklahoma, Massacre: "Tulsa Race Massacre," Wikipedia; "1921 Tulsa Race Massacre," Tulsa Historical Society & Museum," tulsahistory.org; Tim Madigan, *The Burning: Massacre, Destruction, and the Tulsa Race Riot of 1921*, 2001. On search for mass graves, see "Tulsa Searches for Mass Graves from the 1921 Tulsa Race Massacre," *Washington Post*, October 8, 2019.

Detroit history: "History of Detroit," Wikipedia; population statistics from U.S. Census records.

Ossian Sweet case: "Ossian Sweet," Wikipedia; Heather Bourbeau, "Dr. Ossian Sweet's Black Life Mattered," June 17, 2015, daily.jstor.org; an excellent recent book on the case is Kevin Boyle, *Arc of Justice: A Saga of Race, Civil Rights, and Murder in the Jazz Age*, 2004.

General works: Thomas Sugrue, *Sweet Land of Liberty: The Forgotten Struggle for Civil Rights in the North*, 2008; Cameron McWhirter, *Red Summer: The Summer of 1919 and the Awakening of Black America*, 2011.

CHAPTER 7: "INTIMATE CONTACT WITH NEGRO MEN"

McKinley Brown interview: "A Report on Negro Needs in Alabama," Give Unto These (a Chicago-based charity) newsletter, Fall 1931.

Neal Quinn lynching: Associated Press, "Negro Boy Is Killed by Mob in Alabama," Racine, Wisconsin, *Journal Times*, August 6, 1931.

Herbert Hoover quotes: "Before FDR, Herbert Hoover Tried His Own 'New Deal,'" history.com; "State of the Union Address: Herbert Hoover (December 2, 1930)," Infoplease.com/government.

FDR Inaugural address: "First Inaugural Address of Franklin D. Roosevelt," March 4, 1933, Avalon.law.yale.edu. Many versions are available on the internet.

Mary McLeod Bethune and Black Cabinet: "Mary McLeod Bethune," Wikipedia; Charles M. Blow, "Race, to the Finish," *New York Times*, November 12, 2014; Jill Watts, *The Black Cabinet: The Untold Story of African Americans and Politics during the Age of Roosevelt*, 2020.

Boston school segregation case: Opinion at *Roberts v. City of Boston*, 59 Mass. 198 (1849); Stephen Kendrick and Paul Kendrick, *Sarah's Long Walk: The Free Blacks of Boston and How Their Struggle for Equality Changed America*, 2006.

Margold Report: Mark Tushnet, *The NAACP's Legal Strategy against Segregated Education, 1925–1950*, 2004.

Thurgood Marshall and *Murray* case: *Murray v. Pearson*, 169 Md. 478 (1936); "Murray v. Pearson," Wikipedia; Molly Rath, "Desegregation Begins," *Baltimore Magazine*, July 2007.

Lloyd Gaines case: *Missouri ex re. Gaines*, 305 U.S. 337 (1938); "Missouri ex rel. Gaines v. Canada," Wikipedia; James W. Endersby and William T. Horner, *Lloyd Gaines and the Fight to End Segregation*, 2016.

Asa Philip Randolph: "A. Philip Randolph," Wikipedia; Jervis Anderson, *A. Philip Randolph: A Biographical Portrait*, 1973; Daniel S. Davis, *Mr. Black Labor: The Story of A. Philip Randolph, Father of the Civil Rights Movement*, 1972; Andrew E. Kersten, *A. Philip Randolph: A Life in the Vanguard*, 2006.

Beaumont, Texas, race riot: "Beaumont Race Riot, 1943," blackpast.org; "Beaumont Race Riot of 1943," Wikipedia; Sarah Moore, "World War II Prosperity Gave Way to Racial Violence in 1943," *Beaumont Enterprise*, June 12, 2009.

Detroit race riot of 1943: "Detroit Race Riot (1943)," July 3, 2008, blackpast.org; "1943 Detroit Race Riot," Wikipedia; "Race Riot of 1943," *Encyclopedia of Detroit*, detroithistorical.org; Richard Bak, "Detroit's 'Other' Riot," April 25, 2017, hourdetroit.com.

Isaac Woodard blinding: "Isaac Woodard," Wikipedia; John Egerton, *Speak Now Against the Day*, 1994; Michael Gardner, *Harry Truman and Civil Rights: Moral Courage and Political Risks*, 2002; Richard Gergel, *Unexampled Courage: The Blinding of Sgt. Isaac Woodard and the Awakening of President Harry S. Truman and Judge J. Waties Waring*, 2019.

Ada Sipuel case: *Sipuel v. Board of Regents of the University of Oklahoma*, 332 U.S. 631 (1948); "Ada Lois Sipuel Fisher," Wikipedia; William Bernhardt and Kim Henry, *Equal Justice: The Courage of Ada Sipuel*, 2006

Heman Sweatt case: *Sweatt v. Painter*, 339 U.S. 629 (1950); "Sweatt v. Painter," Wikipedia; Gary M. Lavergne, *Before Brown: Heman Marion Sweatt, Thurgood Marshall, and the Long Road to Justice*, 2010.

George McLaurin case: *McLaurin v. Oklahoma State Regents*, 339 U.S. 637 (1950); "George W. McLaurin," Wikipedia; "Oklahoma University Told to Admit Negro; Regents Put Him on 'Segregated Basis,'" *New York Times*, October 12, 1948; "Separate and Unequal: Two Black Student Pioneers Who Were Treated as Social Pariahs at Predominantly White Universities," *Journal of Blacks in Higher Education* 47 (2005).

Books on Blacks in the Great Depression and World War II: Cheryl Lynn Greenberg, *To Ask for an Equal Chance: African Americans in the Great Depression*, 2009; Harvard Sitkoff, *A New Deal for Blacks: The Emergence of Civil Rights as a National Issue: The Depression Decade*, 2009; Richard Rothstein, *The Color of Law: A Forgotten History of How Our Government Segregated America*, 2017.

CHAPTER 8: "I THANKED GOD RIGHT THEN AND THERE"

The accounts in this chapter of the school segregation cases are largely drawn from fuller accounts in two books: Irons, *Jim Crow's Children* and Richard Kluger, *Simple Justice: The History of* Brown v. Board of Education *and Black America's Struggle for Equality*, 1976.

Clarendon County, South Carolina, case: Irons, *Jim Crow's Children*, ch. 3; Kluger, *Simple Justice*, chs. 1 and 13; story of Annie Martin Gibson, interview with author in Summerton, S.C., October 1999; history of Scott's Branch schools, *The Growth and Development of Schools for Negroes in Clarendon County from 1670 to 1966*, Clarendon County Teachers Association, mimeograph, 1997; statistics on Clarendon County from U.S. Census, 1950; trial transcript in *Briggs v. Elliott*, filed under Civil Action No. 2657, U.S. District Court, Charleston, S.C.; opinions of three-judge panel, 98 F.Supp. 529 (E.D.S.C. 1951); 103 F.Supp. 920 (E.D.S.C. 1952).

Prince Edward County, Virginia, case: Irons, *Jim Crow's Children*, ch. 5; Kluger, *Simple Justice*, chs. 19 and 20; Bob Smith, *They Closed Their Schools*, 1965; files of Farmville, Virginia, *Herald*; trial transcript in *Davis* case filed under Civil Action No. 1333 (1951), U.S. District Court, Richmond, Va.; opinion of three-judge court, 103 F.Supp. 337 (E.D.Va. 1952).

Washington, D.C., case: Irons, *Jim Crow's Children*, ch. 6; Kluger, *Simple Justice*, ch. 21; see also Constance M. Green, *The Secret City: A History of Race Relations in the Nation's Capital*, 1967; Carl F. Hansen, *Danger in Washington: The Story of My Twenty Years in the Public Schools in the Nation's Capital*, 1968 (Hansen was superintendent of schools during the integration period).

Delaware cases: Irons, *Jim Crow's Children*, ch. 6; Kluger, *Simple Justice*, ch. 18; state court opinions in *Gebhart v. Belton* and *Gebhart v. Bulah*, 87 A.2d 862 (Del. Chancery Ct., 1952); 91 A.2d. 137 (Del. 1953).

Topeka, Kansas, case: Irons, *Jim Crow's Children*, ch. 7; Kluger, *Simple Justice*, chs. 16 and 17; also see Jack Greenberg, *Crusaders in the Courts: How a Dedicated Band of Lawyers Fought for the Civil Rights Revolution*, 1994 (account of the NAACP legal assault on school segregation); trial transcript in *Brown* case, filed in U.S. District Court, Topeka, Kansas (trial date of October 16, 1951); opinion of three-judge court, 98 F.Supp. 797 (D.Kansas 1951).

CHAPTER 9: "WAR AGAINST THE CONSTITUTION"

Accounts in this chapter of the *Brown* cases and the Little Rock integration case are adapted from Irons, *Jim Crow's Children*; Kluger, *Simple Justice*; and Greenberg, *Crusaders in the Courts*.

U.S. government brief: *Landmark Briefs*, vol. 49, 113.

Oral arguments in Supreme Court: Leon Friedman, ed., *Argument: The Oral Argument before the Supreme Court in Brown v. Board of Education of Topeka, 1952–1955*, 1969.

Deliberations of justices: Kluger, *Simple Justice*, chs. 23 and 24; Greenberg, *Crusaders in the Courts*, ch. 13.

Second round of oral arguments: Friedman, *Argument*; *Landmark Briefs*, vols. 49 and 49A.

Warren's unanimous opinion in *Brown* cases: *Brown v. Board of Education of Topeka, Kansas*, 347 U.S. 483 (1954).

Opinion in *Bolling* case: *Bolling v. Sharpe*, 347 U.S. 497 (1954).

White resistance to integration in Milford, Delaware: "The Milford School Desegregation Crisis of 1954," Delaware Public Archives, Delaware.gov.

Supreme Court opinion in *Brown II*: 347 U.S. 483 (1955).

White resistance to integration in Little Rock, Arkansas: Tony Freyer, *The Little Rock Crisis: A Constitutional Interpretation*, 1984; Daisy Bates, the Arkansas NAACP president, who shepherded the nine Black students through the mob around Central High, wrote a powerful memoir: *The Long Shadow of Little Rock*, 1962; see also Greenberg, *Crusaders in the Courts*, ch. 17.

Oral argument in Little Rock case: *Landmark Briefs*, vol. 54.

Supreme Court opinion in Little Rock case: *Cooper v. Aaron*, 358 U.S. 1 (1958).

Current racial composition in *Brown* case schools: data from National Center for Educational Statistics, U.S. Department of Education, 2019–20.

CHAPTER 10: "TWO CITIES: ONE WHITE, THE OTHER BLACK"

Muhammad Ali and Vietnam War: Bob Okrand, "I Ain't Got No Quarrel with Them Vietcong," *New York Times*, June 27, 2017.

Rosa Parks and Montgomery bus boycott: "Montgomery Bus Boycott," Wikipedia; Rosa Parks, *My Story*, 1992; David J. Garrow, ed., *The Montgomery Bus Boycott and the Women Who Started It: The Memoir of Jo Ann Gibson Robinson*, 1987; Taylor Branch, *Parting the Waters: America in the King Years, 1954–63*, 1989.

CORE sit-ins and Freedom Rides: Marion Smith Holmes, "The Freedom Riders, Then and Now," *Smithsonian Magazine*, February 2009.

Freedom Rides in 1961: Raymond Arsenault, *Freedom Riders: 1961 and the Struggle for Racial Justice*, 2007; numerous accounts in newspapers and magazines in 1961.

Freedom Summer, 1964: "Freedom Summer," Wikipedia; Joel Norst, *Freedom Burning*, 1988; William Bradford Huie, *Three Lives for Mississippi*, 1965; Seth Cagin and Philip Dray, *We Are Not Afraid*, 1988.

Civil rights martyrs: "Civil Rights Martyrs," Southern Poverty Law Center, splccenter. org. I have added additional detail in some of these accounts.

Emmett Till murder: Stephen J. Whitfield, *A Death in the Delta: The Story of Emmett Till*, 1991; Devery S. Anderson, *Emmett Till: The Murder That Shocked the World and Propelled the Civil Rights Movement*, 2015; Mamie Till-Mobley and Christopher Benson, *Death of Innocence: The Story of the Hate Crime That Changed America*, 2011.

Birmingham, Alabama, church bombing: "16th Street Baptist Church Bombing," Wikipedia; Doug Jones, *Bending toward Justice: The Birmingham Church Bombing That Changed the Course of Civil Rights*, 2019 (Doug Jones prosecuted the church bombers); Elizabeth H. Cobbs and Petric J. Smith, *Long Time Coming: An Insider's Story of the Birmingham Church Bombing That Rocked the World*, 1994.

Detroit race riot in 1967: "1967 Detroit Riot," Wikipedia; Sidney Fine, *Violence in the Model City: The Kavanaugh Administration, Race Relations, and the Detroit Riot of 1967*, 2007; Jon Lowell, "Violence on 12th: Street of Nightmares," *Detroit News*, July 24, 1967.

Milliken case and Judge Roth opinions: Joyce A. Baugh, *The Detroit School Busing Case: Milliken v. Bradley and the Controversy over Desegregation*, 2011; *Milliken v. Bradley*, 338 F.Supp. 582 (E.D.Mich. 1972) and 345 F.Supp. 918 (E.D.Mich. 1972).

Supreme Court oral arguments in *Milliken* case: *Landmark Briefs*, vol. 80.

Chief Justice Burger opinion in *Milliken* case: 418 U.S. 717 (1974).

Thurgood Marshall dissent in *Milliken* case: 418 U.S. at 782 (1974).

Boston school integration and busing: "Boston School Desegregation Busing Crisis," Wikipedia; J. Anthony Lukas, *Common Ground: A Turbulent Decade in the Lives of Three American Families*, 1985 (account of Boston busing case); Ronald P. Formisano, *Boston against Busing: Race, Class, and Ethnicity in the 1960s and 1970s*, 2012.

CHAPTER 11: "ALL BLACKS ARE ANGRY"

Kerner Commission: "Kerner Commission," Wikipedia; *Report of the National Commission on Civil Disorders*, 1968; Alice George, "The 1968 Kerner Commission Got It Right, but Nobody Listened," *Smithsonian Magazine*, March 1, 2018, smithsonianmag.com.

Dissimilarity Index: "Index of Dissimilarity," Wikipedia; "CensusScope— Segregation: Dissimilarity indices," censusscope.org (includes DIs for 318 metropolitan areas); "Residential Segregation Data for U.S. Metro Areas," governing.com.

Moynihan Report: "The Negro Family: The Case for National Action," Wikipedia; Daniel Patrick Moynihan and U.S. Department of Labor, *The Moynihan Report: The Negro Family—The Case for National Action*, 1966; Gregory Acs, "The Moynihan Report Revisited," Urban Institute, June 2013, urban.org; James T. Patterson, "Moynihan and the Single-Parent Family," *Education Next* 15, no. 2 (Fall 2014), educationnext.org.

Blaming the victim: William Ryan, *Blaming the Victim*, 1971; William Ryan, *Blaming the Victim*, revised ed. (1976); William Ryan, *Equality*, 1981. See also "Arthur Jensen," Wikipedia; "How Much Can We Boost IQ and Scholastic Achievement?," *Harvard Educational Review*, February 1969; Arthur Jensen, *The g Factor: The Science of Mental Ability*, 1998 ("g" stands for "general intelligence factor"; Jensen argues for a genetic component to account for lower IQ scores among Blacks); see also "Edward C. Banfield," Wikipedia; Edward Banfield, *The Unheavenly City: The Nature and the Future of Our Urban Crisis*, 1970; and Edward Banfield, *The Unheavenly City Revisited*, 1974.

The truly disadvantaged: William Julius Wilson, *The Truly Disadvantaged: The Inner City, the Underclass, and Public Policy* (1987); William Julius Wilson, *The Truly Disadvantaged: The Inner City, the Underclass, and Public Policy*, 2nd. ed. (2012).

Frustration-aggression-displacement theory: John Dollard, *Caste and Class in a Southern Town* (1937); John Dollard, *Caste and Class in a Southern Town,* 2nd. ed. (1989); John Dollard et al., *Frustration and Aggression,* 1939; see also Leonard Berkowitz, *Roots of Aggression: A Re-examination of the Frustration-Aggression Hypothesis,* 1969.

Black rage: Price M. Cobbs and William H. Grier, *Black Rage* (1968); Price M. Cobbs and William H. Grier, *Black Rage,* revised ed. (1992).

Black imprisonment: John Gramlich, "Imprisonment Rate of Black Americans Fell by a Third from 2006 to 2018," Pew Research Center, May 6, 2020.

Trump supporters and race: Emily Flitter and Chris Kahn, "Exclusive: Trump Supporters More Likely to View Blacks Negatively," Reuters, June 28, 2016.

Racial stereotypes: Tobin Grant, "Poll: Most Whites Say Blacks Are Lazier or Less Intelligent Than Whites," Religion News Service, December 8, 2014; see also Juliana Menasce Horowitz, Anna Brown, and Kiana Cox, "Race in America, April 9, 2019," Pew Research Center.

CHAPTER 12: "THE BASIC MINIMAL SKILLS"

School funding disparities: Matt Barnum, "The Other School Funding Divide: States with More Poor Students Tend to Spend Less, Creating Hard-to-Fix Disparities," July 31, 2019, chalkbeat.org; Laura Meckler, "Report Finds $23 Billion Racial Funding Gap for Schools, *Washington Post,* February 26, 2019; "Closing America's Education Funding Gaps," The Century Foundation, July 22, 2020, tcf.org.

Rodriguez case: "San Antonio Independent School District v. Rodriguez," Wikipedia; Paul Sracic, San Antonio v. Rodriguez *and the Pursuit of Equal Education,* 2006.

Supreme Court arguments in *Rodriguez*: "San Antonio Independent School District v. Rodriguez: Oral Argument," oyez.org.

Powell opinion in *Rodriguez*: *San Antonio Independent School District v. Rodriguez,* 411 U.S. 1 (1973).

Marshall dissent in *Rodriguez*: 411 U.S. 1, at 102 (1973).

Texas state court on school funding: "Texas Plan for School Financing Is Found Discriminatory by Judge," *New York Times,* April 30, 1987.

Detroit school testing scores: the data in this section is from the National Assessment of Educational Progress, 2019 test results (website has instructions for finding school districts: nces.ed.go).

Mumford and King high schools: data from National Center for Educational Statistics, 2019–20 school year (website has instructions for finding individual schools).

Data on school preparation: Julia B. Isaacs, "Starting School at a Disadvantage: The School Readiness of Poor Children," Center on Children and Families, Brookings Institution, March 2012, brookings.edu.

EPILOGUE: "ROOTING OUT SYSTEMIC RACISM"

This account of the 2020 presidential election, its violent aftermath, and former president Trump's second impeachment is drawn from numerous articles in the *Washington Post* and *New York Times* during that period. They will soon be supplemented, I'm sure, by a plethora of books.

Trump disbelief in systemic racism: Ruth Marcus, "Opinion: If You Don't Believe Systemic Racism Is Real, Explain These Statistics," *Washington Post*, June 12, 2020.

Biden Plan for Black America: "Lift Every Voice: The Biden Plan for Black America," May 5, 2020, joebiden.com.

Gallup Poll on voter concerns: Lydia Saad, "Gallup Election 2020 Coverage," news. gallup.com; see also "Important Issues in the 2020 Election," Pew Research Center, August 23, 2020, pewresearch.com.

Racial disparities in life expectancy: Dennis Thompson, "U.S. Life Expectancy Drops 1 Full Year Due to COVID-19," February 18, 2021, webMD.com.

Covid-19 death rates by race: "The Color of Coronavirus: Covid-19 Deaths by Race and Ethnicity in the U.S.," APM Research Lab, March 5, 2021, apmresearchlab.com.

Causes of Covid-19 racial disparities: Leo Lopez III, Louis H. Hart III, and Mitchell H. Katz, "Racial and Ethnic Health Disparities Related to COVID-19," *Journal of the American Medical Association*, January 22, 2021, jamanetwork.com.

Accounts of George Floyd's death: drawn from numerous news sources; see especially Manny Fernandez and Audra D. S. Burch, "George Floyd, from 'I Want to Touch the World' to 'I Can't Breathe,'" *New York Times*, March 4, 2021, nytimes.com.

Trayvon Martin and origins of Black Lives Matter: Isaac Chotiner, "A Black Lives Matter Co-Founder Explains Why This Time Is Different," *New Yorker*, June 3, 2020, newyorker.com; Isabella Mercado, "The Black Lives Matter Movement: An Origin Story," Underground Railroad Education Center, no date, undergroundrailroadhistory.org.

General works on racism and its causes and consequences: Ibram X. Kendi, *Stamped from the Beginning: The Definitive History of Racist Ideas in America*, 2016; Nell Irvin Painter, *The History of White People*, 2010; Joe R. Feagin, *Racist America: Roots, Current Realities, and Future Reparations*, 2000; Joe R. Feagin, *Systemic Racism: A Theory of Oppression*, 2006; Stephen M. Caliendo, *Inequality in America: Race, Poverty, and Fulfilling Democracy's Promise*, 2014; Michael J. Klarman, *From Jim Crow to Civil Rights: The Supreme Court and the Struggle for Racial Equality*, 2004; Melvin Oliver and Thomas Shapiro, *Black Wealth/White Wealth: A New Perspective on Racial Inequality*, 2013; Peter Irons, *A People's History of the Supreme Court: The Men and Women Whose Cases and Decisions Have Shaped Our Constitution*, 1999; Paul Kivel, *Uprooting Racism: How White People Can Work for Racial Justice*, 2011; Carol Anderson, *White Rage: The Unspoken Truth of Our Racial Divide*, 2016; Bryan Stevenson, *Just Mercy: A Story of Justice and Redemption*, 2014; Khalil Gibran Muhammad, *The Condemnation of Blackness: Race, Crime, and the Making of Modern Urban America*, 2010; Michelle Alexander, *The New Jim Crow: Mass Incarceration in the Age of Colorblindness*, 2010; Elliott Currie, *A Peculiar Indifference: The Neglected Toll of Violence on Black America*, 2020; Isabel Wilkerson, *Caste: The Origins of Our Discontents*, 2020.

Index

For the benefit of digital users, indexed terms that span two pages (e.g., 52–53) may, on occasion, appear on only one of those pages.